The Blood of Martyrs

The Blood of Martyrs

I
The History of the Christian Church from Pentecost to the Age of Theodosius (AD 397)

Church history unfolded, through the stories that are the inheritance of all believers

Leigh Churchill

paternoster
Lifestyle

First published in 2001 by Paternoster Lifestyle
Reprinted 2002

08 07 06 05 04 03 02   8 7 6 5 4 3 2

Paternoster Lifestyle is an imprint of Paternoster Publishing,
P.O. Box 300, Carlisle, Cumbria CA3 0QS, UK
and Paternoster Publishing USA
Box 1047, Waynesboro, GA 30830-2047
www.paternoster-publishing.com

British Library Cataloguing in Publication Data

A catalogue record for this book is available from the British Library

ISBN 1–84227–077–X

Cover design by Campsie, Glasgow
Typeset by Textype Typesetters, Cambridge
Printed and bound in Great Britain by
Cox & Wyman Ltd, Reading, Berkshire

Contents

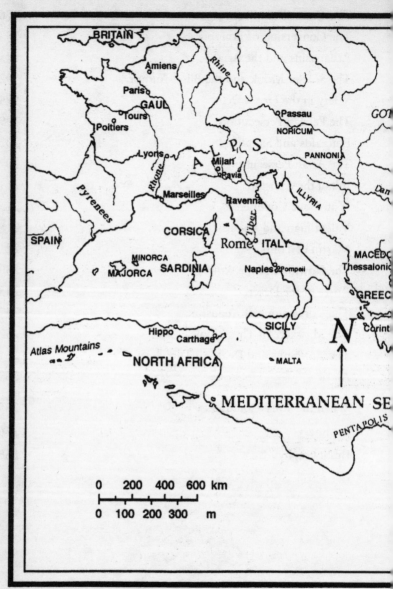

The World of the

Early Christians

In heaven I do think one part of our best employ will be to read the great book of the experience of all the saints, and gather from that book the whole of the divine character as having been proved and illustrated.

CHARLES HADDON SPURGEON

Introduction

Church history will always be one of the most important parts of Christian education. It can equip us for witness, strengthen our faith, clarify questions and inspire emulation. It is nothing less than the story of the hand of our Lord in the lives of human beings, and as such it deepens and broadens our understanding of God's nature and workings.

Church history, however, can be a forbidding subject. A dry catalogue of councils and theologians, controversies and reforms, must always seem rather uninspiring. History must live before it can effectively teach.

From the Bible we can learn God's way of teaching history. The Bible is a treasure trove of inspiring stories: judgements of God and great wars, good and wicked kings, prodigal sons and fearless prophets, visions of God and Satan. The teachings of Scripture come to life in history and parable.

This book follows the example of Scripture in telling the stories of Christian history. Through stories from everyday, and not so everyday, life-stories from the lives of Christians both great and small – the ebb and flow of two thousand years of church history is revealed. It is the author's conviction that a great story can live forever in the imagination, while a string of facts and dates will be as soon forgotten as learnt.

Although the book has been written for teens and adults, many of the stories are suitable for family readings to even younger children. The book covers all the major developments of church history in a personal, fresh and straightforward way that will make learning both easy and entertaining. If you have ever wondered what the real St Patrick was like, or why St Bernard has a dog named after him, read on.

The entire work, complete in four volumes, will be an invaluable resource for families, Christian schools and home educators, as well as for all who would like to improve their knowledge of history and theology. The stories are entertaining for students, and the fascinating detail and depth of treatment will interest any reader. It will be a work not read once only, but one to which the reader will return again and again – forming as it does a veritable encyclopaedia of church history. Those who read these stories will be rewarded with an appreciation of the main currents of the history of our faith in all times and places – something that is very rare today.

The stories assume that the reader is well acquainted with the Bible, so the history of the early church as found in Scripture is here treated quite briefly. The stories from the book of Acts are used mainly to introduce the major themes of church history. They are, of course, the necessary background for everything that follows.

Jesus is the Beginning

The whole of the Christian church is built on a single foundation. Christianity – its Scriptures, teachings and traditions, each of its followers in countless congregations – looks back to its source in the events of a three-year period some 2,000 years ago, when a man named Jesus wandered the towns of a narrow province in a mighty empire. In that brief period a foundation was laid that time cannot wear away or destroy.

It is not the purpose of this book to cover the life of Jesus in detail. Readers will discover the life of lives in the four Gospels. But as Christ's life is the basis and model of all that is good in church history, we cannot embark on the story of two Christian millennia without plainly stating just who and what the master was.

In the eyes of the world, Jesus was a preacher, teacher, healer and prophet. He proclaimed a pure and perfect morality and pointed the way to a wholehearted and intimate walk with God. Even those with no love for the gospel admit that He stands very high amongst the great teachers of humankind. It can be said of Jesus, as of few others, that He taught without fear or favour and rebuked the evils of His time with unbending courage. It was, in fact, His stinging rebukes of the rich and powerful that led to His eventual arrest and execution. Nailed to a Roman cross, the most cruel and protracted form of punishment then practised, Jesus suffered an excruciating death that shocked His friends and foes alike. Indeed the very word 'excruciating', meaning to suffer as though crucified, describes the horror of that event.

If that had been the end of Jesus' story, the great man would have little relevance to today's world. Those who knew Jesus best, however, knew that there was more to the man from Galilee than met the eye.

Throughout Jesus' ministry, His disciples had seen something greater than human in their master. They came to see that Jesus was the Christ, or Messiah, who had been promised to Israel for centuries past. No sooner did they understand this than they were confronted with an even greater revelation. The Old Testament taught that the Messiah would bring a new age of righteousness – but it also hinted at something amazing concerning the promised one Himself. The Christ was to be no ordinary priest or prophet. He was, as the disciples discovered, nothing less than the Son of God.

The crucifixion seemed a plain contradiction of this idea. That the Messiah should die a criminal's death was a hard teaching – that the Son of God should do so was beyond belief. The terrible events of Good Friday scattered the disciples, and the seed of the church would have perished then and there had not the greatest of miracles confirmed them in their faith.

That miracle, of course, was the resurrection. The Son of God had not been defeated by death, but rather He had died to defeat death – that most fearsome of all enemies. The grave, the prison of countless millions of spirits, had proved powerless to hold Christ within its walls. The crucifixion, which had seemed to be Satan's greatest triumph, was in fact his greatest defeat.

The disciples did not immediately understand the full meaning of Christ's death and resurrection. Throughout their lives they would gain ever deeper knowledge of Jesus and His works, and Christians in the many centuries since have still not discovered all that Christ means. These books will explore many of the great realities of Jesus Christ, but we must begin by stating the basics.

Jesus was not *a* son of God, not a prophet chosen by God to carry His message to the world. Jesus was the Father's only begotten Son. He was One with the Father and in Him all the fullness of God dwelled in bodily form. His coming was unique, never to be repeated. He was God incarnate, the eternal Lord made flesh – fully divine, though fully human.

Jesus' life did not begin with His birth in Bethlehem. Before His human birth and from all eternity, Jesus Christ, the second Person of the Trinity, existed in heaven in the presence of His Father and the Holy Spirit. He lived as far from the sorrows of this world and the Roman cross as can be imagined. Eternal and perfect peace was His.

But the world needed Jesus. The human race was crippled with sin and there was only one cure. From eternity it had been decreed that the Son would enter the world to destroy the works of the devil and reconcile sinful human beings with their just and holy Creator.

Jesus' coming opened a new chapter in the world's history, a chapter that Christ Himself called 'the kingdom of God'. Christ's earthly ministry, forgiving sin, expelling demons, healing sickness, was a sign that Satan's power over human beings had been broken. It was only by His death, however, that He completed this work. All humankind was severed from God, lost in sin and deserving of nothing but punishment from the divine righteousness. But at Calvary Christ offered His life to the Father as a substitute, and He Himself bore the penalty for our sin. Salvation from sin's *penalty*, however, is only the beginning. Christ offers to redeem us altogether from sin's *power*, to enable us to experience the rule of God in our lives and to become children of God with renewed hearts.

God's children, redeemed from sin, need a model for the new life they have received. Herein lies another reason for Christ's coming. Jesus' life, as revealed in the Gospels, is our example – a perfect human life given as an ideal to guide and inspire us. Following the road He has laid down, we are privileged to be called the brothers and sisters of Christ, for Jesus came to be the 'First-born of many brothers' (Rom. 8:29).

Jesus' coming is the greatest conceivable revelation of the depths of divine love. Fully knowing the cost of His act, Christ cast off the glorious rights of His divine nature to emerge defenceless and tiny in the Bethlehem stable. In becoming one of us, in walking our paths and suffering our trials, Jesus proved the infinity of His compassion. Mankind is not an accident of history on an obscure planet – we are the centre of God's universe.

The effects of Christ's coming could only be momentous. Sadly, few Christians know even a fraction of the mightiest works of our Lord through His church over the last 2,000 years. Many hardly realize the uniqueness of their church. It might be a good idea, as we enter the third millennium, to let our system of dating remind us that Jesus truly is the centre of history. The terms BC (before Christ) and AD (*Anno Domini*, Latin for 'in the year of the Lord'), accurately represent Christ's significance – His life was the turning of the ages. He gave meaning to all that had gone before and provided a direction for all to come thereafter.

The Coming of the Holy Spirit

During the Easter season we commemorate several of the critical moments in Christ's ministry and reflect on their relevance to our own lives. With 'Hosannas' we salute the King, at Good Friday's cross we witness the terrible wages of sin and in Sunday's empty tomb we rejoice in the certainty of the resurrection of the dead. Ascension Thursday and Pentecost are also worthy of our remembrance, for here the church as we know it really begins. On Ascension Thursday, 40 days after the Resurrection, Christ rose to the Father, leaving His followers with the promise of the Holy Spirit.

'Do not leave Jerusalem,' He said, 'but wait there until you receive power from on high. When the Holy Spirit comes you will be my witnesses in Jerusalem, Judea, Samaria and to the very end of the earth.'

So the Christian church began with an act of obedience to Jesus. The apostles waited in Jerusalem, as Jesus had commanded, until Pentecost. The festival of Pentecost celebrated both the giving of the Law to Moses and the firstfruits of the harvest. So it was an appropriate time for the Spirit to receive these gospel firstfruits and to inaugurate the covenant of grace that was to succeed the old law.

At Pentecost, Jews from many nations gathered to participate in the temple worship. The disciples of Jesus were together as well. They had spent ten days in fervent and expectant prayer, calling on the Lord and waiting for His gift. Early on Pentecost morning, a mighty wind rocked their house. Flickering fire came from heaven and touched each of them and all were immediately filled with the Holy Spirit. They started to talk in strange languages and a crowd soon gathered to see what was going on. Jews from Asia, Africa and Europe heard their own languages being spoken and were astonished.

'These men surely couldn't know my language,' some said. 'Where did they learn it?'

Others began to scoff and, not understanding the strange tongues, said that the disciples were drunk. It was Peter who stepped forward to explain.

'Men of Judea, heed my words. These men are not speaking from fullness of wine, but rather from the fullness of the Spirit of God. Today is the day of which the prophet Joel spoke, promising that the Spirit would be poured out freely upon all the servants of God.

'Listen to our message. Jesus of Nazareth, a man divinely attested by the greatest miracles, you have taken with lawless hands and put to death. You crucified Jesus, but God has raised Him from the dead, for it was impossible that death should hold Him. Of this we all are witnesses. Exalted to the right hand of God, Jesus has received from the Father the promised Holy Spirit and has poured out this power which you see and hear. Repent, accept baptism in His name and you will be forgiven your sins and you too will receive the Spirit, which is promised to all whom the Lord our God will call.'

With many more words Peter exhorted the crowds and that day some three thousand Jews were baptized in the name of Jesus the Messiah. God worked great signs and wonders through the hands of the apostles, and the infant church experienced a season of joy in the days and weeks ahead. There was no distinction between rich and poor amongst the followers of Jesus, as all sold their possessions and gave the money to the apostles, so they could distribute to each believer as he or she had need. Nothing could better show that the church was one family in the Spirit and the Lord added each day to the fellowship those who were being saved.

ACTS 1–2

The First Martyr

But even the best families have their share of problems. Earth has seen only one perfect Man, and the first years of the church were not without conflict. There was the case of Ananias and Sapphira, a couple who held back some of their wealth from the other believers and lied to the Apostle Peter. Their fate is infamous. There was also a quarrel between Christians of different descent – Jews of Jerusalem on one side and foreign Jews on the other, over the unequal distribution of food to their widows. The strife led the apostles to appoint seven servants, or 'deacons', to supervise such matters.

The greatest troubles, however, came from outside the church. It was not long before the leaders of the Jews, the murderers of Christ, began plotting against these followers of their enemy. They had feared that Jesus would destroy their authority and His death seemed to have done little to improve the situation. Something had to be done to stop the whole nation from accepting the Crucified One as Saviour.

The apostles themselves were the first to be arrested and beaten. Far from being silenced, however, the Jews found that the believers actually rejoiced in persecution. In suffering for the gospel they felt even closer to Jesus, because they knew that He also had suffered for them. The leaders were incensed.

'We must destroy them before the whole world goes after Jesus!'

It was one of the seven deacons of the new church, a young man named Stephen, who would be the first follower of Christ to shed his blood in the war of the Spirit.

Stephen was a powerful preacher, and many were led to Jesus through his words and through the signs God performed by his hands. Certain Jews tried to debate with him, but they were utterly infuriated to come out second-best. They were learning the folly of striving against the Holy Spirit – the hard way. Rousing the people against Stephen, these Jews dragged the young preacher before the Sanhedrin and laid charges of blasphemy against him.

'This man claims that Jesus will destroy the temple and change the customs handed down by Moses!'

Permitted to defend himself, Stephen boldly proclaimed the truth about Jesus. The Jews saw his face shine like that of an angel, but they felt his words cut like a sword. The court was enraged, but Stephen seemed quite oblivious as, finishing his defence, he became lost in a vision. Staring above, he saw the cloud of the divine glory, with Jesus standing at His Father's side. Assured of God's approval, he shouted aloud about the revelation, but the Jews covered their ears against the sacred words and lunged forward with a fearful scream. They dragged him outside and began to stone him.

'Lord Jesus,' Stephen cried, 'receive my spirit!'

He fell on his knees and begged that Jesus would forgive his enemies, that they might believe and be saved. Then he fell asleep and died. A Jew named Saul was one of the witnesses to this terrible scene. He, like his compatriots, delighted in the blood of the first Christian martyrdom.

ACTS 3–7

The Road to Damascus

Stephen's death proved to be only the first blow in an all-out war, the first persecution of the church. Saul and other Pharisees went from house to house arresting the believers and almost all were imprisoned or scattered. There was no time to plan and prepare – the only safety lay in fleeing the city immediately. Even this, however, was under God's control. For the believers scattered through the surrounding countryside were able to preach more widely and freely than ever before and the church grew even faster.

Saul learned that many Christians had gone to Damascus and he obtained authorization from the high priest to arrest them there. He would soon find that God had other ideas. Saul had nearly reached Damascus when a brilliant light flashed around him and he heard a voice from heaven.

'Saul, Saul, why do you persecute Me?'

'Who are You, Lord?' Saul trembled.

'I am Jesus, whom you are persecuting. Go into the city and there you will be told what you must do.'

The light disappeared, leaving Saul blinded and his companions had to lead him by the hand into the city. For three days he could not see, and he sat the whole time in prayer, neither eating nor drinking.

God now spoke in a vision to Ananias, a local Christian, telling him to go to Saul. Ananias, knowing of Saul's schemes against the believers, was fearful, but trusting in God he obeyed the message. He went to Saul and laid hands on the blind man's head.

'Jesus has sent me to you,' he said, 'that you might see again and be filled with the Holy Spirit.'

Immediately something like scales fell from Saul's eyes and his sight was restored. He was baptized and afterwards had something to eat.

The change in the enemy of the gospel was immediate and overwhelming. His meeting with Jesus had completely overthrown his personality. Saul craved quiet for reflection and meditation on his vision and conversion, so he left the bustle of Damascus to spend some time in nearby Arabia. When he returned, the whole city took notice.

'Believe in Jesus Christ and be saved!'

'Isn't that Saul, the persecutor of Christians?' all the Jews asked. 'What on earth has happened to him?'

The transformation was unbelievable. How could the power of Jesus be doubted while such a proof walked the city! It did not take long before the Jews saw that they had a new worst enemy.

'We must kill Saul!'

Spies were set at the city gates to capture the preacher, but Saul learnt of the plot just in time. Concealed in a large basket, he was lowered over the city wall by night and soon afterwards he was back in Jerusalem. Once there, however, he found it no easy task to bring the local Christians to trust him.

'Surely this man is a deceiver and plans to spy on us from within?'

But the Spirit's power shone too clearly in Saul for such doubts to remain for long. The church soon accepted Saul and rejoiced greatly at this evidence of amazing grace.

ACTS 8–9

A Mission to the World

'You will be my witnesses in Jerusalem, in Judea and Samaria and to the end of the earth.'

Those had been Jesus' words. The apostles still had little appreciation of the full extent of their meaning.

The Jews had always had a deep sense of their significance as a people. God had chosen their nation out of all the earth and they alone had received the blessing of the Old Testament. They were the chosen race, while every other people they labelled with the name 'Gentile'. The Jews were the people of God, while the Gentile nations were all under the influence of evil spirits – spirits that they worshipped in the shape of idols. Israel was a single bright spot in an otherwise dark world.

A little Jewish light, however, had seeped out to the peoples around them. Even before the time of Jesus, many Gentiles had read the Scriptures and embraced the God of Israel. They saw that the Old Testament made better sense than their own pagan traditions and the Jews cautiously admitted some of them to their congregations.

In the time of the apostles one such Gentile believer, a Roman centurion (a commander of one hundred soldiers) named

Cornelius, lived in the port city of Caesarea. While he was praying one day, an angel appeared to Cornelius in a vision. The angel assured Cornelius that his prayers and generosity to the poor had been pleasing to the Lord.

'Send men to Joppa, to Simon who is known as Peter. He is lodging with a tanner named Simon, whose home is by the sea.'

Cornelius obeyed immediately and the next day, while his servants were on their way, Peter himself saw a strange vision. He saw a large sheet descending from heaven, covered with all types of animals which were forbidden to the Jews, and was commanded to 'Kill and eat.'

'Surely not, Lord? I have never before eaten unclean food!'

'Do not call unclean,' the heavenly voice replied, 'what God has cleansed.'

Peter was so shocked at such a command to break the Law that he asked the same question three times and thrice received the same answer, before the sheet returned to heaven.

An age was ending. The Law, as the Jews had known it for centuries, was now passing away. The food restrictions given through Moses were dead – but the vision also meant something much more and Peter was still thinking it over when Cornelius' men arrived. The Spirit told Peter to go with them and, after the messengers had rested, Peter and six of his fellow believers accompanied them back to Caesarea. When Peter arrived, Cornelius fell upon his knees to show his respect.

'Stand,' said Peter, 'for I am a man just like yourself.'

Peter told Cornelius and his friends about his vision and when he had finished Cornelius described his own experience. Hearing his words, Peter more fully understood the meaning of the vision of the unclean animals.

The Gentiles, of course, did not follow the Law of Moses and the Jews believed that this made the Gentiles unclean. Jews avoided close association with foreigners, for fear that they might be 'contaminated' by them. Even Gentiles who believed in the God of Israel usually stopped short of obeying the whole Law, especially the painful rite of circumcision, and as a consequence their Jewish brothers kept them at arm's length. To the uncircumcised, such as Cornelius, the temple's inner court was taboo and only a very few Gentiles went the whole way to complete conversion and full acceptance into the Jewish communion. It was a culture that the followers of Jesus must obviously break with before the gospel could reach the end of the earth!

Jesus' offer of salvation and cleansing from sin was, and is, to all the peoples of the earth. All who accepted His gift would be clean – irrespective of food taboos and the ceremonies of the Law – and Jew and Gentile would be united in one church. Assured of this through such great signs, Peter wasted no more time. He plainly proclaimed the great facts of the life and promises of Jesus Christ. Even as he spoke the Holy Spirit came upon the Gentiles and they began speaking in other languages and praising God. Any lingering doubts as to the full equality of Jews and Gentiles were swept away and Peter instructed that Cornelius and his family and friends be baptized immediately.

The first Jews to accept Jesus had received the Holy Spirit and spoken in new tongues and the same thing had now happened to the first Gentiles. The church was learning that it had a mission to the whole world – that every people and tongue might offer praise to the true God.

ACTS 10

Paul's Ministry

Many Christians living in the great Greek city of Antioch became involved in this new ministry to the Gentiles. Chief among them was Saul, who soon began to go by the Gentile name of Paul. God had great things planned for Paul, and it wasn't long before his fellow Christians sensed it. During a time of worship and fasting, the Spirit told the church at Antioch that Paul and his friend Barnabas should travel through the surrounding lands on a missionary journey. Since Paul was a Roman citizen, he could travel and preach more easily than most Jews and Christians. Roman citizens enjoyed a wide variety of privileges – including special treatment in case of arrest.

The timing of Jesus' entry into the world was as perfect as everything else in His ministry.

Christ was born in the early years of the Roman Empire, an empire that joined tens of millions – from southern Europe, north Africa and an important part of Asia – under one government. Many areas that were now Roman provinces had been separate countries only a hundred years before Christ, and the fact that these countries had often been at war with each other would have made the task of missionaries very difficult. Also, until only a few years before Christ's birth, the Empire itself had been divided by a succession of civil wars – and the possibilities for travel were severely limited. But all of that was now over. Augustus, the first emperor, brought peace to the Roman realm, and it was during his reign that Christ was born.

Jesus Christ, the Prince of Peace, entered the world in a time of peace. Even the pagan gods agreed. An ancient Roman temple was dedicated to Janus, a god whom the Romans believed aided them in battle. In wartime, the gates of Janus' temple were opened to allow the god to join the army, while in times of peace they were shut to keep the obedient god within. Throughout Rome's bloody history, the Janus gates had been shut only twice – until, that is, the reign of Augustus. Under Augustus, the gates were closed on three separate occasions, the third time for twelve years, and during those twelve years Jesus Christ was born in Bethlehem.

The time of Christ, the era of the early empire, is a period of fascinating contradictions in the Roman world. The peace and prosperity under Augustus were obvious and inspiring realities, but in spite of this there is a strikingly pessimistic streak in leading pagan authors of the time. None denied Rome's splendour, but many believed that political greatness had come at the cost of moral character, and they looked to the future with a nervous eye. Livy, one of Rome's greatest authors, wrote 20 years before Christ's birth that the student of recent Roman history would 'see that it was the relaxation of traditional discipline which made our moral foundations give way and started that decline which has finally brought us to the point that we can neither bear to live with our vices, nor to undergo the therapy they require'.

Emperor Augustus struggled to reform Rome through moral legislation, but his attempts failed miserably. Livy himself, believing that Rome might regain its glory through education, composed a massive history of Rome, some 142 books, which he vainly hoped would encourage reform by stimulating people to model themselves on their more virtuous ancestors. As we shall see, the church would bring the only real solution to Rome's problems.

The Lord had long been preparing the way for these first missionaries. Six hundred years before Christ, the city of Jerusalem had been destroyed by the Babylonians, and in the wake of that terrible event many Jews had settled in foreign lands. This spread of the Jewish people (known as the Diaspora, Greek for 'dispersion') had increased greatly in the decades since Rome had conquered the Mediterranean region, and there were now Jewish communities of various sizes throughout the empire. They were a myriad of doorways through which the gospel might enter the nations.

The first missionary journey was to the island of Cyprus and southern Asia Minor (now part of Turkey). At first Paul and Barnabas spoke mainly to Jews, but they soon found a great many Gentiles coming to hear the new teaching.

Some Jews of Asia Minor, however, were displeased with the flood of Gentiles entering the synagogue, and they began to oppose the apostles. They had been willing enough to hear the missionaries' teaching for themselves, but they were not at all inclined to share the Good News with the Gentiles. They had their own ideas about the Christ and expected a Messiah whose coming would mean blessing to the Jews and destruction to the peoples around them. If they were to have Jesus at all, they must have Him to themselves.

Paul and Barnabas stood firm as the Jewish leaders began to attack their teachings publicly.

'We had to come to you first, but since you will not accept the word in faith and think yourselves unworthy of eternal life, we must turn to the Gentiles instead. For this is the Lord's command: "I have made you a light to the Gentiles, that you might bring salvation to the end of the earth"' (Isa. 49:6).

Many Gentiles heard of this quarrel between Paul and the Jews, and their respect for the apostles grew. They rejoiced in the concern of the missionaries for their salvation, and many more were joined to the church.

Returning to Antioch at the end of two years, Paul and Barnabas rested before undertaking a second tour. In this interval, certain Jewish Christians stirred up trouble in Antioch by teaching that Gentile converts could not be saved unless they were circumcised. This brought them into conflict with Paul and Barnabas, and the apostles soon visited Jerusalem to discuss the matter with the senior leaders of the church. The result was a victory for the missionary party, and a council of the apostles and elders of Jerusalem penned an epistle that acknowledged that the old ceremonial laws were no longer binding on Gentile believers. It was clear that the destruction of the ancient wall between Jew and Gentile would be a difficult process, but charity and understanding could at least make it an eventual reality.

Following this important controversy, Paul embarked on a second missionary journey, this time accompanied by Silas. Asia Minor was again the focus, until one night Paul received a vision of a Macedonian man.

'Come across to Macedonia and help us!'

There was no need for a second invitation. Paul rose early the next day and found a boat that could take him across the Aegean. Europe – this was where God was leading. Preaching first in Macedonia, then slowly making his way south to Athens, Paul cast the first gospel seeds on the soil that was to bear so much fruit in later years.

ACTS 11–17

In the myriad synagogues of the Diaspora, the early missionaries could usually teach about Jesus in much the same way. All Jews were awaiting the Messiah, and the apostles based their ministry on explaining how Christ had fulfilled the Old Testament prophecies and proved Himself to be the Son of God. Teaching Gentiles was different. Paul could not simply preach to them from the Bible. He had to inquire into their own beliefs before he could teach them effectively. He had to learn how they thought and present Jesus in a way they could understand.

Like other missionaries through the centuries, Paul soon found that God had left witnesses to Himself within the pagan cultures. Paul's speech to the philosophers at the Areopagus is a classic example. He found that the Athenians worshipped a multitude of deities, and that in their desire not to miss out on any blessings – even from foreign and unheard-of gods – they had an idol inscribed 'TO THE UNKNOWN GOD'. Seizing upon this title, Paul began to preach to the Athenians in the name of Jesus. He declared that Jesus was this unknown God whose blessing they should seek. He even quoted a pagan poet to illustrate what he was saying. And, as they say, the rest is history.

The New Testament

In the course of his ministry Paul wrote a number of letters to churches and individuals whom he was temporarily unable to visit in person. A collection of these letters, alongside a smaller collection of epistles from other early Christian leaders, is preserved in the New Testament (NT).

Even a cursory glance will give some appreciation of the diversity of Paul's letters and of the wealth of important issues they address. Explorations of the deepest questions of the Christian world-view gave way in a moment to earthy everyday advice and memorable passages – whether on the love of God or end-time happenings – confront the reader on every page. It is hard to remain in the apostle's company for very long without being challenged or convicted and it will strike all observant readers that these letters – with their patterns of conduct for the church, their practical, moral and spiritual guidance for the individual – are anything but dusty historical documents, their significance faded by the revolutions of 2,000 years. Paul's letters deal with universal problems – problems that will always be with us and are as relevant today as they ever were.

An important feature of Paul's writings is a stress on high moral standards. In an age of turmoil, as old boundaries were crumbling and ceremony was being laid aside, some had begun to question whether the Old Testament standards of moral conduct could still be considered relevant. It was almost inevitable that antinomianism, the rejection of moral restriction, should somewhere raise its ugly head. But the great apostle's emphatic response effectively stifled the first stirrings of error.

'Do you not know that the unrighteous will not inherit the kingdom of God? Do not be deceived, for neither fornicators, nor idolaters, nor adulterers, nor homosexuals, nor thieves, nor gluttons, nor drunkards, nor slanderers will inherit the kingdom of God' (1 Cor. 6:9–10).

This stress on morality was especially needful in view of the mission to the Gentile world, a world whose standards were far distant from the teachings of Scripture. In ages past the Greeks and Romans had followed many wise moral teachings, but by Paul's time these traditions were all but forgotten. The Roman Empire to which the gospel was proclaimed was about as debased as can be conceived. The cities teemed with prostitutes of both sexes, the plays in the theatre were full of indecency, and even leading poets wrote filth to divert the drunkards. Violence reigned supreme and the circuses were disgraced by the bloody entertainment of the gladiators, warriors who fought to the death to amuse the depraved pagans.

Once before God had swept away the wickedness of the world with a flood. In a later age He had destroyed the evils of Sodom with fire. In the days of the apostles a new fire was being kindled – the fire of the Holy Spirit. The world would again be cleansed with water, but this time it was the healing water of baptism. Paul's letters show how all people, regardless of their past actions, can begin again on the path of holiness.

In the earliest church, the sayings of Jesus were recorded only in the minds of His followers. This recollection was by no means necessarily vague, for Jesus had left the apostles with the promise that 'the Holy Spirit would remind them of all the things I have said' (Jn. 14:26). It was that same Spirit, however, who in the course of the first century moved four quite different men to commit the story of Jesus' life to paper. Their 'Gospels', like the 21 New Testament epistles, were to be a permanent guide for the church and an encapsulation for all time of the apostolic witness.

Other writers besides the four evangelists composed accounts of Jesus' life (indeed Luke reports that there were many such). But scarcely a trace remains of these early documents, while the four Gospels have spread in an infinitude of copies to every corner of the earth. They are our only source for the life of Jesus, and though none of the four evangelists makes any claim to have presented the whole of Christ's ministry – John tells us that the world itself could not contain a complete account of Jesus' sayings and deeds – the riches they hold are enough to feed the spiritual life of any believer from infancy to life's last moment.

Prior to the composition of the NT, that is, for much of the first three decades of Christian history, the church's only Scriptures were those of the Jewish OT. No doubt the favourite texts of the early preachers were those in the prophetic books which most plainly detail the ministry of the Coming One. One thinks especially of Isaiah and Zechariah. Few OT passages are more striking than Zechariah 3, and we shall take it as an example of the meanings which the early church discovered in the Jewish prophets.

Joshua the high priest stands before the Angel of the Lord (v. 1), clad in soiled garments (v. 3) and accused by Satan. Satan is rebuked for his accusations (v. 2), and the priest is then forgiven by God and dressed in clean robes (v. 4). The Angel then delivers a word from God, a promise to Israel of the coming of God's servant the Branch (v. 8). A stone with seven eyes is set before Joshua, and God promises to remove the sins of the land in one day (v. 9).

What relevance does this strange scene have to the Christian? Remember first of all that the Greek form of the name Joshua is Jesus. This was a fact that the early Christians could never forget, as they used a Greek translation of the OT. Where we read Joshua they read Jesus, just as where we read 'the Anointed' (Hebrew 'Messiah'), they read its Greek form – Christ.

In this passage Joshua stands as a symbol of Jesus, the true High Priest. Condemned on the cross, Jesus is clad in the 'soiled garments' of our sins. Satan's attempts against Him fail and Jesus is dressed in clean robes as a token of His completed work – the restoration of humankind to purity in His Father's sight. The promise of the Branch is Messianic, the Branch having long been understood as a reference to a future leader from David's house. The stone is Jesus Christ, the Rock of Ages, the capstone and the foundation. The seven eyes refer to His complete sight, or omniscience – an attribute that belongs to God alone and thus points forward to the divinity of the Messiah.

With such interpretations, the OT exploded into new life in the hands of the first Christians. It was like a jewel in the rough whose potential beauty had long been concealed. But now, in the fullness of time, it was cut by the nails of the cross at Calvary and showed a thousand new and dazzling facets, each one a unique window into the heart of God.

Each of the four Gospels has its peculiar characteristics and emphases, but it suffices to say that each Gospel contains the apostolic testimony in all its purity. Matthew and John are eyewitness accounts from two of the twelve; Mark is based upon the testimony of Peter; and though Paul did not author a Gospel, much of the substance of his teaching about the Lord is undoubtedly preserved in the Gospel of Luke, his friend and missionary colleague.

Many things prepared the way for the spread of the gospel.

The book, one of history's great inventions, first appears in the time of Christ. It was a revolutionary advance on its predecessor the scroll, both in terms of ease of use and compactness. The scroll consisted of a long piece of papyrus (a form of paper) or parchment (made from animal skins – longer lasting and more expensive than papyrus) which had to be slowly rolled between two rods. The book, by contrast, could be opened to any page immediately, and this speed and ease were important to Christians, who used books frequently and were accustomed to search Scripture at length. Scrolls, as well as being cumbersome, could not contain much information. The longest could fit little more than a single Gospel, while a book could contain all four Gospels plus the book of Acts, and some were even larger than that. They were not as efficient as modern books, however, as the ancient pages were very thick.

Strangely, most pagans continued to use the clumsy scroll for centuries. Rejecting books as a Christian novelty, they were perfectly happy to keep their literature difficult and exclusive. The Jews, to this day, use scrolls of the OT in their synagogues.

Another useful invention, shorthand writing, was probably first used a few hundred years before Christ, but did not become well known until New Testament times. This efficient form of note taking, a system of abbreviations which allowed a scribe to keep pace with the spoken word, enabled the early church to record sermons and speeches accurately.

With two further books, our New Testament was complete. The first was the Acts of the Apostles, the first church history and a sequel to Luke's Gospel. Acts is our only source for the events immediately following the ascension of Jesus. The last, the Revelation of the Apostle John, we will consider later.

The Return to Jerusalem

Paul's third missionary journey, approximately AD 53–7, was longer than either of his earlier expeditions and again concentrated on Asia Minor, Macedonia and Greece. For much of this time Paul was established in the great Asian city of Ephesus. There his ministry enjoyed such success as to spark the famous riot of the Ephesian craftsmen, who were infuriated at the threat to the market for their idolatrous shrines to Artemis (known in Rome as Diana). It was not, however, such Gentile threats which would cause the apostle most trouble in the long run. At the end of this third tour, led by an impulse of the Spirit, Paul directed his steps to Jerusalem rather than Antioch.

One stopover on Paul's journey from Greece to the Holy City was in the city of Troas. When Sunday came and the Christians congregated to celebrate communion, as they have done ever since those days, the great teacher addressed them in the evening and, since he was leaving the next day, continued his message well into the night.

Lamps and the Christian message alike shone brightly in the upstairs room, but not brightly enough to keep a young man named Eutychus awake. While Paul talked on, Eutychus felt his eyelids begin to close – an experience repeated more often than most of us would like to admit in the centuries since! – and he seated himself on a window sill in the hope that the night breeze would revive him. The sermon continued, and finally Eutychus drifted off completely. Slumping backwards, he fell three storeys to the street below. Some ran downstairs, and a loud cry went up when it was found that he was dead.

'Stand back.'

Paul took the young man in his arms and began to pray. The crowd was briefly hushed, but a moment later there were cries of joy all around.

'He's alive!'

Going back upstairs, Paul resumed his teaching and, with their brother returned to them, the congregation was greatly comforted.

Continuing on his way to Jerusalem, Paul visited a number of other congregations. Some of those he visited knew in the Spirit that trouble lay ahead in Jerusalem, and they repeatedly warned the apostle to turn back. Paul, however, was sure of the Spirit's leading. He knew that something important was in the wings and that he must obey the voice within rather than his own fears and his friends' well-meaning advice.

On arrival in Jerusalem Paul sought out James, the brother of Jesus and leader of the local church, and the other elders with him. The elders warned Paul that there was danger not only from the Jewish establishment, but that many local Christians were upset by rumours that Paul had been teaching the Jews of the Diaspora to abandon the Law. They could accept that Gentile converts were exempted from some aspects of the Law, but they could not bear an attack on the distinctive marks of their own Jewish identity.

'There are thousands of Jewish converts here, all zealous for the Law,' they said. 'It will go some way to appease them if you visit the temple and, by publicly observing our customs, show that you also respect the Law.'

Eager to avoid conflict, Paul accepted the suggestion. It was not until nearly a week had passed that trouble began.

Some visiting Jews from Asia Minor recognized Paul. In their homeland they had rejected the apostle and banned him from their synagogue on account of his preaching to the Gentiles. Now they saw him in the street – infuriatingly enough with a Gentile friend! – and later at the temple itself.

'What's this pig doing here?'

'This is the one!' one of the foreign Jews shouted to the crowd. 'This is Paul who teaches everywhere against our people, Law and temple!'

Everyone was astounded – how dare he show his face in the temple itself! Paul was dragged from the temple and beaten and would have been killed on the spot had not some soldiers been quick to the rescue.

'What on earth have you done?' asked their commander. 'Why do these people want to kill you?'

'I beg you,' said Paul, 'let me address the people.' The commander agreed, and Paul stood upon the steps of the army barracks and motioned for silence. 'Brothers and fathers, hear my defence!' When the crowd was calmed, the apostle proceeded.

Paul spoke first of his Jewish upbringing and of his involvement in the first persecution of the church. He recounted his vision on the road to Damascus, and the crowd kept quiet until he came to his last visit to Jerusalem, when the Lord had warned him to flee from the Jews. 'I will send you to the Gentiles instead.' At this they erupted into madness, tearing their clothes and throwing dust in the air.

'No!' they screamed. 'Kill him!'

The commander was amazed at the effect of Paul's words. He bid his soldiers take the apostle away and question him under a flogging so as to extract a confession of what he had done to enrage the crowd, but before the flogging could commence Paul informed his captors that he was a Roman citizen. The commander was told immediately, as it was illegal to flog a Roman without trial and he came straightaway to apologize.

Still keen to discover what had upset the Jews, the commander took Paul to the Sanhedrin the next day. He gained little for his efforts. Paul spoke to the Sanhedrin, but as soon as he mentioned the resurrection of the dead the Jews began quarrelling violently amongst themselves. The Pharisees agreed with Paul that the dead would be raised, while the Sadducees scoffed at hopes of resurrection and the commander was forced to remove Paul before the situation got completely out of hand.

The following night, Paul was encouraged by a vision. Jesus stood beside him.

'Take heart! You have witnessed for Me in Jerusalem and shall do the same in Rome.'

Certain Jews, however, decided to kill the apostle immediately, and more than forty men pledged not to eat or drink until the deed was done. With the help of the priests an ambush was prepared, but the commander learned of the plan in time and sent Paul to safety in Caesarea.

In Caesarea Paul was tried by the provincial governor, but as the Jews did not have a substantial case against him Governor Felix could find no reason to punish the apostle. Afraid of angering the Jews, however, Felix postponed his verdict indefinitely. Ironically, the apostle of the Gentiles was now a prisoner in the city of Cornelius. It is thought that Paul's companion Luke used this relatively quiet time to begin work on his Gospel and the book of Acts.

Felix, however, was intrigued by Paul, and he summoned the

apostle to tell him and his wife Drusilla, a Jewess, about the Christian faith. The governor's personal immorality was notorious – indeed he had seduced Drusilla and caused her to leave her first husband – and when Paul talked about righteousness, self-control and the coming judgement, Felix trembled and dismissed Paul (as many dismiss repentance) 'for a more opportune time'. Hoping, all the same, that the prisoner might offer a bribe to secure his release, Felix spoke with the apostle frequently over the following months. Little could he have imagined that the prisoner's faith would one day conquer the empire he served.

After two years, Felix was succeeded by Festus and the Jews (who we must imagine were more than a little hungry by now) urged the new governor to bring Paul to Jerusalem for a full trial. Again they planned to kill him on the way, but Paul escaped their scheming by using his right as a Roman citizen to appeal his case to Caesar. Under guard of a centurion named Julius, the apostle was soon on his way to the court of Nero.

ACTS 18–27

'Not One Shall Be Lost'

Paul's voyage began with a crossing from Caesarea to Myra in Asia Minor, and there Julius transferred his prisoners to an Alexandrian ship headed for Italy.

Paul's party left Myra in the middle of autumn, near the end of the accepted sailing season. Ships at sea any later were in great danger from the elements, and upon safe arrival at Fair Havens in Crete the apostle warned Julius not to sail again.

'We will suffer disaster if we continue at this time.'

But Paul's words were ignored and it was decided to sail along the coast to Phoenix, a larger port, and winter there. With the first fair wind the ship set out, but in no time the weather changed and the ship was struck by a hurricane-force wind from the island which prevented any return to harbour. The ship was blown entirely off course and its lifeboat was tossed so violently that the sailors had to heave it up on deck.

Ropes were passed under the ship to help hold the hull together during the battering it was receiving, and as conditions continued to worsen overnight and into the next day the crew was forced to take the drastic measure of throwing part of the cargo overboard to lighten the ship and make it ride higher in the water. There was little more they could do. Night fell again, and day followed day, and after more than a week without so much as a glimpse of sun or moon the men gave up all hope of survival. It was then, however, that Paul received a reassuring message. In the night an angel of God stood beside him.

'Have no fear. You will make it to Rome and every man on board will survive this storm. God has granted to your prayers the lives of them all.'

The next morning Paul told the crew of his angelic visitation.

'God has promised to spare us all, though the ship itself shall run aground on some island.'

After two full weeks, the ship came within sight of land. The sailors attempted to make their own escape in the lifeboat, but Paul warned Julius of their intention and the soldiers cast the lifeboat adrift. The ship was further lightened, and all waited with thumping hearts as the beach came closer into view, until with a mighty crash the ship struck a sandbar and the waves began tearing the stern to pieces.

'Kill the prisoners!' some of the soldiers cried. 'If any escape it is we who will be held responsible.'

'No!' Julius commanded. 'Every man for himself. Swim if you can. If not, try to get to shore on planks or pieces of the ship.'

The following moments were terrifying for everyone – especially those who had to cling for dear life to floating boards – so one can imagine the soldiers' surprise to find not a soul missing when they counted the shivering survivors on shore. Some islanders who had witnessed the dramatic shipwreck built a fire to help the people dry and warm themselves.

'The name of our island is Malta.'

Paul was soon busy gathering fuel, but as he put an armful of brushwood on the fire a snake was driven out by the heat and fastened onto his hand. The Maltese, knowing that Paul was a prisoner of the guards, shook their heads gravely.

'This man must be a murderer. He survived the storm, so Justice has sent a viper to kill him instead.'

But when Paul shook the snake off into the fire and kept working with no sign of pain, the islanders quickly changed their minds.

'Surely he is one of the gods!'

Publius, the chief man on Malta, invited the shipwreck survivors to stay with him for a few days. Publius' father lay sick with fever and dysentery and, in answer to prayer and the laying on of Paul's hands, the old man had healing from the Lord. News of the miracle spread quickly, and the sick were brought from across the island. The Maltese were amazed at this power and teaching and, until their departure three months later, on a ship that had safely wintered on Malta, the shipwreck survivors were treated with every honour.

On arrival in Rome Paul was permitted to live in his own rented house with a single guard, and after three days he invited the local Jewish leaders to meet with him.

'I have committed no crime against the customs of our people. It is only on account of my belief in God's promises to Israel that I find myself in chains.'

The leaders wanted to hear more, and a few days later a great crowd gathered at Paul's lodging for deeper discussion. Paul spent the day unfolding the gospel, and many believed and were saved. Some, however, argued bitterly against his words and stormed out when the apostle reproached them.

'The prophets predicted that many would not listen. But understand, God's salvation has gone to the Gentiles and they will listen if you will not.'

It was two years before the emperor brought Paul to trial, but for that whole time the apostle lived in peace in the great city, day by day proclaiming the saving message of Jesus Christ to all who came to him.

ACTS 27–28

James the Just

Paul's escape from Jerusalem had enraged his enemies, and his appeal to Caesar had made the situation even more bitter for the Jewish leaders. They knew that their case would be all but laughed out of the imperial court.

The high priest in Jerusalem at this time was Ananus the Sadducee, a man with a venomous hatred for the church. With Paul gone, he turned his frustration on James, leader of the local church and author of the biblical epistle of the same name. James was popular in Jerusalem, and his holiness and virtue had won him the name of 'James the Just' among Christians and Jews alike. Inspired by such as James, a steady stream of Jews was still entering the church – and this especially angered the Pharisees and Sadducees. When Festus died and the province was briefly without a governor, Ananus and his followers in the Sanhedrin moved quickly.

Ananus brought James before the Jewish court on charges of false belief. Many scribes and Pharisees joined the high priest, but when other leading Jews stood against them and the case became bogged down in debate, Ananus determined on more swift and violent measures.

'Arrest James,' he commanded his followers, 'and bring him to the temple.'

While the command was executed, Ananus summoned an assembly and thousands of Jews were soon crowded beneath the temple wall. Ananus' followers arrived with their captive, and the high priest had them take James to the temple's pinnacle that he might be questioned in full view of the people. Ananus hoped to intimidate the Christian leader into denying his Lord – and with one blow to destroy James' reputation and put Christ's name to public disgrace. It was a foolish hope.

'James,' one of the scribes cried, 'many of our people have gone astray after Jesus the crucified. It is for you, Just One, to declare the truth about this Jesus of whom we hear such foolish talk, that the people might come back to their senses.'

James did not hesitate a moment.

'Friends,' he shouted to the crowd, 'why need anyone ask? Even now Jesus is seated at the side of His Father's throne and He shall soon come again on the clouds of heaven!'

With these bold words, many of the gathered Jews opened their hearts to the Spirit's call. Men and women who had wavered over their response to the gospel now raised their hands in praise to God and almost in salute to James.

'Hosanna to the Son of David!'

The chorus of approving voices was soon drowned out by furious cries from the scribes and Pharisees.

'What have we done?'

Those who had taken James up on the temple began to abuse him.

'Cast him down!' cried the scribes. 'Cast him down that none might dare accept his testimony!'

Some charged at the lone figure, and beating James in the back they knocked him down from the pinnacle.

'So,' they cried, 'even the just man is in error!'

James survived the fall, and when the Pharisees in the crowd saw him lifting himself up they formed a circle and began to stone him. As James got onto his knees, all the while praying forgiveness for his foes, some in the crowd began to abuse the Pharisees.

'Stop! Can't you see that this good man is praying for you?'

But their words were wasted on such men, and one now pushed his way to the fore and struck James dead with a club. One of the church's leading lights was thus extinguished, but James' bold last testimony had imparted the eternal flame of the Spirit to the hearts of hundreds of witnesses.

The violence against James was only the smallest taste of the trouble that was about to come upon the church. There were difficult times ahead – not only for the Christians, but for their Jewish persecutors as well.

EUSEBIUS, *CH* 2.23

Emperor Nero

After two years of patient waiting, the Apostle Paul was released from his Roman detention. It is not certain whether the Jews even dared to bring their false charges to court when the day came, so it is unclear whether Paul was formally acquitted or whether his case was abandoned without trial. Paul spent the next few years on a fourth missionary journey, before he finally returned to Rome itself. Peter was also settled in Rome at this time, and the imperial capital was for a while blessed with the ministry of the two greatest apostles.

There could hardly have been a less inviting place than the Rome that the apostles made their home. Emperor Nero was a monstrosity of evil, hated by his people, and his city was balanced on a knife-edge, dreading equally the continuation of his reign or the turmoil of a revolution against him.

Claudius had preceded Nero on the imperial throne. Married four times, lastly (in violation of Roman custom) to his niece Agrippina, Claudius' reign was disgraced by corruption and violence. Claudius and Agrippina had no children together, but each had a son from a previous marriage – Britannicus and Nero respectively. Agrippina eventually duped Claudius into making her own son official heir to the throne, and this done she promptly poisoned her husband and established Nero in his place.

Claudius may have been a fool, but he was nothing compared to his stepson. Nero is remembered as one of history's most vicious rulers, and one of his first crimes was the murder of Britannicus. He was jealous of his half-brother, the son and rightful heir of Claudius, and he feared that Britannicus, now only thirteen, would become a rival in later years. So Nero determined to rid himself of the threat sooner rather than later.

The Roman nobility had reduced poisoning to a fine art and, wisely suspicious of his imperial brother, Britannicus was accustomed to have a trustworthy servant test all of his food and drink. Even this precaution, however, proved inadequate. At a banquet, Britannicus was served a harmless hot drink. It was tasted for him, but when the youth complained of its temperature an imperial slave added a little cool 'water' and Nero watched with glee as the cup was drained without a second test. Britannicus threw his head back, shook violently, and then stopped breathing altogether.

'Don't worry, it's only an epileptic fit you know,' Nero said with a grin. 'He'll be all right in a minute.'

Everyone else at the table was speechless. They were too intimidated by Nero's presence to do anything, and after a few moments they resumed the meal as though nothing had happened.

Such a crime was nothing unusual for the emperor. Nero's evenings were spent in wild drunken parties, which often ended with the imperial entourage disguising themselves as slaves and going out on the town. They would visit brothels and taverns incognito, before proceeding to ransack shops and beat and rob unwary citizens. Rumours of Nero's conduct spread widely and made the situation even worse, for many other pagans formed their own hoodlum bands and took to the streets in imitation. By night Rome was little better than a war zone, and few dared stop thieves for fear that they might find themselves laying hands on the emperor! This, indeed, was the fate of one Roman senator, who struck back violently when assaulted in a dark street, but in the course of the ensuing scuffle learned his mistake.

'My apologies,' he gasped, dropping his fists. 'I had no idea it was you, my emperor!'

It was a bad move. Nero was quite happy to get into an anonymous brawl in the course of his depredations, and he had often returned home with minor wounds, but an apology he took as a slur on his character(!) and later ordered the senator to commit suicide. Thereafter Nero took more care, and while out and about would keep a contingent of soldiers or gladiators on hand for immediate action. Their orders were to stand back if the fights were fairly even, but to hasten to the rescue if Nero got the worst of it. Such was the society in which the earliest Christian missionaries worked.

Agrippina, no better than her son, was soon seeking a means to dispose of him and rule the empire for herself. Nero, aware of her scheming, was no less anxious to rid himself of this blackest of widows. The first five years of Nero's reign were absorbed in plot and counterplot, though in public the imperial mother and son always pretended to friendship. Both were cautious, and each provided the other with many frustrations. Indeed Agrippina, fearing the poisoned cup that had done away with both her husband and stepson, had for years taken small regular doses of the most common poisons, thus building up a high degree of immunity to their effects.

Such a tragic and brutal cat and mouse game could not last forever, and the final play was Nero's. After making a show of reconciliation and forgiveness, he arranged a night-time boat-trip for his mother on the Lucrine Lake. The vessel was sabotaged so as to sink mid-stream, and a number of Nero's cronies were on board. But, in the final moment, just as the boat went under, the plan was thwarted by one of Agrippina's servants. Hoping to be rescued first and knowing that the dark would disguise her, the girl started to scream:

'Over here! Help! I am Agrippina – the emperor's mother!'

Nero's cronies soon came for her, but instead of pulling her to safety they beat her to death with a couple of oars. Agrippina saw the servant's fate and, realizing that it was intended for her, she swam to safety on her own. Nero soon heard of his mother's narrow escape and in shock abandoned his secret plotting. Instead he openly sent orders, and at his command Agrippina was executed with the sword.

If anything could make Nero worse, this was it. Until now he had committed most of his obscenities in private, or disguise, and had often been restrained by Seneca and Burrus, his chief advisors. Now, however, torn with guilt for his mother's murder, he went right over the edge and became so hideous that many said the earlier years of his reign had been happy ones! Some of his closest friends fell victims to his malice, as did both of the women who shared his throne. Octavia, his first wife, was suffocated and beheaded, and her head brought on a platter to

Poppaea, her cruel replacement. Poppaea herself was reserved for an equally cruel fate and three years later, heavily pregnant, was fatally kicked by Nero. All Rome trembled at the sight of a ruler without affection or restraint.

At about this time, a strange sign made the people of Rome even more troubled. Eight hundred years before the reign of Nero, the city of Rome had been founded by Romulus. Roman lore told how, in infancy, Romulus and his brother Remus had been left lying in the shade of a certain fig tree. This ancient fig was sacred to the Romans, so its sudden and unexpected death at this time was taken as a dark portent. Some declared that it foreshadowed the destruction of the city itself, but when fresh shoots grew from the dead stump soon afterwards new questions arose.

'What does it mean?' people asked. 'Will Rome fall and be born again?'

No doubt the apostles could have told them. While Nero and his people were descending ever further into earthly hell, the apostles were leading all who would listen into a new life.

By now Nero was completely crazed, and he was soon as much despised as he was feared. He broke all traditions of the empire and began competing in the public chariot races, an occupation usually left to slaves, and giving concert tours as a minstrel. Singing and playing the lyre, with insane delight he would drink in the cheers of the mob and the polite but forced applause of the senate and nobility. Progressing from the contemptible to the bizarre, he next established a 'pleasure' zone within an imperial park on the outskirts of the city. Drinking-houses and brothels were constructed, and rich and poor alike were invited to engage in every conceivable species of sin. Hundreds participated in grotesque outdoor orgies.

Even so, Nero's perversity was not satisfied. And, as though determined to show that his evil imagination was not yet exhausted, the emperor next announced his betrothal – to a man! Dressed as a bride and occasionally lifting his veil to peep out at the audience from heavily made-up eyes, the emperor was married with the full traditional service. The Romans had long accepted homosexuality, but even they had never before contemplated the revolting spectacle of such a marriage. But there was more to come.

'Fire, fire, fire!'

This scream was soon ringing out all over the city, as great bursts of flame reduced whole streets to ashes. Nothing could stop this 'Great Fire of Rome', which raged for an entire week and left only ruins behind it. The Romans were stunned, reeling under what they knew must be a divine punishment, until in the chaos of the succeeding days the city was stung into action by a startling rumour.

'The emperor burned Rome!'

'That's right! Hasn't he committed just about every other evil imaginable?'

'I saw Nero watching the fire from his balcony, clapping and laughing!'

'I saw him plucking the lyre, dancing and singing while the fire raged!'

'Nero sent his soldiers to destroy the city. He wants to build a new city and name it after himself!'

The infuriated Romans were soon filling the streets with their cries.

'Down with the emperor!'

Nero was terrified. If he wanted to keep his life and throne, he must find a scapegoat quickly. Who could he blame for the fire?

TACITUS, *ANNALS* 12–15

The First Roman Persecution

It was during this emergency that Nero took one of the most momentous steps in history.

'My hands are clean!' he declared. 'The Christians burned the city!'

And, so saying, Nero became the first emperor to persecute the church. For this his name will never be forgotten – he will always be ranked as one of history's greatest fiends. Perhaps only the names of Herod and Judas Iscariot ring with the same evil suggestions.

'Out with the soldiers, hunt them down!' he commanded. 'We must exterminate them immediately. Death to the incendiaries!'

All Rome knew who the Christians were, and the apostles and their followers had won many souls in the city. It was well known that the Christians didn't believe in the pagan 'gods', and this lent some credence to Nero's words.

'Maybe these strange people actually did burn Rome. They certainly appear to be enemies of our temples and gods.'

Hundreds of Christians were arrested. Some were executed in the Circus, while the majority were taken to Nero's personal gardens to be part of a theatrical display. The Apostle Peter was among them.

At first the believers felt fear and panic but, strangely enough, these violent emotions were calmed when it became clear that there was absolutely no hope of escape or release. The church had long known that a time of testing was at hand, and the Roman believers soon saw that it was to be their lot to take the first draught from the bitter cup. Prayers for deliverance died out, and a new and striking prayer came to birth.

'Lord, make our deaths life to those around us. Give us strength for the battle, that we might conquer fear and show the power of Your name to our enemies. Lord forgive them – let our suffering lead them to You!'

We can only imagine that Peter stood forth amongst his brethren with words similar to those of his first epistle, an epistle written only a few years before this event.

'Live virtuously among the pagans, so that although they accuse you as criminals, they may see your good deeds and glorify God on the day He visits us. Submit to every human authority, whether the emperor or his governors, for the Lord's sake. God's will is that by doing good you should silence the scoffing of fools' (1 Pet. 2:12–15). '. . . if you suffer for doing right you will be blessed' (1 Pet. 3:14).

The scene in Nero's garden can scarcely be imagined. Some of the Christians were tied to posts and set alight as torches, while others were dressed in the bloody skins of slaughtered beasts and thrown to a pack of savage hounds. The crazed pagans clapped and cheered at each new torment, and the emperor himself mounted a chariot and dashed here and there amongst the victims, making theatrical bows and egging the audience on to greater bloodlust.

Such sights, sadly, were nothing new in pagan Rome. The gruesome entertainment of the Circus was the favourite pastime of the imperial city, and the Roman people had long been accustomed to drawing amusement from human sufferings. In a single day, hundreds of gladiators might enter the ring to entertain the masses with their mutual slaughter. The spectacles of the Roman Circus are just one more nightmare from which Christianity has woken the world.

Gladiators were usually either slaves, prisoners of war, or condemned criminals, and they were intensively trained before entering the arena to ensure the most amusing display possible. Every precaution was taken to prevent the escape or suicide of inmates of the training camps.

Seventy years before the birth of Christ, the Romans paid a heavy price for their bloodthirsty pleasures. Seventy gladiators escaped from the training school and, led by Spartacus, began an uprising against their conquerors. The numberless slaves of the Roman citizens took their side and the rebels soon had an army of some seventy thousand.

In a series of battles with the Roman armies, the desperate bravery of the rebels prevailed. They pillaged and plundered the Romans and even forced some of their captives to entertain them with gladiatorial displays. It was three years before the rebels were finally subdued, and by the time this self-inflicted and well-deserved revolution was at an end, many thousands of Romans were dead. The saddest fact of all is that the Romans had not learned their lesson, and the cruel spectacles of the Circus continued just as before.

On this occasion, however, the entertainment in Nero's gardens went somewhat awry. Instead of dreadful groans and curses filling the air, there was an eerie calm amongst the emperor's victims. The crowd eventually became quite subdued, listening with surprise to the martyrs' cries.

'Lord forgive them!'

Nero himself was unnerved. The fiercer the punishments he unleashed upon the Christians, the more fervent became their prayers for his salvation!

'They believe in Jesus the Crucified, do they?' he cried. 'Then crucify the rest of them!'

And so the afternoon and evening of shame and glory came to an end. Peter was amongst the crucified, and tradition says that he was nailed upside-down to the cross.

Hundreds had perished, but Nero's plan had nevertheless been quietly but completely thwarted. The patient and prayerful sufferings of the Christians had moved the hearts of many Romans, and few could now believe them guilty of burning the city to the ground. The crowd returned to their homes that evening with much to think about. Many felt sympathy for the innocent victims and even greater hatred for Emperor Nero.

Christians across the empire had much to think about as well. The church was entering a new stage. The horror in Nero's garden emboldened many enemies of the church to afflict their own Christian neighbours, and in several areas there were small-scale outbursts of anti-Christian mob violence. Calm returned a little more than a year later, but things would never be quite the same again after this first shedding of blood.

Before the situation improved, however, the persecution claimed the life of the Apostle Paul. For some reason Paul had not been arrested along with the rest of the Roman church – he was probably not in the city at the time, but some months later he was imprisoned and beheaded at Rome by command of Nero. His last epistle, 2 Timothy, was written from the depths of a Roman dungeon in the last months of his earthly life.

Nero did not live long to boast of his crimes. He had lost all favour with his subjects, and when a rebel faction acclaimed the governor of Nearer Spain, Galba, as emperor, Nero saw even his own city welcome the revolution. Fearing for his life, Nero fled to a friend's villa about four miles out of town.

Nero soon saw the impossibility of his situation. Cowering in a corner and knowing that his crimes had caught up with him and that his executioners would soon be at the door, Emperor Nero committed suicide.

With Nero gone, the church could breathe a little easier. The empire was thrown into bloody civil wars, as though it was being punished for the violence against the Christians, but the church had peace – or at least as much of that precious commodity as was possible in such times. And, day by day, her numbers continued to grow.

The Jews were far from sharing this peace with the Christians. Jerusalem, the birthplace of the gospel, now started feeling the effects of having rejected the Saviour – the Saviour of Israel and of the whole world.

EUSEBIUS, CH 2.25

Signs of the End

It was only a few months after the murder of James the Just, while the Jewish feast of Tabernacles was being celebrated in Jerusalem, that the assembled people were greatly startled by the words of a simple farmer named Jesus. 'Jesus', incidentally, was a common name among the Jews – it is a Greek form of the Hebrew name *Y'shua*, our Joshua.

While visiting the temple Jesus was seized with a fit of trembling, and his face became dark as he began to cry out in a powerful voice:

'A voice from the east, a voice from the west, a voice from the four winds! A voice against Jerusalem and the holy house, a voice against the bridegrooms and the brides and a voice against this whole people!'

Jesus' friends and relatives tried to calm him, but the 'prophet' burst away from them and ran out of the temple. Crying the same words over and again, he charged through the streets of the ancient city, and for days his startling pronouncement rang incessantly in every quarter of Jerusalem.

At that time the Jews seemed to be well off, and they were enjoying a time of relative peace with the Romans. All the same, this strange happening made many in the city uneasy. It was as though the Jews knew that something was wrong, that a pall of guilt hung over them and that soon there would be a price to pay. As Jesus the Wailer wandered the streets, forever repeating the same cry, the people could not help but be shaken.

So things continued for some months. At festivals the Wailer made himself especially unpopular, for then he would cry out even more loudly than usual. Some of the Jewish leaders had him arrested and flogged, but finding Jesus impervious to their blows they took him to Governor Albinus. The governor ordered that Jesus be flogged until he explained the reason for his actions, but this proved to be impossible. The Wailer was whipped until his back was torn open and his bones laid bare, but with every stripe he made the same cry, 'Woe, woe to Jerusalem!', until finally it was Albinus who gave in. Convinced that Jesus was a madman, the governor ordered his release.

Some of the people believed the Wailer a true prophet and gave him food as he walked the streets. Others struck and abused him, but it made no difference to Jesus. He responded to everyone in the same way, never ceasing to utter his cry.

Other signs soon followed – signs just as ominous. First was a strange star, which appeared in the night-time sky for a whole year. It looked, the people said, like a sword hanging over the city. Later, at the time of Passover, the huge brass gate of the temple's inner court, which normally needed 20 men to move it, was seen to open slowly on its own. The scribes were terrified.

'What does this mean?' they asked. 'Shall God "open" this temple and hand it to our foes?'

But the strangest things of all were yet to come. One evening, near sunset, the whole city came to a standstill. The people were amazed as they stared into the sky. Above the city they saw a vision of the heavenly armies, like those shown to Elisha's servant (2 Kgs. 6), but these heavenly armies were attacking rather than defending them. Then at Pentecost, while the priests offered the evening sacrifice, the temple was shaken and those present froze with fear. A loud noise echoed through the temple and a chorus of voices was heard from above – a sound as of a great multitude roaring in disgust, 'Let us leave this place!'

Was the city of the Jews now forsaken by God?

JOSEPHUS, WAR 6.5

The Jewish War

The worst sign of all was yet to come. It was not a wonder like these, but the appointment of a new governor. Albinus had finished his term in office and the Romans had sent Gessius Florus to replace him.

Earlier governors had been no strangers to corruption and cruelty, but the Jews soon found that Florus far surpassed them all. The new governor was no sooner established in power than the people began to feel his heavy hand upon their purses. Indeed Florus' energies seemed to be wholly directed towards increasing his own wealth through theft and extortion, and within weeks he had made his name an object of hatred throughout the nation. Rich and poor alike suffered under his rule, and many of the wealthier citizens, preferring exile to poverty, fled the province.

The Jews had always had an uneasy relationship with their Roman governors. They resented being ruled by these 'unclean' Gentiles, and conduct such as Florus' only further fanned the flames of their injured pride. For two years they were pushed and provoked, until finally Florus did something that no Jew could suffer in silence. Thieving eyes were turned upon the sacred centre of the nation, and with brazen-faced arrogance Florus ordered his men to remove 17 talents of silver from the temple treasury.

This was simply too much for the people of Jerusalem to bear, and many went up to the temple in tears, praying for deliverance from their governor. The more rebellious began stirring up the people, publicly mocking and insulting the foe. Some went about with a beggar's bowl.

'We are collecting for Governor Florus,' they scoffed. 'The poor old dog obviously has no possessions of his own. Why else would he need to steal for a living?'

Florus could have let the brief protest blow over, but his enormous pride was deeply scarred by such insults and jests. He marched on Jerusalem with a large body of soldiers, and the people were startled to hear that their peaceful complaints had evoked such an ominous response. The Jews gathered in the streets to meet the army with a show of respect and submission, but Florus sent a messenger ahead of him, ordering everyone to return to their houses.

'Do not pretend to friendship with the one you have so foully reproached. You are free speakers and men of mighty jests when hidden in a corner! I dare you now to insult me to my face and prove your worth in the field with the weapons of war!'

The Jews were astounded, and with great trepidation the welcoming party broke up and left the streets empty for the arrival of the Romans. On the following morning Florus ordered the leading citizens to appear before him.

'Bring me all of the culprits in the recent unrest,' he said. 'Do it immediately, or the punishment due to them shall be yours.'

'Governor Florus,' the leaders exclaimed, 'look about you and see that the people are peaceably disposed towards you! Do not be surprised that occasionally some young hothead speaks out of order. It is impossible for us to distinguish the innocent from the guilty, since none will own up to the actions for fear of punishment. It is rather for you to forgive and maintain the peace, than to cause turmoil by searching out a handful of offenders!'

Florus was enraged by these reasonable words.

'If you defend my foes,' he said, 'I shall count you amongst them!'

With that he unleashed his soldiers, sending them on a rampage through the city markets. Hundreds perished in the bloodbath, and Florus had a number of the elders flogged and crucified.

'We are Roman citizens!' some of the elders cried.

'Not in my court!' Florus shouted over them. 'First show respect for your masters, and then we can talk about the law!'

The peace of Jerusalem hung by a thread for the next few

weeks. Florus provoked the Jews in every way possible, and each time he did so they responded with greater rebelliousness. It was a vicious circle, for the more rebellious the Jews, the more violently Florus ordered his soldiers to crush them. Finally a bloody battle broke out in the streets, and the desperate valour of the Jews forced Florus and most of his troops to flee the city. War had begun!

Florus was gone, but a small but dangerous Roman force still remained in Jerusalem, safely shut up within the towers of Herod's palace. A group of Jewish leaders, led by the high priest Ananias, began urging an immediate surrender.

'Stop the fighting before we reach the point of no return. At all costs we must avoid a full-scale war which we cannot possibly win!'

Such words fell on deaf ears, and the leaders of the rebellion soon made it clear that they would not tolerate any opposition to their plans. Some even began to speak of cleansing the city of the 'friends of Rome'. Ananias saw the danger to himself, and the next day no one could find him. The high priest, along with his brother, had gone into hiding in the drains and waterways under the city.

The rebellion spread rapidly through the country. The Jews, tired of subjection to the Romans, were swift to enlist in the rebel cause and several small armies were soon stationed in strategic positions. Jerusalem, of course, was the most important place to defend, and the rebel leaders made a bloodthirsty plan to secure their Holy City.

The rebels did away first with their Jewish opponents. Ananias was among those targeted, and the high priest was soon discovered in the aqueducts and dragged forth to be executed. Messengers were next sent to the Roman soldiers in Herod's palace.

'If you will leave our city immediately we pledge ourselves not to harm you on your departure. Hand over your weapons and you may leave Jerusalem in peace.'

This was too good an offer for the Romans to refuse. Their food supplies were short, and they were greatly outnumbered by the rebels.

'We agree to your terms.'

The Sabbath day was appointed for the surrender, and the Jewish rebels stood by quietly as the soldiers marched from the palace gates, their weapons held in outstretched hands as a sign of submission. The Romans laid down their weapons, but in the instant that they stepped back from them the Jews charged forward with a fearsome scream.

'Don't leave a man alive!'

They didn't – and with this evil and bloody deception Jerusalem was free from the Romans.

It did not, however, appear that this would long be the case. A legion was already on its way from Syria, and in spite of spirited Jewish resistance the Romans were soon in possession of the countryside around Jerusalem itself. The Romans began undermining the city wall, and the rebels were startled to find themselves already on the verge of total defeat. If the Romans could bring the wall down the rebellion would be at an end – but at the very last moment the completely unexpected occurred.

'Retreat!' ordered Cestius, commander of the Roman legion.

Retreat?

Amazingly enough, just when the rebels' plight was becoming desperate, the Romans raised camp and marched away from Jerusalem. The rebels were overjoyed. Was this God's work? Was He going to free them from foreign rule? The retreating Romans were pursued with great slaughter, and an elated Jerusalem was soon strengthening defences in preparation for the next attack.

'We shall crush the Romans!'

But not everyone shared the same enthusiasm.

'We have received a message from the Lord.'

There were still many Christians in Jerusalem, and at this time several men of their congregation became filled with the spirit of prophecy and simultaneously received the same message.

'Flee Jerusalem! God has driven the Romans away to enable us to escape without danger!'

This message opened the minds of the local congregation to

fully appreciate the words of Christ, words pronounced some 35 years earlier.

'When you see Jerusalem surrounded by armies, then you will know that her end is near. Flee the city, for these are the days of vengeance' (Lk. 21:20–22).

Those had been Jesus' words, and the church of Jerusalem was not now going to ignore the advice of her merciful Lord.

It was now one generation, more than three decades, since the Jews had invited God's wrath through the rejection of Jesus Christ. The divine judgement had not been unleashed immediately, and the nation had been granted a long season of repentance – an opportunity to turn with tears to the One they had pierced. Christ's followers had taken the gospel to their Jewish brothers throughout Jerusalem and Judea, and in the power of the Spirit had endeavoured to turn them from destruction. Through scorn and persecution they had persisted, and ultimately their work had borne great fruit. Now, however, after more than thirty years of the Jewish people streaming into the kingdom of God, the number of those called in Judea seemed to be nearing its completion. The outrage against James the Just was the beginning of the end. The hard-hearted people were now being deserted, and their nation itself was going to disappear.

The whole Christian community left Jerusalem. They went east, down to the Jordan, crossed the river and moved on to Pella. Pella was a Gentile town, largely unaffected by the Jewish war, and for the next few years the Christians lived there in peace, praising God for their deliverance. The light of Christ had now abandoned Jerusalem. God had left his ungrateful children to their fate, and the end did not long delay.

JOSEPHUS, *WAR* 2.14–19; EUSEBIUS, *CH* 3.5

The Death of Israel

The rebels made preparations for the coming hostilities throughout the country, and several armies were soon equipped and stationed in expectation of Roman attack. Josephus led the force sent to Galilee, and it was this man and his troops who had to face the first assault of the returning Roman army. They were not long waiting. Vespasian, one of the greatest Roman generals, soon appeared in Galilee at the head of a Roman army some 60,000 strong.

The Jews were utterly unable to take the field against such a force, and Vespasian's march through Galilee met only a shadow of resistance. The terrified Jews fled before the Romans, and soon the only places left to them were a few fortresses. Jotapata, the chief of these fortresses, now sheltered Josephus himself and the bulk of his army.

Unwilling to continue southward without first crushing the frontier forces, Vespasian immediately turned his attention to the capture of Jotapata. He sent a division ahead to surround the fort and prevent escape, and he soon followed in person with the remainder of his army. Jotapata was completely cut off, and the Jews saw that they must conquer or perish.

For several days there were skirmishes outside the fort walls. The Romans were unable to breach the Jewish defences, and the desperation of the Jews made them a formidable opponent. Each day the Jews came forth to fight outside the city, and each evening they retreated to safety. Vespasian soon tired of this drawn-out resistance.

'We must raise the level of the ground outside one of the walls, to enable us to scale it more easily. For that we will need archers and slingers, as well as some heavy catapults, to force the Jews off the wall while our men work below.'

The Romans set to work, and though many were killed laying stones and turf at the base of the wall, the mound slowly grew nonetheless. Forced to find a counter, Josephus ordered his men to raise the height of the wall. They put a shield of ox hides in place to enable the builders to work under the Roman bombardment. Vespasian's mound was soon dwarfed and rendered useless, but the general's frustration was lessened by the certainty that the Jews in Jotapata were in a dire situation.

'They will run out of supplies soon enough.'

Josephus was worried. There was food for the present, but the rebels were extremely short on water. An awareness of this spurred the Romans to attack all the more vigorously.

'They are nearly ours!'

Nearly . . . but, on the verge of defeat, the Jewish commander came up with a strategy to delay the inevitable.

'We must give our clothes a good washing.'

'What? There is hardly enough water to soak our dry tongues!'

'Just do it. I have a plan!'

Imagine the consternation of the Romans to see the Jews drying their washing on the fort wall – water streaming down in dozens of channels from the sopping garments. Obviously the Jews had no shortage of water!

'Now take these fleeces,' said Josephus, 'put them on your backs like this – and . . .'

That night a group of 'sheep' crept down the mountain from the fort, to return a few hours later with water and other supplies! A great success – but it was not long before the Romans perceived the ruse and ensured that none pulled the wool over their eyes again. With this last avenue of supply cut off, Jotapata was doomed and the rebels were soon exhausted. One of their number deserted to the Romans, and from him Vespasian learned the real state of affairs.

'The men are so fatigued that those on night watch can't even stay awake anymore.'

With this information Vespasian's son Titus took a small band of men to the city wall in the middle of the night. Quiet as cats they scaled the wall, swiftly dealt with the sleeping watch, and then signalled for the army to follow.

As the sun rose the fort was filled with Romans, but the slumbering Jews were oblivious to their danger. Even those who had risen early were none the wiser, as a strange fog had filled the fort. All were astounded to hear a blood curdling war cry issuing from the misty streets.

'Death to the Jewish rebels!'

The long-frustrated Romans attacked without mercy, and

within a few hours the rebel army was destroyed. The only
survivors were 40 Jewish leaders, among them Josephus, who
had hidden themselves in a cave. There was no chance of escape
for these men, and the Romans discovered their hiding place a
few days after the massacre.

'Is the Jewish commander Josephus amongst you?' a Roman
soldier called into the cave. 'If Josephus surrenders immediately
he will be spared. Vespasian wishes to meet him.'

'I am here,' Josephus answered. 'I shall do as you say.'

The other leaders were furious.

'How dare you surrender to the Romans! We are in this
together.'

'You are a coward!' said another. 'Take my sword and kill
yourself. Die like a man!'

Josephus saw that there was now a greater danger from his
fellow Jews than from the Romans.

'All right,' he said, 'let us end our lives now, as free men, each
struck down by his equal. We can cast lots to determine who
should kill whom. One by one we will die, until none is left to
fall into the hands of the Gentiles.'

All agreed, and each in turn offered his neck to his neighbour!
A macabre scene indeed, and the blood flowed without cease
until only two remained. One was Josephus.

'What about you,' he asked the other survivor, 'do you want
to die as well? I say we give ourselves up instead.'

The other man agreed, and both left the cave and went over
to the Romans.

Strangely, the Jewish general had been preserved for a special
purpose. As a leader and then as a prisoner of the Romans,
Josephus experienced at first-hand the whole course of the war,
and some years after his release he committed to paper a history of
the period. Without Josephus' testimony we would know little of
the suffering of the Jews at this time – nearly everything in these
chapters comes straight from his work. Only his writings preserve
the details of the divine rejection and punishment of Israel –
information of vital significance to the church, deepening as it does
our understanding of God's ways with His unrepentant people.

With Galilee back under Roman control, the Romans were soon ready for the march south to Jerusalem. Reports coming in from that city, however, told Vespasian that there was no great reason to hurry. Jerusalem was already at war with itself.

'The war is being lost through incompetence!' cried John of Giscala. 'We have nothing to fear from the Romans – not if they sprouted wings could they cross the walls of Jerusalem! – but without a change of leaders, our cause is hopeless!'

The destruction of Galilee had deeply shocked the Jerusalem rebels, and many now wished to see a change in the leadership. John of Giscala was soon at the head of a large faction known as the Zealots, but when he found himself unable to wrest control of the city from the established leaders, he sent a plea for aid to the Idumeans. The Idumeans were descendants of Esau, the Edomites of the Old Testament.

An Idumean army soon arrived at the gates of Jerusalem, but the Jewish leaders, suspecting their purpose, refused to admit them. Infuriated, the Idumeans made camp in the valley below and awaited an opportunity for revenge. The next day brought a violent storm, and when night fell the Zealots seized their chance. Thunder and rain deafened the city to their activity, as they hastily cut through the thick bars of one of Jerusalem's gates. The Idumeans were invited into the city, and the united forces went on a bloody rampage. No one was safe. The people of Jerusalem were robbed and killed without mercy, and the Jewish leaders in particular were hunted down and slaughtered. The Zealots were now masters of Jerusalem.

When news of the Jewish troubles came through to Vespasian, some advised the Roman general to attack straightaway.

'Why?' asked Vespasian. 'Let them kill each other a while longer yet!'

The Romans proceeded to capture a number of smaller Jewish strongholds, but when Vespasian finally decided that it was time to march on the capital, providence stopped him yet again. Word arrived of the death of Emperor Nero, and it was soon followed by reports of the civil wars that were tearing

Rome apart. A succession of hopefuls had risen to clutch at the imperial power but, as the Roman army heard in gruesome detail, none was able to firmly establish himself as Nero's successor. The loyal troops of Vespasian decided upon their own solution.

'Emperor Vespasian!'

The general was not inclined to disappoint his supporters, and taking part of his army he hastened to Rome to enforce his claim. His son Titus was left to finish the work in Israel, and that valiant young man marched on Jerusalem immediately. When the Romans arrived at the centre of the rebellion they found a weary city already on the brink of disaster.

The Jerusalem rebels were now split into three rival gangs, and every day saw savage battles fought between them in the streets and squares. Jerusalem was a very strong city, one that had repeatedly proved easy to defend, but no city is strong if there is war both inside and outside its walls. Jerusalem had a huge store of food and the Jews should never have been troubled by famine even under the longest siege, but in one day of insane and suicidal violence the three gangs managed to burn up the whole grain stockpile. Clearly they were more concerned about harming their enemies than helping themselves. How much easier it would have been if the nation had followed the Man who said, 'Love your neighbour as yourself.'

It was now all of seven years since Jesus the Wailer had first brought his message of destruction to the rebellious people. His words now nearing fulfilment, this strange character daily addressed the citizens from the top of the city wall.

'Woe to this city! Woe to the people! Woe to the Holy House!' he would cry.

For some reason no one dared touch the messenger and so he continued, until the very last days of the siege, when for one moment his message varied: 'Woe to myself also!' And with those words he was struck and killed by a stone from a Roman catapult.

Now that the food supplies were almost gone the rival gangs became even more unbearable. Each day there were riots in the streets, with the Zealots kicking down doors and breaking into any house where they guessed there might be some food. Those caught eating in secret were robbed of their food and beaten or killed; the discovery of so much as a handful of hidden flour could mean death to the unfortunate housewife! The people were soon so famished that they would fill their stomachs with absolutely anything. Hay, leather straps and bits of cloth became top of the menu items, and some turned to cannibalism in their desperation. The streets were full of dead bodies – some murdered, more famished – and the rebels were soon completely unable to resist their attackers. One of the worst famines known to history came to an end when Titus' men came crashing through the broken city walls.

'Jerusalem is ours!'

The Jewish temple was the first victim of the storming of the city. It caught fire accidentally, and although Titus tried to save it the flames proved unstoppable. Deserted by its God, the Jerusalem temple disappeared in AD 70 and has not been rebuilt to this day.

The rebels were soon totally crushed. Tens of thousands were put to the sword, Jerusalem itself was destroyed, and not a single building was left standing. The victorious Romans left only a smouldering ruin behind them, and after selling most of the Jewish survivors into slavery they moved off to hunt down the few remaining rebels who were sheltered in various forts in the south of the land. Masada was the last of these fortresses to fall, and when the Romans finally entered it in triumph they were horrified to find not a single living person inside. Like the Jewish elders in Josephus' cave, the desperate and fanatical rebels had killed their own families and then themselves. With this cruel and repulsive act of murder and suicide the Jewish rebellion was over and the nation itself was all but annihilated.

JOSEPHUS, *WAR* 3–7

The King, the Flies and the Calluses

Following the conquest of Jerusalem the new Roman emperor, Vespasian, commanded that all descendants of the ancient

Jewish king David should be hunted down. Vespasian feared another war with the Jews and thought a member of David's house, claiming to be the Messiah, would be the most likely leader of renewed hostilities. The Jews who had rejected Jesus were still waiting for the Messiah and were sure that he would be like themselves – a bloodthirsty rebel against the Romans! Vespasian had seen enough of their fanaticism not to take any risks.

The years following Jerusalem's fall were crushingly hard for Jews throughout the empire, but for the church these years were comparatively fruitful and happy. Vespasian reigned ten years and his son Titus followed him to the throne. When Titus died young, however, having reigned only two years, his brother Domitian succeeded him and affairs took a turn for the worse.

Domitian ranks among the very worst emperors to disgrace the Roman throne. He had a severe personality disorder, and throughout his life he drew his greatest amusements from the sufferings of others. Indeed no pain was so contemptible that Domitian could not derive some pleasure from observing it, and when there were no enemies on the torture rack the emperor satisfied his passion by catching flies and piercing them with a sharp pen!

Domitian suffered from extreme paranoia, living with a constant fear that people were out to get him. Many were executed for no reason, falsely accused by the cruel imperial coward of plotting against the government. Domitian, like his father years before, commanded the arrest of all descendants of David. And, on learning that Christians pledged allegiance to a King named Christ, he ordered their arrest as well.

Jude, the brother of Christ and author of the New Testament epistle, was, of course, a descendant of David. Jude had already passed away, but two of his grandsons were now arrested and brought before the emperor. They were descended from David and Christians as well – a dangerous combination!

'Do you trace your descent from King David?'

'We do,' the two confessed.

The emperor then quizzed them on the extent of their personal wealth.

'Emperor, we are poor men and own only 39 acres between us. We do all the farming on that ourselves.' To prove their point they showed the emperor their callused hands.

'Are you Christians?' Domitian persisted.

'Yes we are.'

'Tell me about your Christ. What sort of a King is He and where is His Kingdom?'

'Christ's Kingdom is eternal and heavenly. At the end of the ages it will appear upon the earth, when Christ will come to repay everyone according to his works.'

At this even Domitian was satisfied.

'Oh, get them out of here!' he laughed. 'Who arrested a couple of hicks like these anyway? Someone get me a swatter!'

Thus Jude's grandsons survived their meeting with the emperor, and their safe return home was greeted with rejoicing. In time they became great leaders in the church – not only were they relatives of Jesus, but they had been called to witness before the emperor himself.

EUSEBIUS, *CH* 3.20

The Revelation of Jesus Christ

Not everyone got off as lightly as Jude's grandsons under the tyranny of Domitian. Some Christians were killed, including a cousin of the emperor, and many more were imprisoned or sent into exile. Among these latter was the Apostle John himself, the last survivor of the twelve.

The aged apostle was exiled to the island of Patmos, a lonely and windswept rock in the Aegean. No one needed telling that John's death would be the end of an era, and news of his plight underlined the fact that the church was on the verge of losing one of its most direct links with the Lord Jesus – the eyewitness testimony of the twelve apostles. A season for mourning, perhaps, but the apostles' passing could also be seen as a new age dawning. As the church changed there would be new opportunities, new directions pointed out by the hand of God. It had seemed grim to the apostles themselves when Jesus had left them, but God had made it a time of great blessing, with a new dispensation and a new gift.

'Unless I leave you, the Spirit will not come.'

But this is getting ahead of ourselves. John was still alive and well, and God yet had work ahead for His last apostle. It was on Patmos, alone one Sunday, that John was overwhelmed by the Spirit's power and fell into a trance.

'Write an account of all you see and send it to the seven churches of Asia Minor.'

John turned to see who was speaking to him, and with astonishment found himself face to face with the Lord Jesus. It was not, however, the face of Jesus with which he was well accustomed. Christ was appearing to His apostle in a new form. His face, body and dress were a dazzling blaze of white and gold – a revelation in itself of the Lord's power and glory. John was overpowered and fell at Christ's feet as though dead.

'Have no fear. I Am the First and the Last and the Living One. I was dead, but behold, I Am alive for ever and ever.'

The Lord gave John a message for each of the seven churches, and John was then commanded to take heed of a revelation of things yet to come.

For an account of John's vision the reader must turn to the sacred Scriptures. The apostle heard the trumpets of angels rallying humankind to war and unleashing plagues, he saw the angels and saints united in praise before the heavenly throne, and he saw the archenemy, Satan, unwearying in his attempts to destroy humankind until his own final destruction. John's vision ended with a revelation of the new heavens and earth, the promise of God to all His people.

The message of the vision, put in its simplest form, is that God is in control of all things. No matter what dark happenings the future holds, even if events sometimes seem to point out a complete triumph for the devil over the saints of God, the church must wait patiently in expectation of her own eventual victory. From the persecution of Domitian to the present, Christians under attack have received comfort from the message of Revelation.

The last words of John's Revelation mark the end of one of the world's greatest eras. When John laid aside his pen, whether he knew it or not, the sacred ink which had recorded God's words since the days of Moses forever ceased to flow. The Scripture was complete, never to be added to or broken, so long as the earth should endure.

REVELATION

Pride and Unity

Shortly after the writing of Revelation, Domitian was assassinated and the second Roman persecution of the church ended. Nerva, a wise and just ruler, succeeded Domitian, and at his command the prisons were opened and the exiles permitted to return.

The earliest Christian writing that has survived to the present day, outside of the Scriptures, is a long letter from Clement, a leader of the church of Rome, written to the Corinthian church during the reign of Nerva. Clement wrote this letter about AD 96, only a couple of years after John's Revelation. There is little difference in date between the last biblical books and the first non-biblical Christian works; the difference is rather in divine inspiration and apostolic authority.

Though lacking the depth and universality of the biblical epistles, Clement's letter is nevertheless very significant and worthy of study in its own right. It is the first document of an extremely important body of Christian literature known as the writings of the 'Apostolic Fathers'. The apostolic fathers were church leaders from the generation immediately after the apostles, and they were men who had known the apostles personally. The collection of their writings, dating from AD 96 to 155, forms a volume somewhat larger than the New Testament, and their teachings open a unique window into the second stage of the church's growth.

Clement's epistle is a response to a major problem that had arisen in Corinth. The Corinthians, as is evident from Paul's two letters, had a history of volatility, and in Clement's time this turbulence had resulted in disaster. A group of the younger men, arguing that the present leaders were holding the church back, had succeeded in deposing the elders and seizing the reins themselves. The result was strife, division and weakness.

Though Clement's immediate purpose is to urge the reinstatement of the elders, his letter is far more than a simple remonstrance. Recounting the Corinthians' history of charity and devotion, Clement wistfully recalls the universal esteem they had once enjoyed. He speaks of their obedience and humility, their loathing of sin and the depth of their spiritual knowledge. But he laments that when prosperity and rising numbers had been granted them, pride and envy had found a foothold and these sins, running rampant in the persons of the young rebels, were now threatening to sink the local church altogether.

'The worthless have risen against their betters, the foolish against the wise, infancy against maturity. Righteousness and peace have been put to flight, and many are now abandoning their faith and returning to the ways of the world.'

Pride and envy, Clement insists, are the root of Corinth's problem, and it is with these issues that his letter chiefly grapples. He combs the Scriptures for examples of the folly and punishment of these sins, and with illustration after illustration he drives home the need for humility, patience, self-sacrifice, obedience and Christian love – virtues without which the church cannot properly function, or even survive.

'Is there not one Spirit of grace shed upon us? Have we not one calling in Christ? Why then do we divide and tear in pieces the members of Christ, warring with ourselves, in our madness forgetful that together we compose one body?'

Clement reminds the Corinthians of the letters that the Apostle Paul had sent them 40 years earlier. From 1 Corinthians we learn that the people were divided then also, some saying that they followed Paul, others Cephas (i.e. Peter), yet others Apollos. Clement warns against the repeat of such a mistake.

'The guilt of division, if anything, is greater now than in the past, for at least then the people were divided over apostles, whereas today you delight in men of no repute. Your elders were appointed by the apostles or their disciples, and until now the whole congregation has been pleased with them. Is it not a crime to usurp the ministry from those who have long led the church peacefully and honestly? Search Scripture if you will, and try to find an example of men of true piety casting away the righteous!'

Travelling ministers were a very significant part of the life of the early church. The apostles themselves are the outstanding example, but they were supplemented by a varied group of prophets and missionaries who travelled between the towns, establishing churches and ministering to the various fledgling congregations.

A mobile ministry was vital for the nourishment of the first churches, as local leaders could not be raised and trained in a moment, but by the middle of the first century the church was already developing a 'settled' ministry. That is, in each local congregation, trusted and approved men were being appointed to take the lead in pastoral duties – teaching, correcting, controlling church finances, etc. Originally there were only two orders of ministry – the higher responsibilities of the bishops/presbyters, and the secondary role of the deacons.

The terms bishop (literally 'overseer') and presbyter (literally 'elder') have been used since the days of the apostles. At first the two words had much the same meaning, and church leaders could equally well be called by either name. By the early second century, however, the name 'bishop' had taken on a special significance and was coming to be used only for the single most prominent presbyter in a given area. By the middle of that century the distinction had become clear-cut, and the bishop was regarded as altogether higher than the presbyters, thus making three separate orders in the Christian ministry.

The blasphemy of pride, the need for unity, the God-given role of the ministry – these are the vital messages of Clement's letter. Just how true his words were would soon become apparent, for even now the devil was launching a mighty attack on the gospel and it was the elders, the successors of the apostles, who would be God's agents to defeat the enemy. Of that, however, we shall hear somewhat later.

CLEMENT, 'CORINTHIANS'

John and the Prodigal

The Apostle John was among the Christians released from prison at the accession of Nerva, and the beloved apostle's last few years were spent in Asia Minor, encouraging, teaching and appointing new ministers to guide the local churches in the years ahead.

Except for the stories found in the Scriptures, we have very few documents that allow us a glimpse of the daily happenings in the lives of the apostles. There are a number of brief, and often vague, records which inform us that, for example, John's last years were spent in Asia Minor, or that Peter and Paul were martyred in Rome, but we do not have much which really brings these men to life. This makes the few reliable stories in our possession all the more precious – and none is dearer than the following tale of John and the prodigal.

It was soon after the apostle's release that his ministry brought him to an important coastal city of Asia Minor. Here he delivered a stirring address to the local assembly, and when he had finished speaking he singled out one young man from the crowd, a bright and spirited lad. Before the whole congregation, John addressed the local bishop concerning him.

'I commit this young man to your care,' he said, 'and before our Lord and these witnesses I entrust you with his nurture.'

'I accept the charge,' said the minister, somewhat surprised, but willing to follow the apostle's lead nonetheless.

John repeated his charge, and then brought the youth and the older man together.

'It is now time for me to depart. I am already an old man, but God willing I shall return some day and see you again.'

No one knew what had prompted John to act in this way – whether it had been an idea of his own or the spirit of prophecy working through him – and the bishop took the request very seriously. He brought the youth to live in his own home and took great pains with his instruction and guidance over the next few years, until finally the youth received baptism from his own hand. It was then that the presbyter, feeling he had fulfilled

John's charge, relaxed his studious care. He was confident that the young man was now a mature member of the church, sealed and confirmed in his faith by the waters of baptism.

The bishop did not even notice when the youth made some unpleasant 'friends'. At first it was subtle enough. The young man would go out on the town with his new friends, spending his meagre wage on expensive food, drink and entertainment. In time he moved out of the bishop's home, and with no means to support the lifestyle he craved it was almost inevitable that great evil would follow.

'Come on,' said his false friends, 'you need money as much as we do! Get yourself a sword and join us tonight.'

That night he began a new life – the life of a highway robber. Even now the young prodigal's innate strength and ability shone through, and he was soon established as the leader of his band. Making a hidden base in the nearby mountains, the thieves sallied forth by night to rob travellers.

The life of crime was at first a resounding success, and for some time the gang managed to prise the purses and bags from its victims bloodlessly. Eventually, however, they encountered a travelling party that was ready for them. A bloody fight ensued, and the prodigal himself ended up killing two or three people just to save his own life.

Now was the time for repentance, for surrender. Innocent people were dead, and the guilt rested squarely upon his shoulders. It was the very knowledge of the depth of his sin, however, which cut the young man off from any hope of return. He despaired of forgiveness and felt that he could never turn back to face God or his fellow believers. Spurred by his doubts of God's grace he sank to even greater depths, and within a short time was famed as one of the cruellest criminals Asia had seen.

Time passed, and the Apostle John, now close to his death, returned to visit the city. He met with the local bishop, and after talking over many things he startled the minister by asking about the deposit which he had left with him.

'I shall expect to receive it with interest!' he added in good humour.

The presbyter was taken aback and thought that John was referring to a literal deposit of money – money which he certainly did not recall receiving.

'What on earth do you mean?'

'The young man I entrusted to you some years ago,' John explained. 'How is he?'

At that the minister groaned deeply and burst into tears.

'He is dead.'

'How?' said John with great concern. 'What happened to him?'

'I don't mean that he is dead in the flesh,' said the bishop, 'but he is dead to God, which is worse.' He then told the apostle all that had happened since their last meeting.

'A fine guardian you have proved!' John cried. 'Have a horse brought this moment and direct me to the mountain you mentioned.'

The old man rode off alone and was soon caught by guards whom the bandits had stationed in the woods on the mountain's lower slopes.

'Take me to your chief!'

Amazed at this fiery old man, nearly one hundred years old, the bandits could do nothing but obey.

'To the hideout it is!'

The leader came striding out to see this strange intruder, but immediately recognizing John he gave a cry and turned to flee. John chased after him with all his strength.

'Why do you run from me?' he called. 'Rather you should pity me, for I am unarmed and old. Cast out your fear, for there is yet hope of life for you. Christ is still willing to save. I tell you the truth, if it were possible I myself would as willingly die for you as Christ died for all of us. Believe that Christ has sent me to you.'

The young man stopped. His sword fell from his hand, and overcome with tears he stood trembling with his head bowed. He offered no resistance as the beloved apostle took him by the arm and led him past his comrades and down to the town.

'Forgive me Father,' he prayed, 'and forgive me, all of you,' he begged of his brothers in the church.

With many tears and prayers, that day became a day of great celebration and thanksgiving. One who had been dead was now alive.

CLEMENT OF ALEXANDRIA, 'WHO IS THE RICH MAN THAT SHALL BE SAVED?' 42

Ignatius of Antioch

The peaceful reign of Nerva did not last for long. A Spaniard named Trajan, an emperor who opened a grim new chapter in the history of the church, succeeded Nerva.

Emperor Trajan was extremely suspicious of secret societies within his realm. He thought it dangerous to permit his subjects to form any manner of private clubs and pronounced an outright ban on all such organizations. His main fear was that such associations could become building blocks for political opposition, and his suspicion of 'secret' clubs went to such lengths that he banned even voluntary fire brigades!

Along with a myriad of other groups, the Christian church was outlawed. Trajan was worried by the church's rapid growth and by rumours that the enemies of Christ, mainly Jews, were spreading through the empire. These rumours involved the most absurd stories of what went on 'behind closed doors' at Christian gatherings, including claims that Christians practised ritual incest, human sacrifice and cannibalism.

The bizarre rumour of cannibalism seemed plausible to many gullible pagans who were misled by what seemed, to them, one of the most unusual activities of the early church. In ancient pagan society unwanted babies, particularly handicapped infants, were often thrown into the streets to die. This practice, given the darkly expressive name of 'infant exposure', was considered quite acceptable – even by leading pagan philosophers and moralists. The church, of course, vigorously opposed such conduct, and Christians across the empire became known for rescuing and adopting such infants. The enemies of the cross, infuriated by such a striking witness, claimed that Christians took the abandoned infants only in order to devour them in secret rites! The report that Christians took bread and wine as 'flesh and blood' in the celebration of communion added fuel to such wild misrepresentations.

The different regions of Trajan's empire applied the new laws with varying degrees of severity. In Antioch, a major crackdown on illegal clubs took place in about the year 107, and among those arrested was the city's bishop, Ignatius, one of the greatest of the apostolic fathers. The elderly minister was taken before the governor, and when he refused to deny Christ he was sentenced to be transported to Rome to be thrown to the lions in the amphitheatre. The reasons for the execution being removed from Antioch to distant Rome were various, chief among them the desire to prevent rebellion amongst Ignatius' flock and also to spread the fear of a similar fate to Christians all along the route of the martyr's last journey.

The bishop was sent to Rome with a guard of ten soldiers. The long road to the imperial capital passed through many important towns of Asia Minor, and wherever the soldiers halted the local Christians flocked to meet Ignatius. Rather than inspiring terror throughout the region, the bishop's presence became a source of encouragement and inspiration, and he composed a number of letters addressing issues within the local churches. We still possess these letters, seven in all, and they are among the most important writings of the early church.

The main topics in six of Ignatius' seven letters are two different perversions of Christian belief that were afflicting the church in his time. Ignatius' responses to these perversions are highly important – not only because of the power of his teaching in itself, but because his letters show how a very early Christian teacher, a disciple of the apostles, dealt with false belief. The errors that Ignatius tackles are departures from the truth in opposite directions – one moving the gospel towards Judaism, the other towards paganism.

The Judaizers were nothing new. They were, of course, mostly Jewish converts, attempting to force their national customs upon the Gentile church. In Ignatius' day they were still a threat requiring careful attention, but on the whole their influence was waning. Within a few decades of Ignatius' protests against them they were all but gone.

Far more serious was the paganizing threat, and Ignatius writes at length against Docetism, a heretical belief that was gaining ground amongst Gentile converts.

The human body, indeed the whole material world, was viewed very dimly by Greek philosophy. Most pagan intellectuals considered that the mind and spirit of man were virtual prisoners, good in themselves, but chained down and adulterated by their attachment to a physical body. They held that matter was unclean, and those pagans who believed in an afterlife tended to look forward to it as promising freedom from the body. Hence the Athenians were unimpressed with Paul's teaching on bodily resurrection (Acts 17:32).

Misled by these traditions, the Docetists could not accept the teaching that Almighty God would so lower Himself as to enter the world in a human body, and so they taught instead that Jesus Christ was a phantom. His body, they said, had been nothing but an image and the sufferings on the cross were a fraud, a play-act. Ignatius was blunt.

'They say the Lord only seemed to be crucified. I say, rather, that they only seem to be Christians.'

Labelling Docetism a spiritual poison, Ignatius urges his readers to base their understanding of Christ upon the apostolic teaching. For the scriptural facts – Christ's descent from David, His human birth, His cries from the cross – properly considered, make it impossible to conceive of the Lord as some kind of phantom. To mythologize the gospel for the sake of pagan philosophy, to twist Scripture into agreement with the beliefs of the unsaved – this, to Ignatius, marks the death of truth and righteousness. The bishop condemns the tendency of such teachings to divide churches and, like Clement, urges his readers to cling to the safety of the established ministry.

Important as are Ignatius' teachings on false belief, it is actually his seventh letter, sent ahead of himself to the Romans, which is his most famous contribution to Christian literature. It is a starkly new type of writing, a document such as the world had never before known. This seventh letter is a celebration of death – the author's own impending death.

Ignatius speaks of his joy at the prospect of martyrdom and pleads with the Romans to make no attempt to save him from his fate. Suffering for Christ, to Ignatius, is no cause for fear, but rather a gift for which one should be thankful.

'I would sooner die for Jesus' name than reign over all the earth. My desire is the One who died for us; He who rose again is all my care. True life lies before me and it will be no favour on your part to keep me from coming to birth. Allow me to attain the pure light, for I long to imitate the sacrificial passion of my God. If you have Him within yourself you will understand my eagerness . . . My desires have been crucified and no fire requires fuel, but within me I hear the voice of living water. "Come to the Father," it whispers.'

Ignatius' hopes were not disappointed. The bishop of Antioch became one of the church's most famous martyrs, and for centuries his letter to the Romans has proved a great encouragement to others faced with persecution.

Emperor Trajan soon discovered that his policy towards the church was not achieving its purpose. He had hoped that intimidation would destroy the church, but he found the result to be far different. There was a degree of success to be sure, with some who were weak in the faith denying their beliefs to escape trouble, but the emperor found that many more were willing to suffer anything rather than forsake their Master.

Trajan's laws were also making things very messy out in the provinces. Enemies of the church were circulating pamphlets that supposedly named local believers and, regardless of their truth, such accusations had the potential to throw whole towns into turmoil. What was more, Trajan was coming to see that the church was not dangerous politically, and that rumours of evil conduct were complete fabrications.

In a letter from Pliny, one of Trajan's ministers, the emperor's advice on the treatment of Christians is sought:

'I question in person all who are brought before me on a charge of Christianity and to those who confess I give a warning of the appointed punishment and offer an opportunity to change their mind. Those who persist I send to immediate execution, as I think their stubbornness worthy of death regardless of their guilt in other matters . . . Some of those questioned, however, claim to have ceased being Christians many years ago, but even they insist that their guilt as Christians amounted to nothing more than gathering regularly to sing holy songs to Christ as to a God and vowing to abstain from crime and maintain complete honesty. Seeking confirmation of their testimony I put two slave-women, whom the Christians call deaconesses, to the torture, and questioning them closely found no hint of the crimes which rumour suggests, and evidence of nothing but a vulgar and fanatical cult. I have postponed further trials that I might first seek your advice. Am I to punish people simply for bearing the name of Christian, though they be innocent of the crimes supposedly associated with the name? You must direct me.'

Trajan had sense enough to wind back the persecution of the church. He advised Pliny not to actively search out Christians, to ignore anonymous pamphlets, and to execute only those who were publicly accused by their fellow townsfolk and refused to deny the charge. The emperor, unfortunately, lacked sense to see the absurdity of this new policy.

'If we are guilty of a crime,' the Christians pointed out, 'the emperor is in error for not trying to punish all of us. If, however, there is no reason to actively search for us, isn't it the height of folly to kill a token few Christians? We are either criminals or we are not. Simple as that!'

But the emperor was deaf to their complaints, and his appalling policy survived for much of the next two centuries. From his time forward most Christians lived in an uneasy and nervous peace – not suffering open persecution, but constantly fearing that they might be singled out at any time. Although Nero had been the first emperor to attack the church, Trajan was the man who made Christianity illegal.

IGNATIUS, *LETTERS*; THE YOUNGER PLINY, *LETTERS*, BK. 10.96–97

The False Messiah – Bar Kokhba

The Jewish people, especially in the Holy Land, were anxiously waiting. It was now 60 years since their nation had been crushed by the Romans, and still their Messiah had not come to save them. The years went by, the Christians daily gained strength, but still there was no sign of a warrior prince. Then suddenly things changed.

'I am Bar Kokhba,' the new teacher cried out in the streets. 'I am the son of a star of the heavens. I am your Messiah!'

Every ear in Israel listened to the new voice. Could this really be the Messiah?

'I shall lead you. Together we shall destroy the Romans and rule the world!'

This was what they wanted to hear!

'The Messiah has come! Bar Kokhba is the Messiah of Israel!'

The land was ready for war in a moment.

'We lost the last war. We cannot lose again – the Messiah is with us!'

The cruel Bar Kokhba ordered a persecution against all Christians in the land.

'*I* am the Messiah. Followers of Jesus must perish!'

The new leader soon had an opportunity to prove his divine mission. Emperor Hadrian, Trajan's successor, heard of the uprising and a Roman army was quickly dispatched to Israel.

This war was quite unlike the previous one. The Jews were equally determined, probably more so with their 'Messiah' to inspire them, but it was even more clearly a losing battle. The Romans were victorious wherever they went, and the destruction of the Jews was more complete and final than any previous disaster in their history.

Hadrian himself was in the land to celebrate the victory. Thousands of Jews were killed or sold into slavery, and Hadrian ordered a new city to be built on the ruins of Jerusalem. Temples to Hadrian's pagan gods were erected, and the new city was named Aelia Capitolina. The Jews were totally banned from entering it, or even coming within sight of it.

Jerusalem was buried by a new city, Bar Kokhba had proved a liar, not a Messiah, and the Jewish people themselves were in exile. The nation of Israel was completely gone, just as it had been warned.

EUSEBIUS, *CH* 4.6

Marcion and the Gnostics

The early years of the second century were years of rapid missionary growth and martyr courage, whether under the frown of Trajan or of Bar Kokhba. They were also years of great turmoil within the church, as the battle for truth went to a whole new level.

The town of Sinope, on the shores of the Black Sea, was home to a wealthy young man named Marcion. Son of a bishop, Marcion had from an early age sought to assume a position of leadership within his local church. Energetic, arrogant and argumentative, Marcion had little time for the teaching of his elders, and with the passing of years it had become increasingly evident that his personal beliefs were unusual, if not downright dangerous. His relationship with his church was already strained to the breaking point when the young man began openly to attack the Scriptures themselves and bluntly condemn basic Christian doctrine. Marcion would not be silenced, and the bishop was left with little choice but to excommunicate his own flesh and blood.

Marcion was shocked, but not humbled. Eager to re-enter the church, but loath to do so by the road of repentance and submission, Marcion departed for Rome, hoping that the size of the congregation in the great metropolis would enable him to spread his ideas without drawing much attention. He had learned a lesson from his excommunication, but not that which his father had intended. On arrival in Rome he sought a meeting with the church leaders.

'I have moved here from Pontus for business reasons.'

The Roman bishop was surprised that a foreigner should

have come so far without a letter of introduction from his local congregation, and he questioned the stranger closely. Marcion dodged his way through the interview without letting out any hint as to the real state of his case. He even presented the church with a substantial donation. The bishop felt compelled to admit him, though it was not without misgivings.

Marcion's welcome was not to be lasting. He was neither willing nor able to hide the tendency of his thinking for long, and when his blasphemous opinions became evident to those around him he found himself again summoned before the bishop.

'You must leave our church. We will return in full the money that you contributed but, from this moment, you are excommunicated.'

At that Marcion threw caution to the wind and began publicly to preach his own doctrines.

'The God of the Old Testament is not the Father of Jesus,' said Marcion. 'The Jewish religion is a sham, false from the very beginning. Jesus came only to destroy Judaism and He is certainly not the Messiah whom the Jews were awaiting. To understand these things you must read the true bible – my bible!'

With Marcion, the perversion of the gospel that had begun with Docetism had reached its natural conclusion. Rather than simply reject the idea that Christ could have a physical, and hence unclean, body, Marcion attacked the notion that a good God could have been responsible for the creation of such an 'impure' world in the first place. He taught that matter was completely evil and was infused throughout with the spirit of Satan. The God revealed in the Old Testament, said he, was largely responsible for this mess and though He was powerful and just, He was both unloving and fallible. Jesus had come from another God, a truly good and perfect being, and one who was determined to rescue humankind from the present system. The God of the Old Testament was the punisher of sin; the God whom Jesus represented was a Saviour.

To support his wild notions Marcion had made his own 'bible'. The Old Testament, of course, was abandoned in its entirely. Embarrassed by the large number of quotations from the Old Testament, Marcion took a knife to the New Testament as well. He claimed that Paul alone had taught truth, and that the other apostles were deluded followers of the merciless Jewish God. Left with only small parts of ten of Paul's epistles, plus about half of the Gospel of Luke, Marcion insisted that his was the true original state of the Scriptures.

'Get your bible from me. Mine is purer, quicker to read and easier to carry!'

In time Marcion won himself a following in the city of Rome. Something, apparently, had prepared the way for such a teaching, and the cult grew until the master was sending missions to other towns. To understand what had prepared Rome for Marcion, we must take a wider view for a moment.

The great cities of the empire were hives of religious innovation. Beliefs from throughout the known world met in the schools and marketplaces, and cults were forever appearing and mutating. All ranks were drawn by the promise of esoteric spiritual wisdom.

However she might hold herself aloof from the cults and schools, it was inevitable that some of the church's teachings should make it into the common marketplace and, worse, that external beliefs should make their way into the church. The biblical epistles indicate that, even in the earliest times, strange teachings could gain an audience with the immature. Gnosticism was the result – a many-headed movement that, generally speaking, represented an attempted fusion of gospel truth and pagan speculation.

The fundamental feature of Gnosticism was an anti-scriptural devaluation of the created world. Bringing their pagan intellectual baggage to the baptismal font, some Gentile converts could accept the notion of God as Redeemer and Saviour, but not as Creator. To their mind Christ came to save us, not from sin, but from the created universe, and the writings of the movement's leaders are concerned largely with giving an explanation for the origin of 'evil' matter. Unwilling to bow to apostolic teaching, the early Gnostics (*gnosis* – Greek 'knowledge') considered themselves an intellectual aristocracy, privy to a secret knowledge far beyond the ken of ordinary church members. In the eyes of the church they were 'heretics', a word derived from the Greek word for 'choice', reflecting the fact that they rejected God's revelation and chose their own path.

Knowledge was the boast of the Gnostics, and each new teacher promoted a system of his own as containing the true account of the heavenly powers. Freely mutating in the hands of each successive deceiver, it was not long before the new schools lost all resemblance to their great original. Whereas the earliest Gnostics appeared within the church (occasionally, it seems, in secret societies of the 'enlightened'), some of the later groups had relapsed almost completely into paganism. The mildest Docetists went no further than to deny Christ a physical body – whereas the extreme cult of the Ophites cursed His name in their most solemn prayers and honoured as heroes the villains of

---

The heretical groups produced countless volumes of theological speculation, including, interestingly, a number of works that purported to be the writings of apostles and other early church leaders. These forgeries, known as 'apocrypha', mimic the genuine works of Scripture and are in the form of 'Gospels', 'Acts', 'Revelations' and, more rarely, 'Epistles'. With a mixture of biblical quotes and nonsense they seek to strengthen the case for the various heretical systems.

Such works, ironically, served to strengthen and confirm the Christian understanding of the New Testament. The NT books were written piecemeal over about half a century, and it was some time before all 27 (particularly shorter epistles such as 2 and 3 John) were brought together as one and put into universal use. In this unsettled state of affairs heretical writings could make their way into use in particular congregations, and this imposed on second-century church leaders the task of making clear exactly which writings were apostolic and contained God's true 'New Testament'. In the end there was surprisingly little controversy over a subject of such moment. The apocrypha, none of which had managed to become very widespread, were self-evidently spurious, and while the works of the apostolic fathers were held in high regard, none could claim to be on a par with inspired Scripture. The genuine biblical books were in a class of their own from the very beginning – 20 were accepted without a trace of debate, while seven (Heb., Jas., 2 Pet., 2 and 3 Jn., Jude, Rev.), for various reasons, were initially questioned, before their genuineness received universal approval. There was a stark divide between the scriptural books and all other writings, and no other work came close to being admitted to the NT.

Scripture from Cain to Judas (they had their own holy book – *The Gospel of Judas*).

Though each Gnostic had his own peculiar hash, the various cults had certain broad features in common. Matter, of course, was universally abhorred, and to exonerate the supreme God from any involvement in its creation a chain of dozens of lesser divinities was suspended from Him. God didn't make the world – No! – but He made a 'god', who made a 'god', who made a 'god' etc, who made the world! Pagan polytheism was still the core of their thinking, and the Father, Son and Holy Spirit were simply worked into their schemes as three among many. They gave dozens of names to the highest gods, and each Gnostic insisted that it was only through knowing the right names and passwords (which he alone could teach – and often at a price) that one could rise through the various heavens to the highest places after death.

In ethics and morality the Gnostic cults fell into two very different camps. All condemned the body and exalted the mind, but this philosophy was applied in opposite ways.

'The body must be subdued by the mind,' said some. 'Life should be a continual and severe fast, the sooner finished the better, and eating and drinking, marriage, indeed anything involving the body, must be avoided as much as possible. Our mind must hate our body and everything it does.'

Others took another line.

'To gain wisdom we must experiment with evil. Drunkenness, prostitution, gluttony, every sin, is new wisdom. These are sins of the body, not the mind, and as our bodies are already evil it matters not to what use we put them. Moral laws are meaningless, as they were made by our enemy the creator. Our mind must hate our body and degrade it in every possible way.'

This pseudo-Christian mythology created a degree of confusion and uncertainty within the church, but no cult managed to establish itself as a viable alternative to Christianity. The Gnostics, generally, were lacking in organization and missionary vigour, and the various groups more resembled schools of philosophy than churches. Marcion, the first to establish a substantial alternative church, was far more worrying. He borrowed heavily from the Gnostics, but by abandoning some of their more fanciful notions, such as the existence of dozens of gods, he made his system tighter, more compatible (on the surface) with the Bible (or such bits as he deigned to keep), and much more dangerous to the gullible. Thousands were led into error by his pretensions of higher 'gnosis', and Marcionism was soon the greatest challenge confronting the church.

Polycarp was one of the best-loved Christian leaders of his time. Bishop of Smyrna since the days of the Apostle John, he had enjoyed a close friendship with the evangelist. To such apostolic fathers as Polycarp fell the chief responsibility for the suppression of false teachings, and when word of the spreading influence of Marcion reached Smyrna the bishop determined on a visit to Rome. He made the journey sometime in the late forties or early fifties of the second century.

Word of the impending visit created excitement in Rome, but Marcion himself, in his arrogance, was not worried. He actually thought that this would be an excellent opportunity to promote his teaching, and when Polycarp arrived in Rome Marcion was one of the first to greet him.

Polycarp walked slowly through the crowd of Christians that met him on the road into Rome, and he paused to speak with several of them. Coming near Marcion, however, he stopped suddenly. He looked thoughtfully around and then stared intently at the heretic.

'Do you know me?' said Marcion, and it was the first time any had heard a tremor in the proud man's voice.

'I do know you,' said Polycarp, filled with the Spirit. 'You are the first-born of Satan!'

This striking scene was the opening of an extremely successful ministry in Rome, and while Marcion himself was not swayed, the spread of heresy was appreciably slowed. Marcion persisted in his error to the end of his life, though some reports suggest that he repented on his deathbed. Be that as it may, the cult he founded continued to grow even after he was gone, and it was to be several centuries before the last followers of the deluded Marcion disappeared.

Marcion was not alone in questioning the Old Testament; the mainstream church saw its own debate over the Jewish Law.

The New Testament teaches that the ceremonial Law was a preparation for the fuller revelation of Jesus Christ. While the Law was good and holy in itself, it was directed to a particular people in a particular time and place and was not directly applicable to the Gentiles. Opposite wings of the church strayed from this clear teaching. The Judaizers insisted that the ceremonial Law was binding on all, and a faction of Gentile believers responded with the equally unsound proposition that the Law had never been designed to be taken literally, but that the Jews had misinterpreted it. They quoted prophetic attacks on hypocrisy (such as Isa. 1:11 'What do I care for sacrifices? says the Lord. I am wearied of burnt offerings . . .') and from them argued that the Mosaic sacrifices and ceremonies were, properly, only allegory. For example, the ban on pig meat (according to the 'Epistle of Barnabas', an anonymous writing of the early second century) is really a command to avoid men of swinish habits, 'those who forget the Lord in time of affluence, but call on Him when hard times come – just as a pig ignores his master when he is feeding, but squeals again when hunger pinches.' The mainstream church acknowledged the merits of this approach – for the Law really does have a deeper symbolic meaning – but insisted that the allegorical understanding did not nullify the literal interpretation. The pre-Christian Jews were to appreciate the deep symbols of the Law not just by reading about them, but by performing them as well – just as Christians must really be baptized in water, at the same time as appreciating the deep symbolism of this washing away of sins in the name of the Holy Trinity.

In Polycarp's Roman ministry we see an example of the vitally important function of the apostolic fathers. The Greek philosophers had a long tradition of borrowing religious ideas. The pagan world was always willing to add one more god to its system, and there was a great danger that Christians, misled by crafty arguments, would cease to regard Jesus Christ as completely unique and unlike the other 'gods', but merely as one power of good and teacher of truth among many. In an age when many were illiterate, it was all too easy to make wild claims about what the Bible said, or even, like Marcion, to make your own 'bible'. Authoritative and trustworthy leadership was a necessity, and the overwhelming majority of the early church ministers amply vindicated the trust that was placed in them.

But preserving the church from error is one thing – vigorously reaching out to the Gnostics and philosophers and convincing them of the gospel's truth is quite another. The church was growing quickly among all sorts of people – all except the philosophical elite. Evidently the church was in need of some extraordinary missionaries.

IRENAEUS, *AGAINST HERESIES*; TERTULLIAN, *THE FIVE BOOKS AGAINST MARCION*

Justin the Philosopher

At about the time Marcion left Pontus, a young man named Justin took a walk on the beach. Strangely enough, Justin's stroll is famous to this day.

Justin was born in Samaria, to reasonably wealthy pagan parents, about the beginning of the second century. He was an eager and gifted student, and an interest in the study of religion took him to the leading teachers of the land. Like many pagans, he thirsted for a philosophy that could guarantee a deeper knowledge, even a personal experience, of the supreme God.

Justin's first mentor belonged to the Stoical school, but Justin tired of him when he realized that he was learning little of relevance to his quest. He questioned his teacher on this.

'God?' the philosopher mumbled absentmindedly. 'Why would you want to know about God? I know little enough of Him myself and I'm none the worse for it!'

More startled than disappointed, Justin moved to another school.

'Poor fellow,' his second teacher greeted him, 'how unfortunate that you should have wasted your time with a Stoic! We Peripatetics, the followers of Aristotle, are the right teachers for the young. True we are poor simple men, living like birds of the air or beasts of the field, but within we carry rich stores of wisdom. Welcome. Stay with me. I will teach you of God!'

Justin was made welcome and splendidly entertained – but a rude shock awaited.

'Have we discussed fees yet?' the master asked casually a few days later. 'Here is the bill for last week. Board and meals are extra.'

Justin's mouth dropped open at the sight of the bill.

'I thought you lived like a bird of the air?'

'Well yes, but even a bird must feather its nest.'

Disillusioned, Justin next visited a Pythagorean.

'How many years have you spent in the study of music, astronomy and geometry?' the philosopher asked haughtily.

'I have not spent much time on any of those subjects.'

'Then how can you expect to learn what is good and pleasing to God?'

'I don't understand.'

'Poor fool,' the teacher scoffed. 'Only a thoroughly trained mind can receive the highest forms of knowledge. Come back when you are worthy to learn about God.'

Justin was devastated, and impatient of such a roundabout road to God he tried one last teacher, a follower of the Greek philosopher Plato. The Platonists, like the Pythagoreans, believed that only through a long course of study could the mind be prepared for knowledge of God, but they were less exclusive in the students they accepted. Justin set to work with all his energy.

The young man was soon confident in his studies. The Platonists considered that mathematical knowledge and other scientific disciplines were the first elements of divine wisdom. They thought that when their understanding of these had progressed far enough they would achieve enlightenment, their minds becoming one with the mind of God. In this hotbed of worldly wisdom and spiritual pride Justin was soon sure of progressing swiftly to the supreme heights of knowledge. He often went to quiet places to think deeply on all he was learning.

As it happened, on one of these days Justin took a long walk on a lonely stretch of beach. He was deep in thought, trying hard to build himself up for the divine vision, when he was surprised to meet an old man.

'What do you want out here?' Justin asked rudely.

'I am looking for some friends,' the old man replied. 'I might ask why you are here?'

'I am here for privacy. I delight in quiet places where I can study philosophy without interruption.'

'Philosophy! Tell me, why do you study that?'

'So that I can find God.'

The old man smiled and began to question Justin on why he believed that such studies could lead one to God. The young man's answers soon revealed the confusion of his mind. How, indeed, could mere men discover the secrets of God? How could they claim to know anything about God, unless God Himself had told them? Justin had never before considered such questions. The old man explained to Justin that what the Greek teachers were searching for was far beyond their reach. He showed many contradictions in the ideas of the philosophers, and Justin was amazed to find that he had no answer for the old man's wisdom.

But he couldn't accept what he was hearing. He couldn't just believe that the philosophers were wrong. How could life be worth living if people couldn't discover God?

'Young man, life is worth living because we don't have to find God. God finds us.'

The old man went on to tell Justin about the ancient prophets, to whom God had revealed things which men could never have discovered for themselves.

'God finally sent His Son Jesus Christ to teach us things which had been hidden from before the foundation of the world. Only through God Himself can we learn the Truth, and without Him we are lost in confusion. I urge you to pray that God will help you understand the truth of all this. May His blessing be upon you.'

Justin was breathless as the old man walked away. He had just met a man, an ordinary man, whom he could see had a better relationship with God than any philosopher. Things soon began falling into place in Justin's mind. He remembered seeing Christians martyred as a boy and recalled his amazement, even then, at the calmness and bravery of their deaths.

'The Christians are prepared to die for what they believe,' Justin said to himself. 'It's no wonder, if what that man said is true. Oh God, show me what is true.'

Deep down in his heart Justin heard the answer. It was not long before a certain Gentile, still wearing the philosopher's dress, paid a visit to the local church. The erstwhile student was quite surprised to find that he didn't need to pay a fee, and that there were no questions about mathematics or astronomy at the door. He was even more surprised at the teacher of the congregation – God Himself.

From earliest times Christians gathered for worship in private homes (cf. Philemon v. 2 – 'the church which meets in your house'), usually the more spacious homes of the wealthier members of a congregation, and a large dining-hall would commonly be dedicated to the purposes of Christian assembly. In the time of Justin there were still but few regular churches, and it was not until the late second century, when the congregations in many places comprised a significant percentage of the total population, that specific church buildings became common. Even these, however, were seldom purpose-built churches, but rather private residences which had been converted. It was only in the latter part of the third century that widespread construction of buildings for use exclusively as churches began.

Philosophers in those times dressed in a distinctive style and were easily recognizable. Supposed to be wise, they were sought out to settle arguments and explain intellectual problems. Some in Justin's congregation thought it inappropriate for the young convert to continue wearing the traditional dress.

'Is Christ not enough for him? Why should he want to be a philosopher also?'

The philosophers were proud men, and Justin's critics thought the profession of philosophy inconsistent with Christian humility. God, however, had plans of His own for the young philosopher.

The philosopher's cloak, as Justin soon demonstrated, could be a passport to the hearts and minds of men. Stopped in the market, questioned on the meaning of life, Justin had opportunities to share the gospel with the most unlikely people. His *Dialogue with Trypho* records one conversation with a group of young Jews who stopped him in the street.

The Jews abhorred Christians as renegades, apostates from the Law of Moses, and these young men were startled to find themselves speaking with a Christian by accident. At first they scoffed at Justin's faith, but they were so surprised by this new thing, a Christian philosopher, that they stayed to listen even when Justin began to prove to them that Jesus is the Christ. One by one, in the course of a long conversation, the pillars of Jewish prejudice were brought down and the young men were finally brought to see the falsity of the traditions of the rabbis. They left Justin, who was travelling overseas the next day, with the assurance that they would apply themselves to the teaching of the New Testament with all vigour. The philosopher later wrote an account of the conversation as a guide to others.

Justin also won a reputation for his efforts to improve the church's standing in the empire. He could not stand idly by and ignore the laws against the church, but what was to be done?

It was not unknown for people to stand up in court and defend Christians who were on trial for their beliefs. Whether they were Christians or not (and they usually were), they were usually executed along with those they were defending. It was easier just to lie low.

But that was not Justin's way. His *First Apology*, addressed to Emperor Antoninus Pius himself, is an attempt to dispel some of the slanderous myths about the church. He explains Christian faith and practice in detail, urges the rulers to resist the bigotry of the pagan priests, and challenges the emperor to make a thorough investigation into Christian conduct before permitting the persecution to continue.

For this bold (though unsuccessful) effort, Justin is remembered as the leading figure of a movement known as the Christian apologists. The immediate successors to the apostolic fathers, the apologists mark a new maturity in Christian literature. Unlike their predecessors they wrote for universal distribution, for both pagan and Christian readership, and their 'Apologies' are usually addressed to the Roman rulers. Their aims are to exonerate the church from common accusations, to expose the folly of idolatry and to plead the case for the legalization of Christianity.

With the beginning of the philosophical ministry of Justin, there were few in the empire who could make any excuse for ignoring the gospel. Christianity was making itself heard everywhere – from the streets and slums to the Senate and palace.

JUSTIN, *DIALOGUE WITH TRYPHO*; *APOLOGIES*

The Martyrdom of Polycarp

One place where the gospel had long been making itself heard was Smyrna in Asia Minor, one of the cities to which John had sent his Revelation. The famous Polycarp was bishop of this city, and under his guidance the local church had grown quickly. Too quickly, as far as many of the pagan leaders were concerned.

'The Christians are making us a laughing stock!' one priest complained. 'We are hard pushed to get even a handful of people to the sacrifices nowadays.'

'It's not only the Christians who are avoiding the temples,' said another. 'Many followers of the gods are staying away, wondering within themselves whether the idols really are false, as the Christians teach. But what can we do?'

The priests took their complaints to the city authorities.

'You must take a firm stand against the Christians. It's no use to punish a token few every once in a while. If we hit them hard enough the people will return to the temples, fearing that they themselves might be accused as Christians.'

That day Smyrna erupted. The governor agreed to use his powers against the church, and the pagan priests scurried through the town, stirring up the anger of the mob before leading them to the city's amphitheatre. Soon the governor's police arrived with a large number of Christians in tow. The pagans were planning a show to satisfy their hatred.

The Christians, chained like common criminals, were led around the arena to the jeers and howls of the crowd. Some screamed that they be put to death, others clapped their hands and stamped their feet, relishing every moment of the build-up to the bloody spectacle which awaited them. Bizarrely enough, many of these same people had been staying away from the idol temples for months, doubting the priests and confused about which path to follow. Now that the priests had brought them together in a mob, however, it was as though the whole city was controlled by the same evil spirit. Some of those shouting loudest were among those most distrustful of the pagan priests. They felt challenged by the Christians, and in their confusion were glad of the chance to vent their frustration on those who made them feel so uneasy.

Some of the Christians were put to death immediately, but this only brought cheers and demands for more. Wild beasts were led into the arena, and a young Christian named Germanicus was brought before them.

'Curse Christ,' the governor demanded, 'and you will go free!'

Germanicus was silent, and the beasts were restrained while the governor began to wheedle.

'Be sensible. Your whole life is ahead of you. Don't be a fool!'

Germanicus stared the governor straight in the eye.

'Curse my God? Never!'

With that he grasped one of the beasts by the neck, pulled it towards himself, and without another word his earthly life was ended. The crowd was thrown into even greater frenzy by the sight of such patient endurance. None had expected such a witness to the power of God!

'Arrest Polycarp!' the cry began.

'Don't let their bishop escape! He is the cause of these problems in the first place.'

The governor tried to calm them.

'Police will be sent to hunt Polycarp down,' he proclaimed. 'Until he is found we shall have other entertainment.'

The crowd was satisfied with this and spent the next few hours engrossed in the horrid display of martyrdoms.

Among the dozens of men and women tried that day, only

one man proved himself half-hearted. This was Quintus, a visitor from Phrygia. He was a man so sure of his own courage that when trouble broke out he convinced some of the locals to join him in surrendering themselves.

'Only a coward would stay low today. Let us go and die gloriously together!'

Instead of obeying the advice of Christ, 'When they persecute you in one place, flee to another,' Quintus fled voluntarily from safety to the executioners. The boaster was not the only one who trembled when threatened with the beasts, but he was the only one to back down and accept the governor's offer. He swore by Caesar, burned incense to the emperor as a god, and went home leaving the others to die without him. One such coward, however, was not enough to satisfy the mob. Amazed at the display of patient endurance the crowd became even more furious, and for the next few days the city was buzzing with excitement as the mob awaited the arrest of Polycarp.

Polycarp himself had been in the city when the police began making arrests. He had wanted to stay behind to suffer with his people, but his friends had insisted on helping him escape to the country. Polycarp remained in hiding for several days, giving himself wholly to prayer. During this time he saw a vision in which a pillow beneath his head burst into flames. He turned to his friends.

'I shall be burned alive.'

It was soon clear that there was no chance of the police abandoning their search, and Polycarp refused to run any longer.

'I am too old for this sort of thing,' he said. 'God's will be done.'

He awaited the end on a small farm. When the police arrived they were amazed to find that Polycarp greeted them, offered them a seat and asked his friends to prepare a meal.

'The search, I'm sure, was hungry work.'

Indeed it had been, and as the police ate Polycarp stood by them and prayed. It was fully two hours before he was done, as he pleaded for God's mercy on everyone he knew. He remembered all, small and great, by name, and he beseeched the Lord on behalf of the church throughout the world. At the end the old man went cheerfully, leaving the police themselves to lament the evil task which had befallen them.

'Polycarp has been caught!'

The word spread quickly, and the arena was soon full. At the sight of Polycarp Smyrna went wild with delight.

'Polycarp,' the governor thundered, 'swear by Caesar and say "Down with the infidels" or you will be burnt alive.'

'Infidels!' Polycarp pointed towards the crowd. 'Down with the infidels!'

'Don't play with me,' said the governor, red-faced, 'you know what I mean. Curse your Christ.'

'I have served Christ for eighty-six years,' Polycarp replied, 'and He has never failed me. Could you curse such a friend?'

'I have wild beasts at hand and shall cast you to them unless you repent.'

'Call them, for how can I repent of the good and choose the evil?'

'If you think lightly of the beasts I shall commit your living body to the flames.'

'You threaten me with a fire that burns a moment and then goes out. You are ignorant of the flames of the future judgement and of the eternal punishment reserved for the ungodly. Tarry no more, but bring forth what you will.'

The old man's face beamed with joy and grace, and the governor saw that further intimidation would be pointless.

'Have it your way. To the stake with Polycarp!'

The crowd rose to their feet with a cheer, and many ran to grab kindling for the martyr's fire. The Jews as usual were first in line with armfuls of wood, rejoicing at the opportunity to take some part in the bishop's death.

'Burn him! Burn him!'

All was soon ready, and as the crowd hushed in expectation Polycarp turned his eyes to heaven and cried aloud in prayer.

'Lord God Almighty, Father of Your beloved and blessed Son Jesus Christ through whom we know You, God of angels and powers, all creatures, and of the whole race of the righteous who live before You, I give You thanks for this blessing. I thank You that I may drink of this cup of suffering, a cup from which Jesus Himself drank, and I glory in Your promise of resurrection through the power of the Holy Spirit. I thank You that You have counted me worthy of this hour, that I might be presented to You as an acceptable offering from Your flock. For all things I praise You, I bless You, I glorify You, through Your heavenly and eternal Son Jesus Christ, by whom and with whom be glory to You and the Holy Spirit, now and forever. Amen!'

As Polycarp's prayer ended flaming torches were thrown at the dry kindling about his feet, and a great burst of fire shot forth.

For a second the crowd yelled with joy, but deadly silence immediately followed. The fire did not touch Polycarp. Rather, it surrounded him like a ship's sail blown out full stretch in the wind, and the old man stood uninjured in the centre of the blaze. The smell coming from the arena was like that of burning incense or perfume. The governor, more stubborn than Nebuchadnezzar, was first to recover from the shock. He turned on the executioners.

'Don't just stand there, you fools. Kill him!'

The executioners began arguing among themselves.

'You do it.'

'No, you.'

Finally one was pushed forward, and even this brutal ruffian trembled with fear as he plunged his dagger through the wall of fire. The crowd was silent as a great rush of blood flowed from the dagger wound and completely extinguished the fire. Not a soul left the arena that day with any excuse for ignorance as to who were truly the elect of God.

But the hatred of the pagans and Jews was still not satisfied. Some Christians tried to take Polycarp's body for burial, but it was seized from them and burned. The Christians, unfazed, waited until the fire had died and with solemn dignity gathered the bones and ashes and buried them. Though it could mean arrest and death, burial was a solemn duty in which Christians were always loath to fail their brethren.

> Churches congregated annually at the graves of each of their martyrs.
> Referring to the anniversary of execution as a 'birthday', they would repeat
> the martyr's story and give thanks for his life. In some cities the Christian
> cemeteries were enormous underground labyrinths called catacombs, narrow
> tunnels through the rock lined with small burial chambers. As new tombs
> were needed the tunnel was lengthened and new chambers were excavated
> on both sides. Some of these catacombs ran for many miles – the Roman
> catacombs alone, added end to end, would make a tunnel some hundreds of
> kilometres long!

On this occasion the men taking the remains for burial were
completely safe. The bishop's miraculous death had so shocked
the city that the persecution completely ended. And the church
of Smyrna again began to grow.

'THE MARTYRDOM OF POLYCARP'

Justin the Martyr

The church of Smyrna enjoyed a rest from persecution, but
Christians everywhere else were still in danger. There were few
major attacks such as Polycarp's congregation had suffered, but
all the same, day by day, ordinary Christians anywhere in the
empire could find themselves singled out for attack. One victim
was a young Roman woman.

A recent convert from paganism, this young woman had
broken free from a life of depravity and alcoholism. Her
husband, once her partner in sin, she now tried to make her
partner in the new life.

'Jesus can set you free. Only look at me and you will see that
it is true.'

But neither sweet words from the teaching of Jesus nor fiery
warnings of the judgement to come could win her husband's ear.
He seemed not at all pleased with his wife's new-found modesty
and sobriety, and every day his heart became more alienated
from her. The woman, daily confronted with the spectacle of her
partner's wickedness, finally decided that the only way forward

was to seek a divorce. It was a path which her Christian friends were dead set against.

'You must try to stay with him. Perhaps he will change.'

And so things went on, until the husband went overseas and stayed for a while in Alexandria, the Egyptian capital. Affairs were now even worse, and the woman heard frequent reports of her husband's conduct on his travels – stories even more shocking than before.

'I can't bear it. I must get out of this marriage immediately.'

And so she did. Her husband was furious. There was no hint of love in his heart, nor any admiration for her noble efforts to start anew. Thirsting only for revenge, he reported his wife as a Christian and demanded the death penalty.

In this terrible situation the woman lodged a plea for the postponement of her trial. Her husband, who had returned to Rome to witness the execution, was enraged at the disappointment.

'Arrest her friend Ptolemaeus,' he demanded. 'He's the one who converted her in the first place. Rid the earth of these sinners!'

Ptolemaeus was arrested, tried and condemned. Lucius, a spectator in the court, jumped out of his seat when sentence of death was read against him.

'Absurd! This man has done nothing wrong – the wretch who stands as his accuser is the only criminal here and yet you execute Ptolemaeus just for his belief in God! If this is the law of the empire, the empire is utterly corrupt!'

'I suppose you too are a Christian?' said the judge.

'I am indeed!'

'Then you may share your friend's fate. Away with both of them!'

'I can only thank you,' said Lucius, 'for freeing me from a world where devils sit in judgement.'

As Lucius was led out another Christian stood up in protest, and he too soon joined the other two witnesses.

Justin, in Rome at the time, wrote a letter of remonstrance to the Senate. It was a dangerous move, but the philosopher was prepared for whatever should happen.

'Like these three,' he wrote, 'I too expect to be plotted against. As things now stand any man, no matter how notorious his own character, might procure my execution simply on account of my faith. How can this hold with the reputed justice of the Roman courts? I challenge the Senate to talk with us and see for itself whether there are any grounds for persecuting laws.'

The Senate declined the challenge and Justin himself was arrested soon afterwards and, with a number of friends, put on trial for his life.

'What doctrines do you believe?'

'I have endeavoured to become familiar with the doctrines of all the schools,' Justin answered the judge. 'But I have found that the only truth is among the Christians.'

'What say the rest of you?'

'By the will of God we are Christians.'

'By law I offer you a last chance,' said the judge. 'Worship the gods, or you will be scourged and then beheaded.'

'Jesus Christ will accept us into eternal life no matter what you do to us,' Justin responded. 'Shall fear of a human judge make us forget our Saviour, the great Judge of all the world, Jesus Christ?'

'Do what you will,' his friends added. 'We remain Christians and can never bow to that which is no god.'

'Away with them!'

And so from that day Justin has been remembered as 'Justin Martyr, the Philosopher'.

As for the young Roman woman who started our story, Justin's description of her case in his letter to the Senate is all that history knows of her. At her eventual fate we can only guess.

JUSTIN, *SECOND APOLOGY*; 'MARTYRDOM OF JUSTIN'

A Cupful of Magic

'Popular' Gnosticism continued to be a major challenge throughout the second century. Scripture warns of false teachers within and without the church, and the warning is as relevant today as it was in the time of the apostles.

'Have you heard about Marcus?'

That was a hot question among Christians and pagans alike for some years in the middle of the second century.

'The church leaders won't have anything to do with him,' a Christian named Gallus responded when his friend Felix asked him such a question.

'Maybe so, but his new church is growing rapidly in spite of them. Marcus says that the church rejects him because it is corrupt, and that the ministers are jealous of him.'

'How do you know?'

'I've been talking to some of his followers. They've invited me to one of their meetings.' Felix paused. 'Would you like to come?'

So it was that Gallus and Felix attended the service together. They were not alone, borne along by an eager crowd that came at sunset to see the new but already famous teacher.

'Marcus alone has the true gospel,' someone explained. 'The church will not listen to him, but see for yourself the power of the spirit which guides him.'

'No one with Marcus' powers could be a false teacher,' said another. 'His miracles are the proof of his divine mission.'

'Here he comes!'

The long dark room became silent as Marcus came through a thick black curtain and stood on a platform in front of the people.

'God bless you all,' he began. 'May your hearts be opened to receive these mysteries. I, Marcus, have brought down Truth from heaven. I have exposed her that you might see her plainly and understand her fully. To know Truth you must know the alphabet, the magical system of letters that makes all wisdom. Listen, hear the meaning of the letters, and you will become greater than the Creator Himself. You must listen to me and not doubt.'

As Marcus' nonsensical whimsies dragged on Felix whispered to Gallus:

'I'm sorry we came. Let's get out before this nut drives us crazy. This is worse than pagan nonsense.'

'Shh,' Gallus hissed. 'I'm listening.'

Marcus finished his sermon and took up a chalice.

'Now we shall take the communion.'

Marcus began to chant in a strange tongue, on and on and on, until an excited babble broke forth as his spell began to work.

'Look! The chalice!'

The 'wine' in the chalice was frothing and bubbling, even spilling over onto Marcus' hands. Stepping down swiftly from the stage Marcus began offering the cup to his followers. When he reached the second row from the back Felix, who was seated there, stood up defiantly.

'I want no part of this devil's cup!' he exclaimed. 'Come on, Gallus.'

But Gallus ignored him, and a moment later he was taking 'communion' from Marcus.

It was not long before Gallus and Felix ceased to speak to each other altogether. Felix, weighed down with unspeakable guilt, laboured long to retrieve Gallus from his error, but in the end found his friend's ears completely closed against him.

'When your priests have power like that of Marcus and can perform such miracles as he does, then, perhaps, I might believe you. Come on, you saw the wine for yourself. How could you be so blind to true spiritual power?'

Unfortunately Felix did not know how to answer his friend. If he had seen the powder in Marcus' hand, which was dropped into the wine just before it began to bubble, he might have been in a better position. That 'miracle', along with many more in Marcus' repertoire, was performed with the aid of chemicals and tricks that Marcus had learned from the pagan priests of Egypt. Marcus' 'gospel' was actually a dangerous mixture of Gnostic ideas (which baffled the mind) and pagan magic (which misled the senses), and many simple people like Gallus were completely fooled by it. Marcus serves as a warning that miraculous powers, and even seemingly wise teachings, count for nothing. It is in Jesus Christ alone that safety lies.

In the end the trickeries of Marcus did not lead people astray for long, but whenever such a deceiver went out of fashion there was always a new cult waiting to waylay the gullible.

Montanus appeared soon after Marcus. He kept much closer to Christian teaching than did the Gnostics, but this only made him the more dangerous. Where the heresy was less extreme and obvious, the battle to expose it was all the harder.

Montanus was born in a country area of Phrygia in Asia Minor. He came from pagan stock and was himself a priest in the pagan cult of Cybele. He lived a strict and fanatical life, and in his priestly role would rant and prophesy under the 'inspiration' of the idols.

In time Montanus was converted to the Christian teachings and, like many other pagan priests over the centuries, he left his cult for the church. Unfortunately, however, Montanus did not allow the gospel to change his whole inner self, and he soon made himself unpopular amongst his new brothers and sisters.

'The church is not strict enough,' he complained. 'Where is our holiness? Why, I ask you, do so many Christians marry? How can any married man or woman hope to be perfect? The church needs to take a good long look at itself. What about fasting? I wish all would fast as often and severely as I do – for it is through punishing the flesh that we will be truly blessed!'

'Montanus,' his bishop reproached him, 'you must not, like the Pharisees, put great loads on others' backs. Christ's burden is light!'

'I don't put any more on anyone's back than I am willing to carry myself!' Montanus insisted. 'If the people followed me they would be truly holy, so how can I be silent?'

'Montanus, you must stop trying to be a leader,' the bishop replied. 'Maybe when you have grown in Christ you will be better able to teach, once you know how to treat others carefully and lovingly. I'm afraid it seems that much of the old leaven of

Cybele still clings to your thinking.'

Montanus obeyed the bishop's advice for a while, but his resentment continued to fester until finally, at a church assembly, he went right over the edge. He fell to the ground and began raving as though in a prophetic trance.

'I am the Comforter promised by Christ. The new age of the Spirit has come! Listen to me, or be condemned!'

'Montanus, be silent,' the bishop commanded. 'This raving is from Satan!'

'I cannot be silent,' Montanus shrieked. 'I am a true prophet and speak only the Spirit's words. Hear me, all of you!'

Montanus refused to obey the church leaders any longer, and from that day forth preached his new 'revelation' to all who would listen.

'Why languish in the dead letters of Gospels and Epistles? Hear the voice of the Spirit Himself from the lips of Montanus! I am the promised prophet!'

Soon Montanus made his first converts – two women, Priscilla and Maximilla. Both left their husbands to join Montanus and his 'ministry'.

'The end of the world is nigh,' all three 'prophets' declared. 'The new Jerusalem shall be here in Phrygia! Abandon the things of the body, afflict your flesh and prepare for the coming of the kingdom. Be truly spiritual – follow us!'

The local church leaders excommunicated Montanus, but that did not deter many in Phrygia from embracing his cause. Soon the 'Montanists' were spreading the new teaching to the rest of the Christian church.

'The new age has come!'

HIPPOLYTUS, *HERESIES* 6.34–39; EUSEBIUS, *CH* 5.14–18

The Thundering Legion

Montanus' prophecies of the coming end struck a chord with many subjects of the troubled empire. After a long period of peace, the late second century saw the Roman Empire seriously threatened by foreign invasion, and in the fear this generated, some minds were an easy prey to predictions of doom.

The barbarians of Northern Europe were the most significant threat facing Rome. These nomadic tribes moved swiftly and fought savagely – they were hard to catch and harder to conquer. They repeatedly broke through the Roman defences to plunder the northern provinces, and on several particularly serious occasions the emperors had to lead the Roman armies against them in person.

In AD 174, the Emperor Marcus Aurelius Caesar marched against a mighty horde that was laying waste to the region now known as Hungary. After several days on foot, his troops caught up with the invaders late one afternoon. A scout brought the report that the Germans were gathered just over the next hill.

Unfortunately, it was the worst possible timing. The Romans, who had completed a whole day's march without water, had been desperately relying on reaching a fresh supply in the evening. The ranks were thrown into chaos.

'How can we fight? We can hardly walk!'

'We are doomed!'

'Offer up your prayers to the gods,' the emperor commanded. 'All of you!'

The two armies were now in sight of each other, and the Germans looked with delight upon the confusion of the Romans.

'They are ours!'

Most of the Romans began to cry aloud to their deities, some cutting themselves with their swords in an effort to get the attention of the gods.

'Jupiter, deliver us!'

'Mars, fight for us!'

After a few moments of this pitiful supplication the Romans, little heartened, slowly took up their positions and awaited the attack. The emperor attempted to put some spirit into his weary soldiers.

'We must stoutly defend our empire and our Roman name,' he cried. 'Even to die for Rome will be our great glory!'

As he spoke, a few young men left their positions and made their way to the front of the army. A whisper had been passing around one of the legions, the Melitene legion, for a few moments – and soon a stream of men came to join them. The growing group knelt together in the front line, squarely facing the German horde.

'Lord Jesus, forgive us our sins and preserve us from evil,' they prayed. 'Lord, we ask You this day to spare us and these men. None of us can resist our enemies because of our thirst, and we plead that You will grant us Your blessing and restore our spirits. Lord, show Your mighty hand to us all.'

The Germans were puzzled. They looked at the Christians, then at each other. After a few moments of hesitation, they decided to attack anyway.

'Death to the Romans!'

But even as they began the charge the war cry turned to a cry of despair. Lightning flashed forth from heaven, and the startled barbarians were frozen to the spot in dread, before turning to flee in confusion.

'Praise the Lord!' the Christian soldiers cried. They rose to their feet and watched the flight of the enemy in amazement.

Rain came pouring down, and a few soldiers removed their helmets and used them to catch the much-needed drink. Soon all were copying them and the whole army was refreshed and encouraged.

'Don't let the enemy escape!' the emperor cried. 'You have had drink, now give chase. They are ours!'

The Romans were soon hot on the heels of the terrified barbarians, who were struck down in their hundreds over a distance of many miles. Scattered and disheartened, they were chased far from the Roman borders.

EUSEBIUS, *CH* 5.5

War Without, Peace Within

Neither the glorious power of the Christian God, nor the holy lives of His followers, put an end to the attacks of the pagans on the church. Christ's gospel remained illegal, and fierce persecutions could spring up at any time. One of the worst occurred at Lyons in southern Gaul (now France) in 177.

The persecution began with a pronouncement that Christians, as enemies of society, were forbidden to use the public baths or to enter the market place. The local rulers and pagan priests inflamed the mob with harsh words against the church, and there was soon chaos as the common folk took the law into their own hands. Christian houses were plundered and the believers were abused, robbed and beaten in the streets.

To take the violence off the streets the Roman magistrate ordered that the Christians be rounded up and imprisoned. Dozens, confessing to their 'crime', were condemned to the torture.

'Deny your Christ, or you will be tormented until there is no breath left in you.'

'We can never deny our God and Saviour!'

'We shall see!'

About ten of the believers broke down under the threat of physical pain and were returned to the cells. For those who remained steadfast, the torture began.

To keep the fury of the crowd at high levels, the authorities arrested the pagan household servants of the wealthier Christians. These men and women were offered two choices: die under extreme tortures with their masters, or falsely accuse them in public. Most took the latter option.

'Our masters engaged in the most repulsive practices, day and night,' they declared. 'With our own eyes we have seen them devour the flesh of innocent babies. Nearly all of them were guilty of incest. Some of their crimes are too shocking even to mention.'

The authorities, of course, did not believe a word of the accusations, but merely used them to mislead the populace. The plan worked, and even pagans who had once been friends of church members were fooled.

'To think that they pretended to such sanctity and unworldliness, while behind closed doors things like that were going on!'

'I'm glad I never accepted an invitation to their accursed church!'

The governor also tried to force similar 'confessions' from some of the Christians themselves. He first chose Blandina, a woman of great faith, but weak and frail in body.

'Do not give her a moment's relief until she admits to all you suggest to her.'

As it happened, evening came and Blandina was returned to her cell. Each of her limbs was broken, her whole body was contorted with the sufferings she had undergone, but she had remained firm throughout. The shame-faced soldiers reported to the governor.

'It's not our fault! Any one of the tortures we applied to her would have killed a normal man! We don't understand it.'

'Did she not confess to anything?'

'Nothing. She just kept repeating, "I am a Christian and there is nothing vile amongst us," over and over again until it drove us insane!'

The governor next attempted to force a confession from a deacon named Sanctus. Sanctus was tortured indescribably, burned with red-hot plates, but no matter what question the pagans put to him, even when they asked him for his name and birthplace, he gave them only one answer:

'I am a Christian.'

His body swollen and deformed beyond belief by his sufferings, Sanctus was thrown into prison. He was called for again a few days later, the soldiers believing that now, every inch of him tender, he would be an easier prey. It was not to be. What had been swollen, broken and deformed, was now firm, straight and almost healthy looking. Sanctus had recovered from his wounds with incredible speed and, in the words of an eyewitness:

'This second bout of torture seemed to bring him no suffering whatsoever. Strange as it sounds, he seemed better at the end than at the beginning!'

Frustrated again, the governor turned his fury on Biblias, one of those who had denied Christ at the very beginning of the troubles.

'At least she might be brought to confess some crime or other!'

But Biblias, once put to the torture to extort a false confession, seemed to awaken immediately from a slumber of the spirit. Feeling the pains of the rack and imagining the greater tortures that awaited the false witness in hell, she took back her earlier lies and maintained a constant witness.

'Forgive me Lord, for once denying Your name!' she cried. 'I am a Christian – and myself and my brothers and sisters are guilty of none of these crimes you suggest!'

Broken and bleeding from their sufferings, the Christians were thrown into a narrow and stinking dungeon where, chained in tortuous positions, they awaited the end. The pagans spared no one. Pothinus, bishop of Lyons, was more than ninety years old. He had only just recovered from a severe illness and had trouble simply breathing. His pluck was still undaunted, however, and a martyr's zeal still animated his frail bones. He was dragged before the governor in chains.

'Who is the God of the Christians?'

'If you are worthy,' said Pothinus, a glint in his eye, 'then you will know.'

For his answer Pothinus was beaten with the utmost savagery and finally thrown into a lightless and fetid cell, where he died two days later. The prison guards, of all the people in the city, were those most confronted and amazed by the spirit of the Christians. They saw daily the inability of suffering to silence the gospel. Returned to their stocks and chains below, the Christians seemed oblivious to their injuries, and each night the dungeon resounded with cries of praise and worship.

'We praise You Lord! We beg Your forgiveness for our persecutors! May our sufferings show them the truth of our faith!'

Other Christians secretly visited the prison each night. A gift to the guards would get them through the door, and they themselves were hardly less amazed than the pagans by the unfailing joy and love of the sufferers.

'Witnesses for Jesus!' one said to them. 'You little imagine how great a blessing it has been to come and visit you in these days of your testimony to the world.'

'Stop that talk,' some of the prisoners demanded. 'We are not yet beyond the reach of pride, and talk such as that may puff us up to our great detriment. Christ is the true witness. It is unwise to call any witnesses except those whom Christ has already seen fit to bring to Himself, sealing them from all further sin by the blood of their last sacrifice. We ask your prayers and tears that we be made perfect – not your flattering words.'

The Greek word for witness is *martys*, which has come into our language as 'martyr'. This change of meaning reveals the humility of the early church, in their reluctance to call anyone a witness for Jesus unless they had already shed their blood in the battle with Satan. The sufferers were well aware that their power to withstand the devil came from God, not from themselves, and this kept them sure in their humility. Neither did they condemn those who had fallen away at the threat of torture, but instead prayed for them continuously.

'Lord, grant them the same faith and strength which we ourselves have from You, so that none might perish!'

Among the prisoners was a certain Alcibiades. He was one of a growing number of Christian 'ascetics' – people who voluntarily denied themselves all the luxuries of life. Most ascetics refused to marry, fasted strictly and often, and allowed themselves only the poorest clothing and virtually nothing in the way of what we might call 'entertainment'. Alcibiades himself had for some years eaten nothing but bread and water. When the Christians were imprisoned together and their friends brought them food to sustain them through their trials, Alcibiades refused to take anything but his usual meagre ration. Attalus, one of the other prisoners, soon had words with him.

'Alcibiades,' he said, 'the Holy Spirit has revealed to me that you are in the wrong. You are making others unhappy by refusing the food that God has provided for you. Some of our brothers feel that they are being greedy because they take much more than you do. I ask you, are you refusing food out of love? I say, rather, you are putting a stumbling block in the way of the brethren.'

Alcibiades was touched to the heart.

'Thank you for your words,' he said. 'I see that I was wrong to act like that in front of you all. Ever since we were arrested I have been learning, to my surprise I admit it, that I am no better than other Christians. Every day we suffer as one, and now I can praise God wholeheartedly for giving us all the same strength.'

Such tender love and wisdom, in response to such savage persecution, must be one of the most delightfully unearthly spectacles humankind has seen. The howling hatred of the pagans was achieving nothing but the sanctification of the believers and providing encouragement for all future generations of Christians with the story of these patient sufferers.

The governor, in his complete frustration, finally ordered that all should be executed in the amphitheatre, as a spectacle for the people. He included in the sentence even those who had escaped torture by denying Christ – perhaps because of the marvel of Biblias. It was a move that seemed sent directly from God, so greatly did it strengthen the church. The weak were strengthened by the knowledge that there was no way out, even if they were to deny the faith, and the whole city got to see for itself the difference between the constant Christians and those who had originally lied through fear. After a week of torture the former were still bold and cheerful, while the others were almost level with the dust in an agony of fear, though as yet they had suffered but little. They knew their guilt and were weighed down with it as they prepared for their final battle.

'Have no fear brothers and sisters,' the others encouraged them. 'Christ is willing to save even at the last hour!'

Blandina, Attalus, Sanctus and Maturus were the first to be

led into the arena. Blandina was tied to a stake, and to cries of delight from the crowd lions were set loose on the Christians. The three men were mauled and attacked, but none received a fatal wound and their eyes throughout the ordeal were directed at their sister nearby, who was crying forth loud prayers with every breath. Tied to the stake, Blandina looked as though she was hanging upon a cross and the lions, strangely enough, refused to approach her. To the other Christians, it was almost as though they saw Christ beside them in bodily form.

The beasts were eventually restrained, and Sanctus and Maturus were then led around the arena and subjected to a variety of torments. They were at last placed in the iron chair, a device which was heated so as to slowly cook its victim. All of this was fine entertainment to the depraved pagan audience, whose cries became louder and louder as the ordeal continued, until finally the air was almost solid with noise as the pair were executed. It was as though the mob was screaming out its frustration at the unshakeable constancy of the martyrs. Never before had they seen a public execution with such extremes of barbarity and calm resignation.

The governor now discovered that Attalus was a Roman citizen, so he ordered that he and Blandina should be temporarily returned to the dungeon.

'I have determined to show mercy,' he declared. 'Any who will now deny Christ may go free.'

Vain effort! All who had already suffered torture refused the offer, as did all but two or three of those who had originally denied Christ!

'Praise God for your return to the fold!'

The governor, shamed by his powerlessness to break the faithful, now wanted nothing more than to bring the whole affair to a quick conclusion. He ordered that any Roman citizens should be immediately beheaded, while the others should provide entertainment in the arena. Blandina was left for last, and to the end this tiny and frail woman exhorted her brothers and sisters to stand firm under their ordeal. When the day was done there was no doubt as to the victor in this bloody battle. The pagans, unable to conquer in their attack on the Christians' souls, tried at least to ensure a victory over their bodies.

'Burn their bodies,' the governor cried. 'Burn them until only ashes remain and sweep them into the river! We shall see then whether their bodies can rise from the dead – even their God cannot save them from the doom we decree!'

A hollow victory indeed. The mighty Romans were slowly discovering their utter weakness when confronted with the power of God – but how many more believers must suffer before the pagans abandoned their useless struggle?

EUSEBIUS, *CH* 5.1–3

The Doctor of Heresies

Nothing better proved the divine authority of the church than that she maintained her strength and vigour though confronted with enemies on every side. If the original commission of Jesus, carrying the light of the gospel to a perishing world, was not enough, persecution and the war with heresy had come to make the life of the church almost a continual round of warfare. It would have been hard to find a hotter centre of the church's varied battles than Lyons itself. Thousands had been rescued from the grasp of Satan, the church had emerged victorious from the worst persecution yet seen, and to cap it all the new bishop, Irenaeus, was soon to become one of the greatest ever warriors against heresy.

It was appropriate that the city of Rome, site of Justin's martyrdom, should inspire Irenaeus to his work. Justin's two great goals had been the defeat of the heretics and the conversion of the philosophers, and when he died both tasks were still barely begun. Irenaeus was to be his first great successor in the assault on heresy.

A native of Asia Minor and disciple of the illustrious Polycarp, Irenaeus had moved to Gaul as a missionary. Polycarp himself had been a disciple of the Apostle John and thus

Irenaeus, like many Christians in the late second century, knew the precise details of the chain that linked him to the apostles. He had the privilege of conversation with a man who had learned the teachings of Jesus from the lips of John himself and, as we shall see, it is little wonder that such a man should be anxious to war with those who sought to pervert the testimony of the apostles.

During the persecution in Lyons Irenaeus was sent as a messenger to the church of Rome. A great shock awaited him in the capital city. In Lyons the name of the Gnostics was scarcely known; in Rome Irenaeus saw evidence of heresy everywhere.

'How can you bear it?' he asked the Roman leaders. 'These heretics must make it extremely difficult to get the true gospel message across.'

'It is hard,' one confessed, 'but that is only what one must expect in the capital. Every crackpot comes here to test his ideas on the mob, and Rome is virtually the first stopping place for each new heresy. We just have to live with it and fight on as best we can.'

Irenaeus felt stirred in his heart. He wanted to help the Roman church battle these wolves, but for now he had to return to his own suffering brethren. When he returned to Lyons, Pothinus had already been dead for some weeks and Irenaeus was chosen to replace him as bishop. He was now too busy to give the problems of Rome a second thought. But not for long.

'Turn to the God of Marcion!' the new missionaries proclaimed. 'Come and learn the true Christian doctrines!'

In the wake of the persecution, the heretics of Rome had arrived in Lyons. Irenaeus himself was almost pleased.

'I had felt a call to this mission,' he told his friends. 'Now I know with certainty that it is the Lord's intention. This evil must be confronted before it goes any further.'

Irenaeus has often been called the doctor of heresy. Like a medical doctor – sitting with patients, studying and describing symptoms, striving after cures – such were Irenaeus' long labours amongst the heretics. Christians considered the Gnostic teachings with horror and repulsion, and most avoided the heretics like the plague. While such conduct was safe for the church's purity, it was not much help to those 'infected' with the various deceptions. One was needed to sift patiently through the heretical writings, to analyze their errors and provide adequate answers. Irenaeus' great work, *Against Heresies*, explains and refutes the multitude of Gnostic systems in five large books. It proved a turning point in the war with heresy and long remained a chief weapon for those who hoped to witness to the Gnostics.

Interestingly, in recent times, many scholars questioned the honesty and accuracy of this great Christian leader and cast doubts on the details of Gnosticism given in Irenaeus' writings. They claimed that Irenaeus had falsely represented Gnosticism and that he was either ill-informed or deliberately exaggerating the flaws of the various systems. These modern scholars felt free to invent their own theories about Gnostic beliefs, as the original Gnostic writings had long since disappeared. Such doubts evaporated in wonderful fashion earlier this century, when archaeologists uncovered a large Gnostic library. Irenaeus' work now has the respect it deserves, and the bishop of Lyons has been proved entirely accurate in his description of the heresies. He is just one of many Christian leaders unjustly attacked by sceptical modern historians.

Irenaeus, Against Heresies; Eusebius, CH 5.4

The Catechetical School of Alexandria

The second task that Justin took up was that of converting the pagan intellectuals. He himself inspired several philosophers to accept the truth of Christ, and his pupils continued the work after him. It was a start – however small.

Athenagoras, an Athenian Christian of the late second century, wrote a philosophical work in defence of the gospel, and in the tradition of the apologists sent copies to the pagan emperors Marcus Aurelius and Commodus. A second book by the same author explained and defended the resurrection of the body, an idea that most philosophers found very hard to accept.

Such works were significant, but still there was something missing.

An Alexandrian named Pantaenus was about to be called to fill in the gap. What the church needed was its own school of philosophy.

Pantaenus had been a Stoic philosopher prior to his conversion, but like Justin had discovered that peace with God could not be found in man-made systems. In time he became a skilful teacher of Christian truth, and a group of the younger Alexandrian Christians formed around him. Philosophy was a major interest of educated young men in the empire, but prior to Pantaenus most Alexandrian Christians had been very wary of it. The example of the Gnostics had made them fearful of the whole discipline, and Christian youths had been largely deprived of this dimension of education. Pantaenus was to change all that.

'Many of the ideas of the pagan philosophers are right and true,' Pantaenus would say. 'Many more are simply wrong. Rather than ignore the whole discipline on account of its errors, Christians, illuminated by the Scripture, must try to sort the right from the wrong. To do so will be to reinvent philosophy itself.'

The Alexandrian Christians already had a school, a 'catechetical school', and Pantaenus was soon entrusted to lead it. Under his supervision it was quickly established as the most important Christian school in the empire. But what was a 'catechetical school' in the first place?

From the very beginning the whole Christian church has been a type of school, existing to teach and train the world in the ways of God. Early on, however, Christians saw the need for specific schools for new converts. We will have to go back more than a century from Pantaenus to understand why.

In the early days, most people who converted to Christianity were already familiar with the Law of Moses. Some were Jews, while others, like Cornelius the centurion, were Greeks well versed in Jewish belief. They knew the promises and precepts of the Old Testament and were awaiting the Messiah. When they accepted the teaching of the apostles about Jesus, they were baptized and became full members of the church immediately.

The mission of the church began to change in the second half of the first century. Most converts were now Greek and Roman pagans, people who had known little of God and had often lived amidst the darkest sins. For these people to fully appreciate the gospel, it was necessary that they be thoroughly instructed in scriptural truths and principles. To fail in this regard would be to risk them entering the church with the web of pagan sin still clinging to them.

To keep good discipline and ensure the proper training of converts, the church began to make new schools. They were intended mainly for the largely illiterate lower classes and, instead of being baptized immediately, converts were made to wait for up to three years. During this interval they were called catechumens, 'Christians in training', and were required to attend regular lessons. Step by step they were taught the basic Christian doctrines and then tested on their knowledge by question and answer sessions. (Educated converts, able to search the Scriptures for themselves, were usually admitted to baptism more speedily.) Catechumens attended the regular church services but did not participate in the celebration of communion until after their baptism. The catechetical schools were run in believers' houses and in church buildings. Nobody paid to learn, and nobody was paid to teach.

The schools were a brilliant innovation, but under Pantaenus the one in Alexandria became something quite different. New converts continued to come for basic instruction, but they were now joined by older believers, coming to hear explorations of the deep things of Scripture, discussions of the relevance of philosophy to the gospel, and defences of the faith against heresy. Before long everyone in the city was talking about the theological school, Christian and pagan alike, and Christian students were flocking to Alexandria from the rest of Egypt and from other lands as well.

Pantaenus, however, was not one to sit back and take it easy as master of the new school. When he saw that one of his students was competent to take the reins, he obeyed a new call that had been growing in his heart.

'Brothers, I must leave you, for I have been called to other service.'

Called to India no less. It was an age in which few missionaries ventured beyond the empire, and this fact made Pantaenus' journey all the more notable. Unfortunately for this history, however, his work there is almost a blank page to us! All we know for certain is that over the next few centuries a strong church became established on the west coast of India – at Pantaenus' role we can only guess.

One of Pantaenus' foreign students, Clement, took over the running of the school. An Athenian by birth, Clement is known to history as Clement of Alexandria – after the city that was graced with the fruits of his mature ministry. He is mainly remembered for his three major writings, the *Exhortation to the Greeks*, the *Instructor* and the *Tapestry*. The first is an attack on pagan mythology, an exposé of all that is corrupt in the old idolatry and a plea for the Gentiles to listen to the voice of truth made incarnate in the person of Jesus Christ. The second is a guidebook for Christians, giving advice for daily life in the midst of a sinful world. The third is a miscellany, a collection of interesting facts and teachings – intellectual proofs of various doctrines, arguments against the heresies, explanations of difficult passages of Scripture – in short, a collection of brain food and a snapshot of the teaching of this first great school of Christian theology. The three books read together were designed to lead the pagan from the very basics of the gospel to the deepest speculations of the second century church.

The church now had a school fit to handle the great intellectual tasks ahead. A loud challenge was being sounded to the whole empire.

'The only way forward is with us!'

EUSEBIUS, *CH* 5.10–11; CLEMENT OF ALEXANDRIA'S WRITINGS

The Golden Ladder

The way forward, however, was not without challenges of its own. Montanus' false prophecies had spread widely, and the Phrygian now had a considerable following. His teaching was disseminated by a fanatical band of missionaries (the master himself did not venture beyond Asia Minor) and was added to from time to time by new prophets, mainly women, who arose in congregations where Montanism had gained a foothold. The Montanists believed that the words of their prophets were of equal authority with God's revelation in Scripture and they made countless written collections of their prophecies.

Except in Asia Minor, where the prophet himself had been excommunicated, the Montanists were at first regular church members, and most Christian leaders made little effort to restrain the movement. Montanus, after all, was not teaching obvious heresy – he seemed rather to be asking all believers to live like the 'best' Christians already did. Many congregations became sharply divided on the teachings, and it was hard for the average believer to know which way to go, as there were holy and respected people on both sides. The greatest catch of Montanism was Tertullian, the leading author in the North African church of his day. In his earlier years Tertullian wrote several important works against paganism and heresy (he is best remembered for the immortal words 'the blood of martyrs is the seed of the church'), but in later life he wrote severely against the mainstream church itself, urging all Christians to embrace Montanistic strictness.

But how was it that many respected Christians became Montanists?

From the days of the apostles, different Christians have followed different paths. God has a unique plan for each of us. The Apostle Paul said that some of God's people would marry and raise families, while others, remaining single, would be called to other works. He also taught that Christians should not judge each other over the food they eat, but that each should eat with thanks to God for his own sustenance.

Most Christians in the early church fasted regularly. In many areas it was customary to fast twice a week, most commonly on Wednesday and Friday, until three o'clock in the afternoon. Other than this, Christians did as the Spirit led them. Most married, ate a normal but temperate diet and observed short, regular fasts.

Some, however, as we have already seen, adopted an ascetic lifestyle. Denying themselves in various ways, heroically striving for godliness, it was almost inevitable that some of these ascetics should begin to pride themselves on their achievements and to think themselves better and holier than other Christians. A few even began to argue that the church should make new laws, insisting that God would pour out more abundant blessings if all believers were to adopt ascetic practices. When Montanus said the same thing and pretended to divine inspiration, they were sitting ducks.

'A new age has come. God permitted marriage at first, but only as a concession to our weakness. We must now become more spiritual.'

The numerous writings of Montanus and his fellow prophets contained a great many new rules and regulations. All Christians were exhorted to remain single for life, second marriage for the widowed and divorced was totally banned, and a great many compulsory fasts were introduced. On some days the Montanists were allowed to eat nothing but dry food, on other days all but radishes were taboo! The Montanists urged that Christians guilty of any one of a wide variety of sins should be excommunicated for life, with absolutely no hope of restoration to the fold, and one of Tertullian's later works condemns mainstream Christians for everything from permitting second marriage to eating sweet fruits and bathing.

Delighted to accept a 'revelation' that assured them that they really were better than everyone else, many ascetics rallied behind the Montanist banner. It was soon evident that no church could afford to ignore the challenge. After much patient delay and passionate debate, Montanism was declared a heresy and its adherents were excommunicated.

Many Montanists were shocked back to their senses by this stern condemnation; others broke away to form separate (and mostly short-lived) churches of their own. Amidst the conflict and pain, however, Montanus' ministry can be said to have done one good thing for the church. After testing this spirit and finding it false, the church knew for certain that the age of scriptural revelation was at an end. Never again would a voice be trusted which claimed to be superseding the teachings of the Bible.

Even before their excommunication, many Montanists had become quite extreme in their conduct. They did not preach; they verily raved at the pagans in the street, threatening whole cities with hell if they failed to give ear to Montanus. They also made new laws concerning persecution.

'Jesus said to flee persecution, but His word no longer applies. From now on real Christians must not flee, but should rather goad their enemies to the attack! Anyone who denies the teaching of the Holy Spirit is a coward!'

Their antics ensured that a chance to try these ideas soon arrived.

The church had recently enjoyed fairly peaceful times. Emperor Septimius Severus had previously turned a blind eye to the Christians, and there had not been a major persecution for many years. In 202, however, the emperor's attitude to the Christians changed and a bloody persecution began. It is probable that the Montanists had made Severus think poorly of all Christians. What would happen, he might have asked himself, if the whole church embraced Montanism?

Amongst the most renowned victims of this persecution was one Perpetua, a young mother from North Africa, who was arrested along with her friends Felicitas, Revocatus, Saturninus and Secundulus. Perpetua wrote an account of her experiences while imprisoned, and her story begins in her own words:

'When we were first accused as Christians my father made a great fuss, trying to make me deny it. I knew that he did so from love, but I knew also that the devil was using him to tempt me.

'"Father," I said to him, "is the thing on the ground beside you a jug, or is it something else?"

'"It's a jug of course," he replied.

'"You wouldn't call it anything else, would you?"

'"Of course not. It's a jug."

'"Just so I cannot call myself anything but a Christian. Please stop telling me to lie."

'My father flew into a rage at this and tore at my face, but he was soon stopped and taken away. After this I was pleased not to see him for a few days, not because I feared him, but because I hated to see him so unhappy.

'Over the next few days we were kept in the cells, and during this period some ministers came and gave us baptism, for until that time we had been catechumens. The Spirit spoke to me at that time and told me to seek for nothing but the grace of bodily endurance.

'We were later removed to the dungeon, and that was truly terrifying. It was totally dark and miserable, a darkness which one could *feel*, but even so I was more worried for my baby than myself. I didn't even know where he had been taken.

'After some time below, two deacons from our church convinced the guards to let us all go up to a better part of the prison for a few hours. That was a great relief, and I was even happier when some friends brought my son to me. The little one was now weak with hunger, and my friends pleaded for me that I might be allowed to keep him in the dungeon with me. This was granted, and when my mother and brother visited I asked them to take care of the child if I was killed. My brother, who was still a catechumen, was very emotional.

'"Perpetua," he said, "ask Jesus for a vision. I'm sure he will reveal to you whether this imprisonment will end in death."

'So that evening I wrestled in prayer with Jesus, and while I slept my prayer was answered.

'I saw an enormous golden ladder, reaching right up to heaven, with swords, hooks and all manner of weapons fixed to its sides. Some who climbed carelessly, or without looking upwards, were torn to pieces by them. I saw a huge dragon crouching at the ladder's foot, terrifying the climbers and trying to deter them from the ascent.

'Suddenly my friend Saturus raced past me. He had not been arrested with us, but had freely surrendered himself when he heard that his best friends had been taken. "If we can't be together in life," he had said, "at least we can be together in death."

'Saturus reached the ladder and began climbing. He didn't once look back and he reached the top with great speed.

'"Perpetua, I am waiting for you," he called down. "But beware the dragon's bite!"

'"In the name of the Lord Jesus Christ I will fear no harm," I cried, and the dragon trembled in fear as I trod upon his head and began my own ascent.

'Upon reaching the top I found myself in a beautiful garden. A man dressed as a simple shepherd was milking a sheep there, surrounded by thousands of people dressed in white robes.

'"You are welcome, daughter," he said, smiling at me, before offering me some cheese from his sheep.

'As I put it in my mouth, everyone standing about said "Amen", and I woke up at that moment with an indescribable sweetness in my mouth. I knew then that my time in the world was short and that Jesus was calling me to a better place.

'It was not long after this that we had to testify in court. My friends confessed with joy, but when they came to me my father appeared, carrying my son.

'"At least have pity on your child," he pleaded. Hilarianus the judge also scolded me.

'"Spare your father's grey hair, spare the infancy of your boy and offer sacrifice for the emperors."

'"I cannot."

'"Are you a Christian?" asked the judge.

'"I am a Christian."

'The judge was infuriated, and while condemning us all to be thrown to the beasts he ordered my father also to be thrown down and beaten in front of me. For me this was the most painful thing of all, but once we had returned to the dungeon there was not a single one of us who was not in high spirits. We were greatly encouraged as we talked about our glorious privilege of suffering for Jesus.

'My father took my baby home from court with him, and I sent a message asking him to bring him back. He refused, but God defeated his stubbornness. I was soon told that the child no longer wanted the breast, and my own milk dried up at once and caused me no pain.'

Following this Perpetua records three more of her dreams, and finally a vision that Saturus himself saw of the friends being carried to heaven. Her own writing ends here, but after her death the story of the friends' last days was finished by a fellow Christian who had witnessed their end.

Conditions in the prison were so bad, he tells us, that Secundulus actually died before the day of execution came.

'Only one thing saddens me,' Secundulus said to his friends, 'and that is leaving you to gain glory without me!'

It also seemed that Felicitas would not be sent to the amphitheatre along with the others. She was pregnant, and the day set for the execution was some time before her baby was due. The authorities were planning to delay her execution until the baby was born, but three days before the exhibition the group joined in prayer that Felicitas might not be separated from them. Immediately following the prayer vigil, Felicitas began labour and delivered her baby, a healthy girl. She was only eight months pregnant. Hearing her cries as the child was delivered, a servant of the prison keepers taunted her.

'If you sob now, what will you do when you are thrown to the beasts, a punishment which you have despised and treated as nothing by refusing to sacrifice?'

'Now it is I that suffer,' Felicitas answered. 'Then you will see that it is another who suffers in me.' The child was soon taken from the dungeon by a Christian sister, who raised her as her own.

At last the day came, and the friends were led into the crowded amphitheatre. As they passed before Hilarianus they called aloud:

'Today you judge us, but God will soon enough judge you.'

The crowd was infuriated and demanded that the martyrs be flogged, but they were only further enraged to hear them cry, 'We are flogged gladly, and happily suffer as our Lord did!'

'To the beasts!'

Saturninus, while in prison, had said that he would happily take his stand against each of the beasts in turn, and so it now transpired. He and Revocatus faced a leopard and bear in turn, and when a wild boar was brought forth it actually turned on its master and gored him so severely that he died the following day. The amphitheatre was in confusion by now, which was not uncommon when the crowds wished to see the Christians tortured. God did not spare His children from their martyrdom, but He strengthened them for the contest and often made the spectacles with the beasts look nothing but ridiculous. By the end the mob had usually seen something to make them really think, even if the failure of their 'entertainment' only made them the angrier at the time.

A fierce cow was released against Perpetua and Felicitas, and when the crowd had seen enough of this punishment the cow was restrained and the martyrs were called back to the sidelines. Felicitas had been badly injured, and Perpetua helped her up and led her back to the gate. Rusticus, a catechumen, encouraged the women when they came close to the crowd, but Perpetua blinked and shook her head at his voice.

'I don't know when we are going to be led out to that cow.'

'But it has already attacked you!' said Rusticus in amazement. Only by pointing to wounds on her body and tears in her clothing, could he bring Perpetua to believe him.

Saturus was now led out to face a leopard, and having received a premonition of this fate while in prison he understood that the end had come.

'I have survived all the beasts so far,' he told a soldier beside him, 'but God has shown me that one bite of this animal will end my life.'

A moment later his words came true, and as he was bleeding to death the crowd taunted him.

'Saved and washed, saved and washed!'

These words were a common mockery of the dying martyrs,

as the mob knew that Christians believed themselves to be saved and washed by the blood of Jesus. Saturus, oblivious to them, returned to the soldier.

'Remember my words and my suffering,' he said. 'Give me that ring from your finger.'

The startled soldier obeyed, and in Saturus' trembling hand the ring was soon covered with blood. The martyr handed it back to its owner.

'Stained as it now is,' he said, 'keep it so as a memory of me. May this day and our suffering, be to you the beginning of life.'

With that he collapsed and entered eternal life. Perpetua now realized why Saturus had climbed the ladder first in her dream.

'Enough,' cried the crowd. 'Finish the rest of them with the sword!'

And so it ended.

'THE MARTYRDOM OF PERPETUA AND FELICITAS'

Origen

The persecution was especially furious in Alexandria. Believers from across Egypt were carried to the capital to be executed; many local Christians fled to neighbouring provinces; services could only be held in strictest secret; and the great catechetical school fell silent. Watching it all was a sixteen-year-old named Origen. Day after day he saw the martyrs led to execution, but rather than being intimidated he was filled with excitement by the spectacle of their quiet courage. The sight of injustice and sense of danger made him only the more earnest in preaching the gospel.

It wasn't chance that made Origen eager to serve God. His father Leonides had ensured that the word of God was the first love of his life. Before setting his son to study the various subjects that formed a standard education, he had made sure that Origen was full of the higher truth of the Bible. Even when he was a pre-teen, Origen would puzzle his father with questions, searching deeply into the meaning of Scripture.

Now, with trouble blazing, Origen refused to keep his faith safe and silent. In all company he witnessed to the gospel without reservation, and he was often in danger of arrest. His mother begged him to calm his zeal, rightly worried that she would lose him, but in the event the persecution was not to claim Origen, but another equally close to her heart. It was her husband Leonides who was arrested and imprisoned, and when Origen returned home one evening to the news he immediately determined to join his father in gaol and death.

'On trial tomorrow! He won't be alone.'

Origen's mother could not bear to lose her husband and eldest son at one stroke, so while Origen took a few hours sleep that night she hid all of his clothing. Exasperated, Origen did the only thing that was left to him.

'Take heed not to change your mind on account of us,' he wrote to his father. 'May we meet again in heaven.'

Origen's mother not only lost her husband, but all of Leonides' property was confiscated as well. This was standard government practice – an extra torment to the martyred men and an extra temptation to deny Christ. With no husband and no property, their wives were reduced to an extremely pitiful condition.

Try as they might, however, the authorities could not deprive the martyrs' families of the favour of heaven. The Lord took care of Leonides' wife and seven sons and Origen himself, the eldest, was taken into the home of a wealthy Alexandrian woman. This woman, though a respected Christian, was host to a heretic named Paul of Antioch, her son by adoption. Many came to the house to hear the heretic's teaching, but in spite of his youth and needy circumstances Origen refused to associate with the false teacher and avoided even his benefactress' prayer meetings.

From this uncomfortable situation Origen was soon delivered. He continued his studies with great fervour, and within a few months was able to leave Paul's den and establish himself as a tutor in Greek literature and philosophy.

The bishop of Alexandria was now struggling to put the local church back in order. Clement had fled Egypt and established a school in another city, and when Bishop Demetrius cast his eye about for a replacement, he found none fitter than a certain seventeen-year-old tutor in Greek philosophy!

'Put aside these heathen subjects. You are young, but if God wills you to take this position you need not fear the opinion of men.'

Origen, who had spent time under Clement's tuition, was already well respected by his fellow students. He embraced the charge with his customary vigour, and it was not long before the teenager had established a solid reputation throughout the church and even beyond. Under Clement the school had attracted a number of pagan students, and in spite of the persecution (which was by now only sporadic) some of these began to return. Drawn by the reputed sanctity of the Christian teachers, most having already suffered disappointments at the hands of money-grubbing pagan philosophers, these youths were willing to leave the beaten track in order to gain true wisdom. They were not disappointed in their choice of school, and many were led to Christ through the example of their fellow students and teachers. Others, though greatly challenged, dared not embrace the cross at the high price it carried.

'My family would disown me, I could never get a job in the government, and I might well lose my life! God forgive me, but I just can't risk all that!'

EUSEBIUS, *CH* 6.2–3

Potamiaena and Basilides

Many did run that risk, however, and they were in an especially dangerous position during Severus' reign. The main concern of the Roman authorities was to slow the spread of Christianity, so recent converts were hit with the utmost severity. Catechumens were usually the first targets, and several of Origen's students were martyred.

A young man named Plutarch was the first of Origen's pupils to suffer martyrdom. Several others soon followed him, but the most famous of them was Basilides, one of those students who had not dared to make a public profession of Christ.

Having enlisted in the Roman army after leaving Origen's school, Basilides was stationed in the city of Alexandria. One of his first assignments was in a security force for the city's main court. Basilides' comrades were pleased at the assignment, a relatively easy one, but ominous feelings welled within the new recruit's chest notwithstanding. His forebodings were realized when two Christians were led in for trial and Basilides saw that he must be witness to their trial and torture.

The Christians were a mother and daughter, Marcella and Potamiaena. The younger woman was subjected to severe tortures and then offered the choice of being handed over to the gladiators for bodily abuse, or immediate release if she would curse the name of Christ. After a moment's pause Potamiaena thought of a way she might possibly avoid either option.

'I'll give you a curse if you demand it,' she said. 'A curse on the gods who have made you a demon!'

At that the court was in uproar, and the judge ordered her immediate execution.

'Immerse her in burning pitch!' He turned to Basilides. 'You take her!'

Basilides stood a moment in stunned silence, but seeing the danger in the judge's burning features he took Potamiaena by the arm and led her away. The bystanders began to insult and strike at the condemned woman, but Basilides, his chest heavy as stone, pushed the crowd back and drew his sword against them. The martyr saw his kindness and caught his eye with a smile.

'I thank you for being a friend to me,' she said. 'Thank you for your courage.'

'I have no courage,' Basilides said with tears in his eyes. 'You are the brave one.'

Potamiaena's smile grew, and she shook her head.

'I need no courage, for I know that I have almost reached my heavenly rest. When I see my Lord I shall petition Him on your behalf. I can offer you no reward, but He has promised to bless all who help His little ones.'

A moment later Potamiaena was dead, and her mother soon followed her to the place of execution. A few days passed, and Basilides was called upon to swear an oath by his fellow soldiers. To their amazement, the recruit refused.

'I am a Christian and may not swear.'

At first the other soldiers took it for a joke, but when they realized that Basilides was serious they dragged him into court. Basilides boldly confessed Christ before the judge and was sent to prison to await execution. The local church, hearing what had happened, secretly sent men to the prison to find what was going on – for no one in Alexandria knew anything of this new believer!

'Three days after her death,' Basilides revealed, 'Potamiaena appeared to me by night. She placed a crown on my head and told me that she had prayed to Jesus for my soul and had been promised that I would come to her soon.'

'Let us not waste a moment,' said one of the visitors, and straightaway the believers baptized their new friend. The next day, praising God and publicly proclaiming his amazing story, Basilides was beheaded. Many others at that time saw Potamiaena in dreams, and the whole church was greatly encouraged in the midst of its suffering.

EUSEBIUS, *CH* 6.4–5

Three Liars

The persecution lasted several more years, but the situation slowly improved after the death of Severus in 211. The Alexandrian school's influence continued to spread, and Origen's teaching ministry began making serious inroads among Gnostics and pagan intellectuals. A pivotal Gnostic convert was Ambrose, a wealthy man, who became a sponsor of Origen. Ambrose employed seven secretaries to whom Origen could dictate his writings, a similar number of copyists, and specialist calligraphers in addition. Such an office was a scholar's dream come true in an age when all was done by hand, and this guaranteed swift distribution of the master's works.

At this time a curious controversy was played out in the church of Jerusalem. (It will be remembered that Jerusalem was officially known as Aelia Capitolina at this time, the city having been rebuilt by Hadrian in the wake of Bar Kokhba.) Three dishonest members of the local congregation caused the trouble. Guilty of serious crimes and fearing that their bishop suspected them, these men determined to turn the tables on their adversary. To discredit any testimony Bishop Narcissus might make against them, or perhaps to remove him altogether, they boldly accused the bishop himself in a church assembly. We do not know the nature of their allegations, but whatever they said was greeted with disbelief. Narcissus was a well-loved and respected old man, and the three men were shouted down by the congregation and accused of lying. They responded firmly.

'Doubt me if you will,' said the first, 'but may I burn to a cinder if what I say is not true!'

The second liar fell on his knees and spread his arms to heaven.

'May my flesh be smitten like Job's if I bear false witness!'

'May the Lord take my sight if I have told a lie,' said the third.

But even these grotesque oaths could not convince the brethren. All waited dumbstruck as Narcissus rose from his seat.

'What can I say? I can only call God as my witness against these men. May He who is strong to save defend me!'

Narcissus, visibly upset, left the church. He could not be found the next day. Had he fled for shame at being caught out?

'We told you so!' the liars boasted, and in secret they celebrated their victory together.

But not for long. Narcissus had rested his case in the hands of One well able to set things right.

'Fire! Fire!'

The slumbering city was awakened to see the house of the first liar all ablaze.

'It was the strangest thing I ever saw,' a neighbour declared. 'Only the tiniest spark fell from a passer-by's torch, but within a second or two the whole wall was burning. I tried to put it out, but it caught hold so quickly that I could hardly do a thing. It was as though the whole house was covered with oil, or something!'

The house burned to the ground, and the liar and his family died in the blaze. This was only the beginning.

'Oh, agony!' cried the second liar, sobbing as he trudged through the city market. 'Get a doctor! Help me!'

The city was shocked, only a few days later, to see this man covered with horrible sores from his head to the soles of his feet.

'Lord forgive me!' the third conspirator cried. 'Lord spare me!'

He called the church together and confessed everything.

'It was us, the three of us!' he said trembling, a wild look on his face. 'Narcissus is innocent and we are guilty. Oh, forgive me! Please, all of you, pray that God will not take my eyes!'

With his eyes rolling in terror, he was looking all about him, as though expecting an avenging angel to appear any moment! For days he was in total despair, wailing for his sins and cursing his folly. Soon he did go blind, both eyes ruined in the course of his continual weeping. Justice had been done, but no one knew where Narcissus was to tell him the good news. Jerusalem could not wait for its absent bishop forever, and after a decent delay the neighbouring bishops ordained a minister named Dius as Narcissus' successor. When Dius died he was replaced by Germanio, and Germanio himself was eventually succeeded by Gordius. While Gordius was bishop, the totally unexpected occurred.

'Narcissus!'

The venerable old man had returned, as though from the dead, and all the people, not least Gordius himself, urged him to resume the bishopric.

'We must tell you what has happened – you will hardly believe the fate of your accusers!'

'Oh, I will believe it all right,' the bishop smiled. 'I left my case in capable hands.'

'Where have you been?' the people asked in amazement.

'Here and there,' he said, 'living in desert places, living like a prophet of old on the simplest fruits of the earth. The cave has often been my home and the locust my meat!'

In spite of his great age, Narcissus remained with his flock for several years more. As though making up for lost time, he lived to be almost one hundred and twenty years old, a witness of God's ability to justify His chosen ones before men and to deliver them from evil.

EUSEBIUS, *CH* 6.9–11

The Banker of Rome

There were far more serious problems for the early third-century church than the criminal foolery of the three liars. A new form of heresy was gaining strength in Rome, a heresy far more subtle than any of its predecessors. It goes by a variety of names (Patripassianism, Sabellianism, Modalism), but in essence it is quite simple.

'There is One God,' said Sabellius, a leading teacher of the new heresy, and so far all Christians agreed with him. 'Yet we know that Father, Son and Holy Spirit are all God,' he continued, and still all agreed. 'How can that be?' he added, and here his brethren sniffed danger. 'If God is One, how can we believe that three distinct persons are God? Surely they cannot be so distinct as we have imagined?'

Sabellius believed that the Trinity existed only in the appearance of God, not in God's deeper nature. Instead of seeing the Father, Son and Holy Spirit as three separate persons, Sabellius taught that God simply showed Himself at different times in three different ways. He taught that God showed Himself as Father when giving the Law to Moses, came to earth as Son in the second stage, and since then has played the role of Holy Spirit.

'Jesus Christ, the Son of God, no longer exists. Rising to heaven He disappeared back into the Godhead, as He was no longer needed.'

How different this is from the true Christian faith, which

looks forward to spending all eternity in the company of the Son of Man who bears the scars of His infinite love for us, 'The Lamb, looking as if it had been slain!' But the heretical teaching got even stranger, with the most bizarre implications.

'Jesus was not the only one nailed to the cross, the Father and Holy Spirit were also. When Jesus prayed, He was speaking only to Himself. Father, Son, Holy Spirit – they are simply three masks which the One God wears.'

Which probably sounds pretty confusing. In fact the bishop of Rome himself was confused. Zephyrinus had become bishop during the persecution of Severus, and he did not know what to do about Sabellius.

'I am only a simple man,' he complained. 'I don't know how to handle such questions as these.'

Unfortunately, Zephyrinus appointed a certain Callistus to deal with the difficulty for him. Callistus, a cunning type, used the opportunity of the troubles to gain power within the church. He tried to get everyone on side, making a friend of Sabellius, but then turning around and pretending agreement with the teaching of the mainstream leaders as well. Hippolytus, a gifted teacher (and student of Irenaeus), was leading the fight against Sabellius, and he stood forth boldly against Callistus' duplicity. The church was balanced on a wire until the death of Zephyrinus, when Callistus replaced him as bishop. This was too much for Hippolytus and many others to bear. Callistus tried to placate them by excommunicating Sabellius, but it was not enough.

'Sabellius himself is not our target,' said Hippolytus. 'It is his ideas we oppose and yours, Callistus, are no better. Indeed it is you who has been encouraging him.'

Undeterred by this opposition Callistus established a school of theology to spread his own peculiar doctrines, a system similar in its main features to that of Sabellius. At this, Hippolytus and his followers broke away from the Roman church in protest. The heretical bishop's closet was already well stocked with skeletons, and Hippolytus ensured that they did not remain hidden.

'It is a disgrace for us to call this man bishop. He has got where he is only by playing on Zephyrinus' gullibility.'

The accusation was in fact quite true.

Many years earlier, Callistus had been the servant of a wealthy Christian named Carpophorus. Carpophorus was involved in the banking business, and trusting in Callistus as a fellow believer he had made him his financial manager and put him in charge of a great deal of money. Callistus operated a bank in the city market, and many Christians, relying on the reputation of Carpophorus, deposited funds with him. All was well, until a Christian client once attempted a large withdrawal.

'Come back some other day!' Callistus hissed. 'I just don't have any cash on hand right now.'

This was true – for the bulk of deposits had already been put to Callistus' own use! It was not long before word got back to Carpophorus.

'He won't let you get at your money? I will look into this myself as soon as possible.'

Rumour of the planned investigation threw Callistus into a panic. He quickly closed up shop and made for the port, but he was spotted on the way by some of the very people he had robbed.

'Goodbye,' he called cheerfully. 'No time to stop right now!'

'He doesn't look like he's up to any good!' one decided, and promptly reported to Carpophorus.

'Running in the direction of the port!' exclaimed Carpophorus. 'Let's get to the bottom of this right now!'

Callistus was by now strutting about on the deck of a ship, which sat at anchor in the middle of the harbour.

'A free man at last!' he chuckled to himself. Going to the rear of the ship he laughed aloud at the Roman shore, so soon to be forever left behind.

'You really pulled a good one!' he congratulated himself. 'You really . . . What is that?'

He had spotted Carpophorus, standing at the prow of a rowboat that was closing in quickly. Callistus immediately turned to the sailors at work on deck.

'Can't you go any faster?' he cried. 'Come on, raise the anchor, set sail!'

Seeing that his cries were to no avail, Callistus gave up all hope and dived into the deep.

'Man overboard!' the sailors roared, and they jumped into lifeboats and tried to fish Callistus from the water.

'Stop it! Get away from me,' Callistus gasped. 'Leave me to drown!'

But the sailors dragged him on board in spite of his struggles, and soon the sodden 'banker' was handed back to his master. Carpophorus returned to Rome with his prize catch, and with just severity sentenced him to hard labour.

With the passage of time, however, old wounds faded and certain Roman Christians began to nag Carpophorus on behalf of his servant.

'Callistus is truly repentant,' they insisted. 'He says that he is owed a substantial amount and shall be able to claim it once he is released in order to repay the people he defrauded. You have nothing to lose, and everything to gain, by showing mercy.'

Carpophorus eventually gave in to their sincere but misguided appeals and permitted Callistus' release.

'You may be right about his repentance, but I still don't trust him. I will send two men to ensure that he really does repay what he owes.'

'Thank you so much, my brothers!' Callistus exclaimed upon release. 'You have shown the world what forgiveness is all about, and you won't regret it! I'll just be off now to claim that money. I'll see you shortly!' Callistus strode away towards the busy market but was annoyed to see that two men were trailing him. 'And who are you?' he demanded.

'We will take you to Carpophorus as soon as you have claimed the money.'

'Oh, will you now,' Callistus grimaced, seeing that he was still in a fix. 'Well let's have a bite to eat first, your shout! You see I don't have any money on me yet. I was just released from degrading hard labour, after all!'

The two guards looked at each other and shrugged. 'I guess so,' one said, 'I have a little money on me.'

'Good man,' Callistus slapped him on the back. 'Here's an

eating house right now. It's been a while since I had a good meal!' It was a while before he finished this one.

'We really must be going,' one of the guards complained as his purse was finally emptied.

'Don't you worry about that,' Callistus said. 'I'll pay you back for this fine meal when I get at my money. Just be patient!'

Callistus was soon leading his two guards on a long march around the city.

'You do understand of course,' he apologized, 'it's been a long time since I was free to walk the streets of Rome. As you might recall, I've been imprisoned. I can't quite remember my way. Ah . . . ' he pointed to a side alley and looked very serious, 'now that looks familiar.'

But nothing could shake his companions. Several times Callistus tried to lose them in thick crowds, or by quickly slipping off into dark lanes, but still they remained hot on his heels, never more than a few paces away. Finally Callistus hit upon a desperate solution. It was the Jewish Sabbath, and passing a synagogue he made a sudden break from his guards and dashed inside.

'Down with the Jews! Death to the Jews!'

You might imagine that it was not long before he was thrown onto the street and given a beating! The guards ran off to inform Carpophorus, and by the time they returned Callistus and the Jews were arguing in front of the city prefect.

'This man abused us in our own synagogue!'

'Prefect Fuscianus,' said Carpophorus, 'don't trust this rascal. He abused the Jews so that he might escape from my hands. He is trying to get away without repaying a large sum of money he owes.'

The Jews, thinking that Carpophorus was lying to get a fellow Christian off the hook, became even angrier. They demanded that Fuscianus punish Callistus immediately, and the prefect decided in their favour. Callistus was given a flogging and then sent to a prison camp in Sardinia.

It was a few years later that a concubine of the emperor Commodus, a God-fearing woman named Marcia, wished to perform a good deed for the church. She asked Bishop Victor of Rome for a list of those believers who had been imprisoned for their faith. Victor gave her the names of those imprisoned in Sardinia, and Marcia successfully pleaded their case with the emperor. She received a letter of emancipation for the captives and immediately sent her servant Hyacinthus to execute it on the island. Callistus, of course, was not on the list, for Victor knew his character, but when the prisoners were gathered ready for departure Callistus discovered what was going on.

'Please, take me with you,' he pleaded. 'I also am a Christian. I must have been left off the list by accident.' And so he continued to beg and grovel, until Hyacinthus was moved to permit his release also.

Bishop Victor was not at all pleased to see Callistus' return, but he could not bring himself to return the poor wretch to Sardinia. He sent him to Antium instead.

'You can hardly remain in Rome,' said the bishop. 'Carpophorus still lives here, and so do many others you have robbed.'

'How will I live?' Callistus cried. 'You can't send me to starve in Antium. Surely you don't want me to turn to crime!'

'I will grant you a monthly allowance of food,' Victor said. 'But you must go to Antium and stay there.'

In Antium Callistus got up to his old tricks again, and it was there that he managed to make a friend of the minister Zephyrinus, who later succeeded Victor himself as bishop of Rome. And, as noted above, this was the route by which Callistus rose to a position of power, finally becoming bishop himself.

Even as bishop, however, Callistus could not win. The true believers, led by Hippolytus, attacked him as a heretic. The Sabellians also condemned his teachings, claiming that he had perverted their system in order to make it more palatable to the church. When Callistus died, after a reign of less than five years, his school and teaching collapsed and the church reunited to fight the battle with heresy.

Hippolytus himself followed in the footsteps of his teacher Irenaeus, and among many other books he wrote a major work

"I am not ashamed of the Gospel'

Roms 1:11-17. In the face of shame
I will _not_ be ashamed.

Three reason why we can become
      ashamed of the gospel:

1. World see's it as foolishness
2. Gospel offensive world
3. The world despises those who
   proclaim the gospel.

Reason why we should not be
ashamed
1. Gospel is good news
    entrusted to us
1 Cor 9:16
Roms
2. Gospel is the only way "om1"
3. Gospel is the power of God

Callistus may not have been a good example, but there were other church leaders who had once been slaves. This reveals something significant about the church. Christians, believing that all are created in the image of God, denied that slavery made one a second-rate person. The attitude of pagan society could not have been more different. Roman law allowed masters to kill their slaves without giving any reason for their conduct, and it was generally accepted that even women might use brutal tortures on their female slaves if the mood took them. For the vulnerable, history has seen no greater boon than the growth of Jesus' church.

against all of the heresies, including those of Sabellius and Callistus. In gratitude for his services the Roman Christians built a statue in the teacher's honour, with a list of his books engraved on it.

HIPPOLYTUS, *HERESIES* 9.6–7

Philosophers and Fiends

The mission of the Christian philosophers to the pagan world was not without its troubles. By the late second century many pagan philosophers, startled by the challenge, were rallying in an attempt to silence the new school.

A Cynic philosopher named Crescens was one of the first to lock horns with the church. He publicly debated with Justin in Rome, but when the searching questions of the Christian exposed his complete ignorance of Scripture, rather than study the subject more closely and return for a second bout, this 'lover of wisdom' (the literal meaning of 'philosopher') adopted the easier method of lobbying the courts to take sterner measures against the believers, Justin in particular. Sadly, his efforts were successful.

Better informed on Christian belief was Celsus, author of a lengthy work designed to 'expose' and refute the gospel.

'Why would God want to come to earth?' he asked. 'Obviously not to see what is going on down here – for He knows everything already! It is inconceivable that the great and holy God could assume an unclean body. He no more cares for mankind than He cares for apes and maggots.'

Celsus scoffs at the hope of resurrection and labels those who believe such things 'mindless worms'.

'The Christians make most of their converts amongst the superstitious and ignorant lower classes. They are a mob of uneducated slaves, beneath contempt. They can convert women easily enough, but no man of any sense will have a bar of them. Picture them, these Christian slaves, sitting out on the porch and discussing the deep issues of theology! How could they conceivably know anything of God – wiser than their masters I presume! No indeed, for as soon as the master comes they go silent. Such a contemptible mass of folly could only be inherited from that worst of nations – the Jews!'

Celsus dared not mention the growing number of Christian philosophers in his scurrilous book – it was easy to sneer at slaves, a bit harder to attack the likes of Justin. The pagan did not see, however, that his own words were the clearest proof of the gospel's glory. Christianity was raising the Roman slaves to wisdom, raising them up from the contempt in which the likes of Celsus had always held them. The gospel was a divine wisdom that reached out to every man who was not too proud to confess himself the equal of a woman, a child, a slave.

The spite of Celsus did nothing to halt the Christian march. A more formidable pagan foe appeared in the second quarter of the third century. Neoplatonism, a new school of philosophy, attempted to construct a new religion from all that was best in the pagan world. For it was becoming obvious that Rome, as it was, could never defeat the church. In their bid to revitalize Rome and strengthen paganism against the Christian attack, the Neoplatonists encouraged good morals, distanced themselves from idolatry and embraced all sorts of magical arts in the attempt to harness miraculous and healing powers. Plotinus and other Neoplatonist leaders even spoke of Christ as one of their religious heroes.

'Jesus' teaching is true and good. He is one of many good men who have come to show the way to God, but the Christians err in believing Him to be the Son of God. Nonsense! He is no greater than many of our Greek holy men.'

Some Neoplatonists went even further, composing mythological histories about famous pagans of the past.

'Why accept a Jew as your Saviour? Apollonius, the Pythagorean philosopher, has just as much claim to your worship. He raised the dead, cast out demons and healed sickness. Moreover, if you worship a pagan saviour, we will not throw you to the lions!'

Indeed it seemed that the empire was going quite mad. Satan was pulling every trick in a last-ditch effort to slow the spread of the gospel. Where the sword was failing, mimicry might succeed. Vain hope!

Origen's ministry was highly important at this time, and his skill in argument became legendary. At Ambrose's urging he wrote a major work that cut the arguments and snipes of Celsus to pieces. And when he once attended the lecture theatre of Plotinus, the greatest Neoplatonist, the mere sight of him virtually scared the false teacher from the room.

'That's enough for today,' said Plotinus. 'I have nothing more to teach you.'

The Alexandrian school, with its polished and articulate defence of the gospel, dealt Gnosticism (whose higher 'knowledge' now looked absurd by comparison) a blow from which it never recovered. This ensured that, as the gospel slowly conquered Rome, it was freed from pagan addition and perversion. The church was now toe to toe with the greatest pagan minds, and her blows were raining down fast and hard.

The attitude of the emperors towards the church fluctuated greatly during the third century.

The persecution that began under Septimius Severus slowly wound down, until by the time of Alexander Severus (222–35) the church was entirely at peace with the authorities. Alexander employed a number of Christians in important posts and, inspired by the gospel teachings, even placed statues of Abraham and Christ in his personal shrine (where they sat rather uncomfortably beside his idols). His mother was also

Origen's ministry did the church great good, but after his death the teacher became a highly controversial figure.

In his efforts to defeat Gnosticism Origen was often forced to tread upon new ground, to come up with Christian answers to problems which had never before been examined. Most of his work was sound, but with such a huge volume of writing as Origen produced, in areas so new, there were bound to be problems. He had few predecessors in Christian philosophy to refer to, and so (in his early writings) he too often allowed the ideas of the Greek thinkers to direct his understanding of Scripture – a fact that has made most Christians treat his writings with caution.

Origen's reputation, however, has suffered most from a story about his early years as a teacher. Origen, unlike most pagan philosophers, took on female pupils, and this caused a great deal of scandal in Alexandria. To silence the slanderers who accused him of immorality, and with a mistaken interpretation of Matthew 19:12, 'some have made themselves eunuchs for the kingdom of heaven', Origen castrated himself. Many have doubted the truth of this story, but it does seem to be based on fairly solid evidence. Regardless, we can be assured that if the story is true Origen repented of the deed in later life, for his commentary on Matthew expressly states that literal castration is a false interpretation of the text in question. Origen's extreme application of the passage has been a graphic warning to later ages of the dangers of false interpretation of scriptural hyperbole (i.e., exaggerated figures of speech). And, though the story of this strange act has harmed his reputation, to be fair to him, we should at least remember that castration was not nearly so unusual in those days as it is now. A few pagan philosophers are reported to have done the same thing, and eunuchs were a common feature of ancient society.

favourable to Christianity and once had a personal interview with Origen.

In this atmosphere the church found itself flooded with new converts – but not everyone was convinced that all was as well as it seemed. Origen himself wrote that persecution had in some ways been a blessing, forcing a complete and perpetual reliance on Jesus, and he questioned how many of these 'easy' converts would have the courage of their convictions if trouble returned.

His question was answered by Alexander's successor Maximinus. Maximinus hated Alexander bitterly, and one of the ways he avenged himself on the deceased was by punishing the religion Alexander had favoured. Hippolytus was one of the first martyrs, and Origen's friend Ambrose was among those imprisoned.

Bishop Pontianus of Rome also fell victim. He was succeeded by Anteros, but when Anteros died only a month after his ordination the Romans had to again summon a church assembly. Fabian was among those who travelled to Rome from the country for the fresh election. He was not even a contender for the position but, just before the casting of votes, as names were being suggested, a dove descended amongst the believers and settled on Fabian's head.

'Fabian!'

No one was more surprised than Fabian himself, who was immediately and unanimously elected.

But with the death of Maximinus peace returned again and, as Origen had predicted, the church appears to have emerged from the troubles even stronger. Some of those who had been lukewarm had fallen away, but many more now emerged from the forge with a new zeal and devotion. The church's rapid growth continued, and about ten years after Maximinus' death a new emperor, Philip the Arabian, showed himself even more favourable towards the Christians than Alexander Severus had been. It seemed inevitable that an emperor would embrace the faith in the not-too-distant future; it was equally inevitable, however, that the forces of the old pagan culture would not die quietly.

The last years of Philip's reign saw an unprecedented round of festivities throughout the empire, with the official millennial celebrations of the founding of the city of Rome. Most Christians refused to involve themselves with the pagan festivals, and this provoked many idolaters against them. As the year 1000 in the Roman calendar (AD 247) came and went, the excitement and fears associated with 'big round numbers' were much in evidence. And, with frequent reports of barbarian attacks on the frontiers, emotions ran hot in all ranks of society. Towards the end of Philip's reign a mob persecution spontaneously erupted in Alexandria – it was but the slightest taste of what was to come.

Decius (249–51) followed Philip on the throne. The persecution that he authorized, the Decian persecution, was something far beyond anything the church had previously suffered. Earlier persecutions had aimed at slowing the church's growth and had mainly concentrated on the major cities. The persecution under Decius was empire-wide and aimed at the church's complete destruction.

'The empire is faltering,' Decius lamented, 'and nothing seems to slow the barbarian advance. How have we angered the gods? Surely it must be this new religion and its insults to our traditions!'

Superstitious pagans all over the empire agreed. All it required was a whiff of imperial approval, and mob fury blazed forth as never before. Hundreds of Christians were seized and stoned, their possessions were stolen or burned, and within weeks the Roman cities, stained with blood and filled with smoke, looked as though the barbarians had already destroyed them! The mobs, the emperor and the Neoplatonists joined arms in the most brutal assault that a religious group had ever suffered.

Fabian of Rome was one of those cruelly killed by Decius. Origen, now almost seventy, was imprisoned and horribly tortured.

'If we can force blasphemy from Origen, the Christian rabble will be devastated!'

The pagans, however, were to be disappointed, for the great teacher survived his ordeal to outlive Decius himself. Stories of courage and suffering abound from all over the empire. One heroic Christian woman, Bona, was dragged by her pagan husband to an idol temple.

'You will sacrifice whether you like it or not!'

'I must obey my God even before my husband,' she replied.

'Then we shall see who is the stronger!' said her husband, holding her hands and performing the sacrifice with them while Bona struggled against him.

'My husband's hands, not my own, are performing this abomination!'

'If you refuse your husband's kindness,' said the judge, 'you can see how well you prefer hard labour! Away with her!'

In the African city of Carthage a group of believers was stoned and burned by the mob. Other Christians, as usual, were quick to collect the bodies for burial, and with them was a girl whose parents had been among the martyrs. The girl wept loudly when she found her mother's body, and her friends encouraged her to return home.

'No. I will see my poor father first,' she insisted, but a moment later her tears were lost in a cry of joy. 'He's alive!'

Her father Numidicus was in a terrible state, but with careful attention and much prayer he recovered quickly. Cyprian, bishop of Carthage, was astounded at the man's survival and later ordained him as presbyter.

'He has remained among us,' he wrote in one of his surviving letters, 'that the Lord might add him to our ministry, sadly depleted as it is by the death of some and the falling away of others.'

Numidicus was not the only Christian to have a marvellous escape from death during this persecution.

EUSEBIUS, *CH* 6.21–41; CYPRIAN, *LETTERS* 18, 34

Dionysius and the Wedding Guests

Early in the persecution the pagans sent officers to arrest Bishop Dionysius of Alexandria. The bishop, though aware of his danger, refused to flee.

'Someone must remain to guide the church. I shall stay and accept God's will.'

So for four days Dionysius waited for the officers to arrive. The officers, for their part, searched everywhere for him. They blocked the roads, examined the rivers and wandered through the fields. In fact, they did everything but search the branches of the trees around his residence – but they couldn't find the bishop anywhere.

'The Lord has struck them with blindness! The only place

they haven't looked is in my house. I suppose it is a rather unusual hiding place.'

Dionysius was one of Origen's two most famous students. The other was Gregory Thaumaturgus, bishop of Neo-Caesarea in Pontus. Thaumaturgus means 'Wonder Worker', a name Gregory acquired on account of a series of great miracles under his ministry. Although few details are recorded, Gregory's work as bishop of Pontus was evidently one of the great successes of missionary history. 'When I arrived here,' he said shortly before his death, 'there were 17 Christians in the region. Now there are about the same number of pagans.'

That night, however, the Lord spoke to Dionysius and commanded him and his friends to flee. For a time the bishop was a 'wanted man', sheltered by his congregation as he moved from house to house, until one day at about sunset he was speaking with friends in the front room of one such refuge when the door flew open and several soldiers charged in.

'Arrest them! That one is the bishop – take care he doesn't escape.'

'You have nothing to fear,' Dionysius said. 'No one will attempt to escape.'

'Take them to Taposiris. We will keep them at the barracks tonight.'

Timothy, a young Christian who had been staying with the bishop's group, was out when the soldiers arrived. He returned after dusk to find the house guarded by soldiers and apparently empty. He caught his breath, turned on his heels and fled into the night.

'Lord, spare my friends! Deliver them from harm!'

'Timothy!' a voice boomed behind him. 'Whatever are you doing out here?'

The young man nearly leapt out of his skin, but he looked about in the dark to see the familiar face of Gaius, a Christian from a farming area near Alexandria.

'Oh, hello,' Timothy managed to pant. 'What are you doing here?'

'I'm on my way to a wedding feast,' Gaius said. 'I'm a little late, but that's no matter as the celebrations usually go on all night. The real question is what are you doing, running around out here in the dark?'

'I've just come from the house where the bishop has been staying. It looks as though he's been arrested. Soldiers are guarding the house.'

'Where do you imagine they've taken him?'

'Probably to Taposiris.'

'Well,' Gaius paused, 'it seems the only thing for you to do is to come along with me now. There's no good in wandering around on your own.'

The pair soon arrived at the feast and received a cheerful and rowdy welcome.

'All right, that's enough,' Gaius began. 'We have some very bad news. This young man believes that Dionysius has been arrested and taken to the barracks in Taposiris.'

The whole party was momentarily silent, before with one movement and one shout all burst for the door and ran into the night. It was not long before Dionysius and his friends and guards were shocked by a fearful noise. The barracks door was beaten down and the duty soldiers, greatly outnumbered, took to their heels. Dionysius was left lying upon a bare couch, clothed only in a linen garment.

'If you are thieves,' the bishop called, 'you may take my clothes which are beside me here, but I apologize that I've nothing better to offer you. I am here under arrest.'

'Get up bishop, we're here to rescue you. Come quickly!'

'Oh, no!' Dionysius cried. 'You will only make things worse. Go, leave us!'

'We've already scattered the guards,' said the wedding guests. 'Come with us!'

'If this is your idea of help you may as well cut off my head for yourselves! I can't come – it would just further inflame them against the church. Now we are really breaking the law, attacking barracks and freeing prisoners!'

'Don't worry bishop,' someone said, as he and two others

lifted Dionysius between them. 'We know what's best!'

'You are breaking the law,' Dionysius cried, throwing himself onto the floor. 'Leave me to my fate!'

'You take his hands, I'll take his feet!'

And with that, Dionysius was 'rescued'. The bishop was hastily carried out of town and, seated on an ass, he was conveyed to a hiding place in the Libyan desert where he remained until the end of the persecution. Many others fled to the mountains and deserts at this time, and not a few disappeared in the wilderness without a trace. Others, sadly, escaped such a fate by compliance with the authorities. One man, who was on the verge of denying Christ, was saved in an odd manner.

'Sacrifice to the gods,' the governor demanded, 'or you will die.' The man stood uncertainly. 'Sacrifice now!'

The man was about to go forward when he and everyone else noticed that four of the court soldiers and an old man, standing near them in the crowd, were making strange gestures. They were grinding their teeth, shaking their heads and signalling to the fearful believer. When they saw that they had not gone unnoticed by the bystanders, all five charged up to the judge together.

'Come on brother and join us,' they said to the waverer. 'We are also Christians!'

At that there was silence, and the governor himself visibly trembled.

'Then it is death for you also,' he finally managed. 'Away with them.'

The Decian persecution sparked debate on an important question – whether those who had sacrificed, the 'lapsed', should be allowed to return to the church. A Roman named Novatian argued that they should not, that by their actions they had declared themselves unworthy of the fellowship of saints, and at first many agreed with him. Novatian pointed to Christian leaders of the past who had expressed similar opinions, and he called upon the church to ensure that the standards of former ages were not allowed to slip. As the diabolical Decian persecution wore on, however, and more people became guilty of the offence, the debate became more earnest. Perhaps, it was pointed out, some past leaders had shared Novatian's view, but that was when the church was smaller and persecution less severe. In time the spirit of forgiveness conquered, and it came to be accepted that after a period of penance for their sins, the weak should be restored to the fold.

A group of hardliners, however, refused to accept this charitable idea. Under the leadership of Novatian they formed a small breakaway sect and, ignoring all pleas for peace from the mainstream church, they were soon established in many cities of the empire. They not only forbade the lapsed to return to their churches, but they insisted on the permanent excommunication of all those guilty of any manner of major sin. They were the first group to break with the church purely on a question of discipline.

One of Dionysius' letters tells the story of a man who had sacrificed from fear. His name was Serapion, he was old and had lived a pious life, but since his weakness he had been excluded from his church. His brethren were at that time in agreement with Novatian, and Serapion's pleas and assurances of repentance fell on deaf ears.

Serapion fell seriously ill and lay for three days in a coma. Awaking on the fourth day, he called for his grandson.

'I cannot die until I have been accepted by my brothers. Go quickly and ask the priest to come to me,' and with those words he again became unconscious. His grandson ran with haste to the priest.

'You must come quickly. Grandpa's dying and wants you to forgive him.'

'I'm sorry, but I cannot come,' said the priest, 'for I too am ill. I will, however, give you some communion bread for your grandfather. That will give him courage to die.'

The boy returned to his grandfather immediately, and as he opened the door Serapion again stirred.

'You are come,' he said. 'The priest could not come with you, but do as he told you and then let me die.'

In amazement the boy placed the bread in his grandfather's mouth, Serapion swallowed, and the next moment was gone. To Dionysius, the story was God's own answer to Novatian.

'God accepted Serapion, whatever men might say.'

Another, unrelated, problem also became prominent at about this time. The success of the mission to the heretics had raised the question of what was to be done with those who had received baptism into a heretical group. Should they be baptized a second time when they entered the true church?

Some attacked heretical baptism as a mockery and said that no spiritual benefit could flow from a ceremony performed by a rebel against God. Taking this view to extremes, others even suggested that baptism performed by a minister guilty of secret immorality, a wolf within the true church, was worthless. But if this was the case, how could anyone know for sure that their own baptism had been valid? How were they to judge?

Again, thankfully, common sense was victor and the church eventually united in the belief that baptism is a gift of God and not of the minister who performs the ceremony. It was agreed that baptism into the name of the Trinity was valid regardless of the minister's standing before God. If, however, baptism had been into the name of a false god of some sort, the ceremony must of course be repeated.

Emperor Decius, meanwhile, after two years as emperor, two years of bloody persecution, went to war with the Gothic barbarians.

'I have spilt rivers of Christian blood at the foot of the idols. The gods will grant me victory over all my foes!'

The gods showed their power, or lack of it, in a decisive manner, when Decius himself perished on the field. Gallus, who rose to the throne in his place, at first permitted the Christians to live in peace, but with barbarians still attacking and a terrible plague stirring, the superstitious pagans were again blaming the Christians for all their woes. As Tertullian had said half a century earlier: 'If the Tiber rises too high, or the Nile too low, "The Christians to the lion!" is the cry.'

In another of his letters Dionysius writes, 'Gallus was too foolish to perceive what had caused the fall of Decius. His reign was relatively prosperous until he attacked the church, and he seems not to have understood that war on the men of God meant war on their prayers for his peace and welfare.' No wonder that he also was dead, murdered by his own soldiers, after reigning less than two years.

EUSEBIUS, *CH* 6.40 – 7.5

The Stirrup and the Stuffed Emperor

Valerian succeeded Gallus, and for the first three and a half years of his reign the church enjoyed a welcome peace. It seemed, in fact, that Valerian was more favourably disposed towards the church than any of his predecessors, and it was soon widely known that a great part even of the imperial household were professing Christians. All was well, until Valerian fell under the spell of an Egyptian by the name of Macrianus.

Macrianus was a talented general, and Valerian had raised him to a high position in the empire. The danger for the church, however, was that Macrianus was a leader amongst the Egyptian magicians. Valerian used divination and sorcery in seeking answers to the empire's troubles, and under the tuition of his general he practised all manner of rites in the hope of revealing the mind of the gods. The abominable pair even used human sacrifice to seek a 'sign', but when repeated attempts failed to bring a useful message Macrianus laid the blame squarely on the church.

'The gods are displeased with the emperor. Your household is full of unbelievers, and you will receive no aid from heaven until you remove them. I have had long experience of such things in my home country. A Christian need only enter our shrines and the angered gods depart immediately.'

Valerian could well believe the magician's words, for it was widely known that the 'gods' were not at all pleased at having Christians for company. For centuries the pagans had received messages through the temple oracles, and inspired by the gods of prophecy their priests and priestesses would issue warnings and make predictions, often in a state of trance. Christians, sure that such people were demon-possessed, often visited the temples to pray that the Lord would silence the spirits and, as Macrianus complained, their prayers were effective. It is a challenging fact to our sceptical age that even leading intellectuals of the early church believed that a Christian who entered a temple and failed by his mere presence to silence the oracles was a false believer. They held that the powers of darkness were incapable of enduring the Spirit's presence.

Urged on by Macrianus, the superstitious emperor dismissed all Christians in his employ and soon afterwards, in AD 257, he issued a decree for the exile of church leaders.

A number of Alexandrian ministers, including Bishop Dionysius, were among the first to be tried. Together they were exiled to a miserable desert place called Cephro, and it was no small testimony to the love of their people that word of the calamity inspired many Christians to follow them. The savage inhabitants of Cephro attacked and stoned these Christian exiles upon their arrival.

'Be brave, little flock!' Dionysius encouraged them. 'God can open a door even here!'

And so He did. The gospel had never before been preached in Cephro, but Dionysius' flock shared their faith with the local people. They soon saw a new church born in the barren place and, as though God had sent them there for this very purpose, the authorities moved the bishop elsewhere immediately after the church was established. His new home, Colluthion, was an even more dangerous place than Cephro, but it was closer to Alexandria, and Dionysius could there receive regular visits from the Christians of the capital. He remained in Colluthion for the rest of the persecution and was able to conduct his ministry almost without interruption.

The Egyptian bishop was more fortunate than most, since he was out of the way in exile when the persecution worsened. It didn't take long for Macrianus to see that threats of exile would accomplish little.

'Emperor, we must stop toying with the Christians. They are too stubborn to bow at the threat of exile – we must use brutal force.' And, with Macrianus in control, the empire soon plunged into a persecution even bloodier than that of Decius.

By the third century there were many levels of official responsibility in the church:

- Bishops guided a major church and were superintendents for an area
- Presbyters (i.e., priests) pastored a smaller congregation
- Deacons were the chief assistants to the bishop
- Deaconesses worked with female Christians, doing tasks that it was improper for male deacons to perform – e.g., home visitation to single women and assisting in the baptism of women
- Subdeacons were aids to the deacons
- Readers read the Scriptures to the congregation
- Exorcists were gifted in the casting out of evil spirits and assisted at baptism

There were also singers, church janitors and other minor roles.

Xystus, bishop of Rome, was one of the victims of this persecution under Valerian and Macrianus. But the story of his martyrdom is overshadowed by that of his deacon, Lawrence. As Xystus was arrested, Lawrence followed him in despair.

'Will you really leave me fatherless?' Lawrence cried. 'As deacon I have served you in all things. I have always laboured by your side in the church. Do not now take it upon yourself to suffer for Jesus alone!'

'Have no fear of that,' said Xystus. 'In three days you will walk the path which I now follow.'

The bishop was executed, and immediately afterwards Lawrence was called before the governor.

'I hear that the followers of Christ are generous in their gifts to the church,' he said. 'Hand over the church treasures and your life will be spared.'

'As you wish,' said Lawrence, 'but I must ask a few days to collect them.'

'Excellent. You have three days.'

Handing the church's property to the pagans was of course the last thing in Lawrence's mind. Instead, he distributed the church funds among the poor and lame and, accompanied by a crowd of the recipients of this charity, presented himself before the governor on the third day.

'I have collected the church's treasure as you commanded.'

'Splendid! Let me see.'

'Here they are,' said Lawrence, indicating his companions. 'The treasures of the church!'

The governor was enraged at the disappointment.

'That's enough of your humour. You will not die any ordinary death!'

Lawrence was sentenced to be slowly roasted on hot coals, but the governor watched in frustration as the deacon endured his punishment with complete calm. Just before he died the martyr sat up, almost chuckling at his tormentor's confusion.

'I am just about done,' he said. 'Whether I am better well done or raw, you will have to decide for yourself!'

Bishop Cyprian of Carthage was another victim of this persecution. At first he was exiled, but on the night of his arrival in exile the Lord warned him of his eventual fate.

'Last night,' he told his friends the next morning, 'before I had even fallen asleep, I saw a vision. A youth of enormous height led me to the courthouse. A judge was seated there and he looked at me sternly and began to write. The tall young man stood behind him and, reading the judge's writing, he began to look troubled. Without a word he mimed the blow of a sword, and from this I knew that I had been sentenced to death. When I understood this I begged the judge to grant me a day's delay, and he again began to write. From the look on his face I knew that he had granted my request, and the young man also signalled that I had been allowed one day. It was all so strange that even now I don't know quite what it means. I do know, however, that I will be beheaded and that I have been granted a postponement before it happens.'

It was not until one year later that the exact meaning of the day's delay was proved. Until then, the exiled minister continued his work of leading and encouraging the church by letter and word of mouth, waiting for the sentence which he knew was to come. Exactly one year later, on the anniversary of the vision, Cyprian was executed. Many had encouraged the bishop to escape and even offered hiding places, but Cyprian was not interested.

'I have already received my sentence,' he told them. 'For some reason I must remain. It is part of God's purpose.'

Hands stained by the blood of the empire's best citizens, Valerian confidently gathered an army for the invasion of Persia. The result will hardly surprise. Valerian himself was captured and taken in chains to the Persian king.

'Greetings, mighty emperor! Be not cast down, for I have an honourable job to offer a great but fallen ruler!'

The emperor was pushed onto his knees, and in this abject position he implored his insulting foe with a look of grovelling hopefulness.

'You shall henceforth be my stirrup! Surely you will consider it an honour to be the support of the king of Persia!'

For the rest of his life Valerian was the cruel Persian's personal slave. When mounting his horse King Sapor would tread on Valerian's neck to lift himself, and when the emperor finally died Sapor had him stuffed and put on display in a Persian temple.

Gallienus, son and successor of Valerian, had sense enough immediately to issue a new law. He ordered an end to persecution, returned church buildings that had been seized, and effectively made Christianity a legal religion for the first time in its history. It was a great victory to be sure, but not all of the empire was thereby freed from persecution.

Macrianus and his two sons had survived the disastrous war with Persia. Indeed they had done more than survive, for in the heat of battle it was Macrianus who had manoeuvred Valerian into danger and permitted him to be captured. He prevented the soldiers from mounting a rescue operation and, following the battle, had himself and his sons proclaimed as emperors. For about a year they controlled much of the eastern part of the empire, and wherever they reigned persecution continued. One victim was a young soldier, Marinus of Palestine.

Marinus was summoned before the tribunal to receive a military promotion, but before the magistrate could speak another soldier burst in and halted proceedings.

'It is not right for Marinus to be raised to this position. It rightfully belongs to me.'

'On what grounds?'

'On the grounds that Marinus is a Christian and refuses sacrifice to the emperors.'

Judge Achaeus was disturbed and turned to Marinus in surprise. 'Is this true?'

'I am a Christian,' Marinus confessed.

'You must deny your faith this moment.'

'I cannot do that.'

'You have three hours to change your mind,' said Achaeus. 'This is no small matter, and we are not just talking about your promotion. Refuse worship to the gods and you will be beheaded. Consider carefully.'

Marinus, his joy turned to sorrow, slowly left the court, and news of his plight spread swiftly. Theotecnus, the local bishop, came to speak with him. Taking Marinus by the hand, he led him to the church. He pushed back Marinus' cloak and exposed the sword that hung by his side, and then placed a copy of the Gospels on a table before him.

'Decide.'

Marinus did not pause a moment, but put forward his hand and grasped the Gospels.

'Be strong,' said Theotecnus, with a sad but firm smile. 'Hold on to the promises of God. Go in peace and pray for strength to accomplish what you have chosen.'

When the three hours were up Marinus returned to Achaeus in high spirits.

'I have considered and cannot do as you ask. Jesus is my Lord now and forevermore.'

Immediately he was led out to execution. A wealthy and respected Roman senator named Astyrius was present at the martyr's death, and coming forward without a word he lifted the lifeless Marinus onto his shoulder and departed. There was a gasp of surprise from the crowd, but none dared speak against a senator, and Astyrius returned home and prepared a public and fitting burial. It was not the only time this man had set himself against the pagans.

Jesus' conquest of death is nowhere more evident than in the ancient Christian cemeteries. The tomb inscriptions brim with confidence and joy in God's love and the promise of resurrection. They make a stark contrast to the contemporary pagan cemeteries. Most pagans viewed death as dark, mysterious and miserable, and the hope of even those with some belief in life after death fell far short of the Christian expectation. Interestingly the early Christians, like the Jews, always buried their dead – while their Roman pagan contemporaries commonly practised cremation.

In the cemeteries we see many examples of the artwork of the ancient church. The favourite symbol was the fish – the letters of the Greek word 'fish' (*icthys*) stand for the words 'Jesus Christ, God's Son, Saviour', and the fish also recalled the miraculous feeding of the crowds and the apostles as 'fishers of men'. Another favourite artistic symbol was the Good Shepherd. In an age when the church was so often defenceless, and Christians were like lambs for the slaughter, the idea of Christ as shepherd was very dear. The most popular non-biblical writing of the early church, incidentally, was an allegorical fiction called 'The Shepherd' by the apostolic father Hermas.

The springs at the foot of Mt Panius were a pagan religious site, and on a certain feast day each year a sacrificial beast would be cast in. To the wonder of the crowds, instead of floating it would completely disappear.

'The gods have eaten it!'

Visiting the site on this day, Astyrius was filled with sorrow.

'God of all the earth,' he cried, looking up to heaven, 'in the name of the Lord Jesus I ask You to expel this demon and cure these people of their delusion.'

'What?' the pagans began to mumble. 'What's that?'

It was the sacrificial animal, which had gently floated back to the surface. From that day forth, the priests were never again able to summon their demon. Wherever they went, Christians like Astyrius were destroying the powers which had misled the world for centuries.

EUSEBIUS, *CH* 7.10–17; PRUDENTIUS, *MARTYRS' CROWNS* 2; 'THE LIFE
AND PASSION OF CYPRIAN'

War and Plague

In the wake of Valerian's capture, the empire was torn apart
with civil and foreign war. Besides Macrianus and his sons there
were at least another dozen pretenders to the throne. The
barbarians also inspired by Persia's success, thought that the
empire was theirs for the taking and were attacking with
renewed vigour. The devastation in Alexandria was such that
Bishop Dionysius wrote that it seemed the Nile had again turned
to blood!

One imperial pretender, established in the Alexandrian
citadel and surrounding city district, suffered a long siege from
the troops of Gallienus. There was no way out for the citizens,
many Christians among them, who lived behind his defensive
lines. As the pretender's supplies ran short they were hit with
severe famine. Caught between the sword and starvation, a
Christian minister named Anatolius got a secret message out of
the city to Eusebius, a Christian of high standing who knew
Gallienus' general personally.

'Food is scarce and we are beginning to starve. Ask the
general if he will permit us to desert the city in peace.'

Eusebius took the message to the general, who agreed
immediately.

'Leave as soon as you can, and you will be perfectly safe.'

At that Anatolius called a meeting of the rebel leaders.

'The enemy will allow us to surrender,' he told them. 'We can
save the lives of the whole city if we submit now.'

The leaders were unimpressed and professed their readiness
to fight to the death.

'You could at least allow some to leave,' Anatolius argued.
'There are many old people and children here, many men and
women who are useless for the army. They eat our food but

can't help us fight, and if they stay will only waste valuable resources. I vote that we allow them to depart in peace.'

The Alexandrians agreed to this motion, and Anatolius swung into action. He gathered all who could not fight and then gathered more and more besides. As a great crowd marched from the city to safety the rebels were amazed.

'What a good idea that was,' said one. 'I had no idea there were so many women in the city!'

In fact all of the Christian men, and many of the pagan men also, had just marched out to the enemy wearing women's clothes. The emaciated refugees were received by Eusebius, and under his careful attention were restored to health; the rebels, reduced to a handful, soon surrendered.

But the troubles of Alexandria were not finished. With the defeat of the rebels a dreadful plague began, and the city was again full of the dead and dying. The pagans fled from their sick friends and relatives, even throwing the dying into the streets in an effort to escape contact with the illness.

Things were totally different for the Christians. They nursed the sick with joyous zeal and gave the dead fitting burial. Many caught the disease from those they cared for, but even this could not deter them. They were used to suffering, and it mattered not whether they were attacked by emperors or diseases. They would still do the works to which their Master had called them.

What could the Romans do? They had savagely persecuted the Christians for generations, but the gods were not any the more favourable to them. The barbarians still attacked, pretenders still arose, and plagues still decimated cities. How could Rome find peace?

Gallienus, of course, tried something different, and at the start of his reign he made peace with the church. He was no friend to Christianity, but he could see that, if the last decade had proved anything, it was that persecution was clearly not the way to make heaven propitious. For the next 40 years a succession of emperors followed him in respecting the rights of the Christians and, as the liberated church went from strength to strength, the Emperor Aurelian (AD 270–75) actually had to reprimand the Roman Senate for neglect of the idols. He scornfully remarked that they seemed to think they were in a Christian church, not in the city of all the gods!

Aurelian himself was the only emperor of the period to plot against the church. Hoping to stem the rising tide of conversions, he drew up an anti-Christian edict, but he died suddenly before it could be put into effect. As the years went on, many pagans began to think that the gods had finally lost. It was undeniable, even to those who hated Him – there was a power in this Christ!

Many pagans were prepared for the gospel by elements of their own culture and religion, for no people has strayed so far that God has not left many 'loose threads' in their culture – hints and ideas which can be used by Christian missionaries to link in with the gospel story. Pagan Rome, for example, was already familiar with the idea that above their many gods there was only One supreme God, and their mythology contained more than one tale of the death and resurrection of a god. But perhaps the most striking 'thread' of all was a prophetic poem by Virgil, pagan Rome's greatest author, written some 40 years before the birth of Christ. Striking and enigmatic, the fourth Eclogue moved many educated pagans (the great Constantine among them) to give the teaching of Jesus careful attention. The whole still repays a careful reading – the more striking lines include the following:

'The final age has come and the great cycle of centuries is born anew. The Virgin returns, the golden age of Saturn [the Roman father of the gods] returns, and a new generation comes from on high. Look favourably on the boy, he with whom the race of iron ceases and a people of gold is created throughout the world . . . Every vestige of sin shall dissolve and leave the world free of dread and the boy, with the life of a god, shall rule a world at peace . . . Cattle will no longer fear lions, as the child's cradle pours forth flowers, the serpent and the poisonous plant perish and every field becomes a bed of spices . . . The ground will no longer be worked with sweat and tears . . . and the fleece of the lamb shall be blood red upon its back.'

Was the church going to grow gradually until paganism all but disappeared? How long would it be before one of the emperors themselves was converted?

EUSEBIUS, *CH* 7.21–32

Mani and Paul of Samosata

Now that there was peace with the pagans the devil could only attack the church from within. His first move was to raise up two of the most dangerous heretics yet.

Mani the Persian (also known as Manichaeus) was by far the most successful of the two heretics. His thinking was heavily influenced by the Zoroastrians and the Elkesites – and to explain who these groups were, we must step further back in time.

Several centuries before the birth of Christ, the people of both the northern and southern kingdoms of Israel had been exiled from their homeland and carried in chains to the lands across the Euphrates. There they had lived under foreign domination – first under the Assyrians, later under the Babylonians, and finally under the Medes and Persians.

As is well known from Scripture, some Jews rose to high office in the governments of their oppressors and were outspoken in their opposition to their masters' idolatry. Less widely appreciated is the fact that, shortly after the prophet Daniel's death, the Persian kingdom officially abandoned idolatry and promoted a new religion that in certain features resembled Jewish monotheism.

Just how much the success of this new religion, Zoroastrianism, is attributable to the influence of Hebrew prophecy is impossible to determine. The teaching of Zoroaster, certainly, was quite different from both Judaism and the traditional paganism of Persia. Like the Jews, the self-proclaimed Persian 'prophet' taught the worship of one God and condemned the use of idols, but beyond this the differences are more striking than the similarities. Zoroastrianism is dualistic rather than strictly monotheistic. That is, it worships only one god, but believes also in a second, evil, god, who is the source of all misery and sin. The rejection of idolatry also was partial, for though Zoroaster abandoned gods of wood and stone, his followers practised fire-worship, believing fire to be the symbol and holiest gift of the good god. In ceremonial law

Zoroastrianism was even further astray, for while the Law of Moses promotes cleanliness and health, Zoroastrian laws aim mainly at protection from evil spirits. A main ingredient of these ceremonies is *gomez* – the Persian name for ox urine! Zoroastrians consider this revolting stuff exceedingly holy and frequently wash in it and drink it to make themselves 'clean'!

Our interest now, however, is not in the perversities of Zoroastrian practice, but in their basic idea that the universe is divided between two diametrically opposite deities. This idea had already exerted an influence on Gnosticism, and it now became the foundation of a new perversion of Christian teaching.

Mani, born about AD 220, was raised in the midst of Zoroastrian culture, but as a child his family converted to the sect of the Elkesites. This cult, a strange mixture of Jewish and Gentile errors, followed a 'holy' book (like the Mormons in modern times) which they claimed was given to their founder by an angel and (like Marcion) used a cut-down version of the Bible.

At the age of eighteen Mani left this obscure cult and began to formulate a religious philosophy of his own. A decade later, claiming divine inspiration, he undertook a preaching tour of the eastern lands.

Mani's teaching has been described as Zoroastrianism with a Christian varnish. He accepted Zoroaster's fundamental dualism, but borrowed from the Elkesites the name of Jesus and a few biblical books. He despised the created world and taught extreme asceticism. He claimed that the disciples had falsified the teaching of Jesus and that he, Mani, was the Holy Spirit whom Jesus had promised (Jn. 14:26) would remind the world of His teachings. He taught that Zoroaster, Buddha and Jesus had all come from the good god to show the way of truth, and that the new Manichaean faith had come to unite the various religions in one.

In the east Mani found a ready audience among Zoroastrians and heretics. The church, however, was largely deaf to his entreaties.

'We cannot accept your prophecies. We believe in Jesus Christ and His apostles and cannot accept teachings contrary to the Scriptures.'

The land of Mesopotamia bordered on Persia, and Mani decided to try his hand with the church there. To his disciple Turbo he entrusted a letter for Marcellus, a famous and wealthy Mesopotamian Christian.

'Carry this to Mesopotamia immediately. You need no money for the journey, as you can stay with the Christians along the way.'

Mani knew that the Christians had many hostels for travellers but, unfortunately for Turbo, he didn't know that in obedience to 2 John 10 they were careful to exclude heretics.

'May I have a bed for the night?'

'Who are you and where are you from?'

'I come from Mani, a master among the Christians of Persia.'

'Sorry, but we know of no such Christian leader. You cannot stay here.'

For several days Turbo had to go without food or a bed at night. He would never even have made it to Marcellus without a change of story.

'Who are you?'

'I am Turbo. I am carrying an important letter to Marcellus.'

'Ah,' said the hostel keepers. 'A friend of Marcellus! Come in, come in!'

Thus Turbo reached his destination and finally met Marcellus, whom he found in conversation with Archelaus, the local bishop. Marcellus accepted the letter and read it aloud:

'From Mani, an apostle of Christ and all the saints and virgins who are with me, to Marcellus, my dear son.

'Grace, mercy and peace to you from the Father and the Son. May the right hand of light keep you safe from the world's wickedness. Amen.

'After hearing of your love and generosity with delight, I was saddened to learn that you hold a faith perverted from the truth. On this account, appointed as I am to be the teacher of mankind and showing mercy, as I do, to those who hold foolish doctrines,

I have determined to write that I might save yourself and your friends from error – chiefly the horrid belief that there is only One God. If you care for your eternal salvation I suggest that you send word by my messenger, that I might come and correct you. Consider carefully my words, most honourable son.'

'The rogue!' Archelaus cried in amazement. 'Who is this that seeks to change Christ's gospel?'

Marcellus instructed his servants to bring food and drink for Turbo. 'Do not worry, bishop,' Marcellus said, 'I will send for this Mani and you can question him in person.' Marcellus dictated a brief note and offered it to Turbo. 'Would you be so good as to take this to your master?'

'I beg you, sir,' Turbo whimpered, remembering his journey. 'Find another to take it. I've no desire to go back, or indeed to have the least thing to do with Mani ever again!'

'I understand,' said Marcellus, 'you may stay with me. I will send one of my servants.'

Marcellus' servant found Mani on the Mesopotamian border. The letter was delivered, and though the 'prophet' was pleased by the invitation, he could not help feeling that Turbo's failure to return boded no good. With considerable unease the prophet proceeded on his way.

Turbo, meanwhile, was interrogated at length by Archelaus on the teachings of Mani. The bishop was astounded at this mishmash of false wisdom, a curious confusion of heretical and pagan errors, but he was not nearly so astounded as was Turbo himself to hear from his hosts the true gospel teachings.

'I too wish to become a Christian!'

News of these strange goings on filled the whole town with excitement. Upon his arrival Mani tried to find Turbo, but failing in this he sought out Marcellus instead.

'Greetings. I am Mani.'

Marcellus was momentarily lost for words. Dressed in high heels and a coat of many colours, a huge Babylonian book under one arm and an ebony staff in the other hand, wearing trousers with one red leg and the other green as a leek, Mani was quite a sight.

'I have eagerly awaited your coming,' Marcellus managed. 'I shall summon our bishop, who is keen to have words with you and some other respected men of the town.'

All was soon prepared.

'Mani and Archelaus,' said Marcellus, 'I think that the truth will best be revealed if you face each other in public debate, and I have requested four men to sit as judges of the discussion. They are followers of the pagan religion, they have no sympathy for either of your views, and will be impartial in awarding the victory. Mani may begin.'

'Brethren, as a disciple and apostle of Christ, I have come to free you from the foul errors of Archelaus, a man who leads you astray like dumb animals . . .' thus began a lengthy exposition of Mani's beliefs.

With a plethora of spurious arguments (mostly along the lines of 'how could a good God make a bad world?') and many misused scriptural quotes, Mani endeavoured to prove that there must be two gods, who are mortal and eternal enemies. Once the basics of his position were out on the table, the debate quickly heated up. From the length of the surviving record it seems that the confrontation must have lasted some hours. The argument passed endlessly between the two speakers, until finally Mani's contortions were lying in disarray, exposed for the lies they were.

'Archelaus has won!'

Children standing nearby began to throw rotten fruit at the 'prophet'.

'An offering for your evil god!' they called.

Others joined them, pelting stones at the foreign teacher, until Archelaus broke away from those congratulating him and stopped the violence.

'Christ has had a victory today,' he said. 'It is a joyful day. Let us not end up with blood on our hands!'

Mani was not going to stay around to congratulate, or thank, the bishop, and removing himself from sight with all haste he departed, never to return. Turbo, overjoyed with the victory of his friends, made his new home in Mesopotamia and in time became a deacon of the church.

But Mani was not to be stopped so easily. He next stopped in a small town some distance away.

'Here, I will have better luck. I'm not likely to run into the likes of Archelaus in this backwater.'

The prophet began preaching his wares at the local market. None could answer him, and some simple folk became his disciples. The local Christian minister, Diodorus, was horrified and sent Archelaus a full report of the Persian stranger. Astounded that Mani had dared show his face again, Archelaus wrote back with details of his own encounter. He gave the rural priest many suggestions on how to handle Mani in argument, and Diodorus was soon ready to debate with the foreigner. Mani was most perturbed at this development.

'Where did this country bumpkin learn all this?' he said to himself, as he slunk away to lick his wounds and come up with a new plan. 'I can still beat this one,' he decided. 'He seems fairly simple. I'll fix him tomorrow!'

The next morning Mani challenged Diodorus to another public debate, but just as he started his speech, who should appear but Archelaus! The bishop strode past Mani and greeted Diodorus.

'I sent the letter,' he said, 'but then thought it might be better if I was here to deal with things in person.'

Diodorus was overjoyed and breathed a sigh of relief. Mani himself almost fell over, and for a moment the only sound was the grinding of his teeth. 'How can I get out of here?' he muttered under his breath, though out loud he pretended that the bishop's arrival meant nothing to him.

Archelaus began the debate this time, and the result was the same as before. In fact, the bishop was still talking when Mani made a run for it, and burning with frustration made his way back to Persia.

But the false prophet's problems were not over even then. Some Zoroastrian priests complained to the king of Persia that Mani was trying to pervert *their* religion, and the monarch had Mani and many of his followers executed and the false prophet himself stuffed and displayed (clearly the king had a taste for taxidermy). Mani's ignominious end, however, did not signal the end of his cult – but more of that later. Such, at any rate, was the story of the Persian prophet. The other heretic of this time was Paul of Samosata.

In 260 Paul became bishop of Antioch, one of the empire's greatest cities. Soon after his ordination, however, strange rumours began to spread about his teaching.

'Paul is teaching a new doctrine, and much of his flock has swallowed it whole. He says that Christ was not truly God on earth, but that He only became a divine being after He ascended to heaven.'

Troubled by this report, a number of Christian leaders came to Antioch to see for themselves what was going on.

'Christ only "a sort of god"? We will see about this!'

A synod was held, Paul was put to the question, and with tensions running high the bishop denied all accusations. Eventually his testimony prevailed.

'I believe nothing but the apostolic truth.'

The other bishops departed and left Paul to rejoice in his victory.

'They won't be back in a hurry – now's the time for some real changes!'

He wasted no time. Paul ordered the construction of a huge throne for his church and then employed a number of bodyguards to accompany him continually.

'You can't be too careful,' he said.

He next formed some of his followers into a choir and composed new hymns for them.

'This is what we will be singing in church from now on.'

The congregation was amazed at Paul's new throne – more so at his sermon.

'Silence please. These are the beliefs of our church, so listen carefully.'

Paul now assailed his flock with a baffling hotchpotch of heresy and scriptural misinterpretation and when he finished speaking his followers, strategically positioned around the church, cheered and threw their handkerchiefs in the air. It was a rather disappointing spectacle, as no one else joined the show of appreciation.

'What's wrong with you?' the bishop thundered. 'As bishop, I demand a little more respect! I tell you there are going to be a few other changes around here as well. I have decided to replace the old hymns to Jesus with a number of new ones I have composed myself. Listen carefully to the choir and see how quickly you can pick up the lines.' Paul turned on his throne to face the choir. 'Sing!'

'God of heaven,' the choir burst forth, 'thank you for the teaching of Bishop Paul!'

'Louder!' he cried, slapping his thigh.

It shouldn't be surprising that a new synod was soon summoned! This time Paul was exposed and excommunicated, and one Domnus was appointed in his place. But the heretic was not to be beaten so easily.

'I care nothing for your decrees,' he cried, stalking out of the synod. 'See if you can remove me by force! I am bishop whether you like it or not!'

Queen Zenobia of Palmyra had recently seized control of Antioch and, befriending the Arabian queen, Paul had been appointed as her governor.

'I am not only the bishop,' he boasted, 'but I am the governor as well. How dare anyone excommunicate God's chosen ruler!'

For about four years, Paul and Zenobia kept their places. When the Emperor Aurelian put down the Arab rebellion, however, bishops from all over the empire made complaint to the victor.

'The church voted long ago that Paul of Samosata should be deposed, and until now he has only kept his place by force.'

'Rome is the royal city,' said the emperor. 'The bishops of Rome and Italy shall decide the matter, and I will act on their verdict.'

The Italians did not hesitate a moment, and Paul of Samosata was sent fleeing from his city in disgrace. Heresy had lost yet another battle, and the true faith continued to thrive in Rome.

'THE ACTS OF THE DISPUTATION WITH THE HERESIARCH MANES';
EUSEBIUS, *CH* 7.27–30

Gregory the Illuminator

The Roman emperors were not going to have the honour of being the first rulers to accept the gospel as their religion.

The late second century had seen Abgar, king of Edessa, become the first ruler to embrace Christianity. Edessa, however, was a tiny kingdom – little more than a single city – and still a century later no larger realm had followed it. But the time had come.

The kingdom of Armenia occupied a precarious corner of the world. It was situated between the two great rivals, Rome and Persia, and its king was usually controlled by one or the other of these powerful neighbours.

Christianity had entered Armenia very early, but most of the population remained pagan by the middle of the third century, a time at which Armenia suffered one of the most devastating attacks in its history. The land was overrun by the Persians, and the conquerors attempted to compel all, pagan and Christian alike, to accept Zoroastrianism. Internal treachery compounded the foreign troubles, and when a noble named Anak assassinated the Armenian king and was himself struck down by the king's attendants, the Armenian cause was utterly lost. The only option left for the leading citizens was to flee the country.

One refugee was Tiridates, an infant son of the assassinated king, who was sent to Rome and educated there in the traditions of Roman paganism. Another refugee was Gregory, son of the assassin Anak, who took refuge in the Roman province of Cappadocia and was there befriended by the local church and eventually converted to the gospel.

The Persians held Armenia for many years, but they were finally expelled by the Roman Emperor Diocletian. The Romans established Tiridates on the throne of his fathers and, when news of this turn of affairs reached Cappadocia, Gregory could not resist the desire to return to his homeland.

'Christ calls me back to my people.'

Soon arriving in Armenia, Gregory began publicly to proclaim Christ's message. In a short time many were converted, and it was not long before the king himself heard the 'Good News'.

'Gregory has dared return! Arrest him immediately, as the son of an assassin and as an enemy of the gods.'

The unfortunate missionary was dragged before the king, and after severe tortures he was thrown into a narrow dungeon.

'Let him rot there!'

For nearly fifteen years Gregory remained in a cold and lightless cell. Indeed he would most probably have starved to death on the pittance he was provided had not a Christian widow secretly brought him food during his imprisonment. Fifteen years! Would God not act on behalf of His herald and His church? It seemed not, and there were worse things yet to be feared from Tiridates' rage.

'I want this foreign religion rooted out. The friends of Gregory must be compelled to return to their old allegiances – to myself and to my gods!'

But sometimes God moves in mysterious ways. A beautiful young woman, Hiripsime, once caught the king's eye.

'I desire that woman as my wife.'

Tiridates needed to say no more – Hiripsime was immediately brought before him. Her response, however, astounded him.

'How could I marry the murderer of my people?'

'Murderer? I am the king of your people – what madness are you speaking?'

'My people are the Christians,' said Hiripsime, 'and their blood is on your hands.'

'Don't be a fool,' Tiridates menaced, 'I am offering you something that other women would die for!'

'I would *rather* die!'

'Then you shall!' said Tiridates, slamming down his fist. 'Execute her at once!'

Murder is easy for a *king*, but not so easy for a *man*. When the day was done Tiridates went to bed feeling quite uneasy. He managed to sleep, but after much tossing and turning he awoke in terror about midnight, shaking all over as he remembered his dream.

'A demon came and turned me into a wild beast, a boar,' he whispered to himself, 'and Hiripsime was there, accusing me for my cruelty!'

The memory of Hiripsime now became a cruel torture to Tiridates, and madness slowly spread over his mind. Day and night the king was a nervous wreck, and it was not long before the whole land saw the dark change. One day the king's sister approached the throne and spoke to Tiridates in private.

'My royal brother, may I share with you a dream which I had last night?'

'I don't know,' said the king in fear. He looked down at his trembling hands and became silent.

'I saw a man with a shining face, who told me that there is only one cure for the king's sickness.'

'Yes! What?' Tiridates cried, springing forward and startling everyone. 'Tell me this moment!'

'He told me that Gregory must be released from prison. Only then will there be healing.'

At that the king slumped back into his throne and closed his heavy eyelids.

'Do it.'

Pale, thin and almost brittle in his frailty, Gregory was soon brought in before the king.

'What do you want?' he asked quietly.

As the situation was explained, a small but sad smile came over Gregory's face. He fell on his knees and began to pray.

'Lord, relieve this man of his illness. I know that he has persecuted Your little ones, but I pray that You will forgive him and let him feel the wonder of Your salvation!'

The king was soon restored to health, and after discussions with Gregory, and with his own household, the whole royal court was baptized. It was the year 301, and the first major ruler had become a Christian.

Gregory was installed as 'catholicus', or chief bishop, of the Armenian church. Together king and bishop destroyed the pagan temples of the land, and Gregory and a number of eager missionary colleagues began the enormous task of spreading the Christian teachings throughout Armenia. It was a work of many decades, but with the aid of a king it was a far different proposition from that which faced the Christians of the empire.

Gregory is to this day known as the 'Illuminator', the man who brought the light of Christ to a whole nation. At his passing in 325 there were few alive who could claim to have achieved so much for the conversion of the world to the Christian faith.

AGATHANGELUS, *HISTORY OF TIRIDATES*

The Diocletian Persecution

But what was going to happen in Rome? Were the emperors going to accept the gospel?

Many Romans thought so. Even the wife and daughter of the Emperor Diocletian became believers. There was peace for more than forty years – long enough that most Christians could not even remember what persecution was like. But a change was soon to come.

For the moment, the church's main problems were internal. Heretics like Paul of Samosata were one problem, but even worse were the more subtle deceivers who had crept into the flock. By now some cities were almost entirely Christian, and in most Roman cities Christians accounted for anything from a sixth to a half of the population. The position of spiritual minister to such large groups made the bishops very powerful men, and it became evident that some were entering the church, and then the ministry, in the hope of gaining such authority for themselves. The higher positions in the church were soon disgraced by worldlings, squabbling amongst themselves in a shameful pursuit of leadership and power.

A time of testing was again at hand. The cross was going to triumph over Rome, but it was not going to be the triumph of human beings. God was going to put His church through the furnace and expose what was really in the heart of all who called themselves Christians. This testing would be Satan's last chance to destroy the church, before pagan Rome itself was destroyed.

Emperor Diocletian was the man behind this last persecution. His twenty-year reign had seen many other major changes in the government of the empire.

Prior to the rise of Augustus Caesar, the first emperor, Rome had been a republic with many democratic features. When the early emperors changed this system, they had to be careful not to make the alteration too abrupt. The very name of king was hated in Rome (hence the adoption of the title 'emperor' – which had originally been a title accorded to victorious generals) and for many generations, realizing that moves against tradition could provoke rebellion, the emperors kept up a public pretence that they were little more than leading magistrates. It was only under Diocletian, three hundred years after Augustus, that the last signs of the old democracy finally disappeared. Faced with widespread discontent and insurrection, Diocletian sought to secure greater respect for the imperial power by the introduction of changes that are sometimes referred to as the 'Asian ceremonial'. He assumed royal dress (gem-encrusted robes and shoes, whereas previously the only distinguishing garment of the emperors had been a purple robe), and like the rulers of the ancient Asian kingdoms of Babylon and Persia, he expected his subjects to fall on their faces before him and to grovel out their requests in a posture of abject humiliation.

Diocletian performed an even more radical action when he split the empire into separate principalities. The troubles of the times required more attention than was humanly possible from any one emperor, and Diocletian divided the empire into four parts, each of which was to be held by a different ruler. Two of these rulers, himself and Maximian, were emperors (both assumed the title of 'Augustus'), while the other two, Galerius and Constantius, shared the imperial power, but were effectively understudies to their older colleagues (they were dubbed 'Caesars'). Diocletian's idea was that when the emperors died the Caesars would succeed them, and new Caesars would be selected. It was an interesting system in theory, but a failure in practice. All four rulers ended up at each other's throats, and things were so wild at one stage that there were six emperors, all at war amongst themselves! But not yet – while Diocletian was at peace with the church, the empire enjoyed internal tranquillity.

It was Galerius the Caesar, a violent and superstitious man, who was chiefly responsible for the new persecution. Addicted to all the excesses and sins of pagan culture, Galerius had an immense loathing for the church which was slowly destroying the old ways. He complained to his superior, Diocletian, without end.

'Are you a coward?' he blustered. 'Why don't you have some stomach and stand up to the church? Christianity is an enemy to our religion, our culture, and our empire itself. It must be crushed!'

Persistence finally paid off. Diocletian released an edict ordering the destruction of church buildings and the removal of Christians from government positions. No sooner was it posted than the individual believers began to show their true colours. Those strong in faith and Spirit suffered punishment for the name of Jesus without hesitation, while the half-hearted gave in without a struggle. But Galerius was not satisfied.

'Too mild! You will never get through to these fanatics without much tougher measures than those.'

The emperor was soon brought to agree. In Nicomedia, where Diocletian himself lived, the local Christians were not at all deterred by the first wave of persecution. As soon as the new laws were displayed in public a respected Christian nobleman tore them to pieces.

'Unjust laws will perish!'

Diocletian ordered the protester's immediate execution, and when a fire broke out in his palace soon afterwards the emperor suspected that it might have been started by Christians angered at the new laws. When another fire occurred 15 days later he decided that it could not be an accident, and that someone was definitely trying to get him. He was right, but that someone was actually Galerius, who was starting the fires to turn the emperor more sharply against the Christians. His scheming was again successful.

Diocletian issued a second, harsher, edict against the church, and this was soon followed by a third. Tension continued to build until April 304, when a fourth edict carried the situation to its inevitable conclusion.

'All Christians are to be executed immediately.'

The ink was no sooner dry than a thousand city streets were stained with blood. The empire exploded into the most savage persecution yet seen, and men and women alike were rounded up and killed in great numbers. Diocletian encouraged his governors to invent new varieties of torture to afflict the stubborn faithful, and the empire was darkened with the disgusting spectacle of a mighty emperor throwing all his energies into making the lives of his subjects a hell on earth. The groaning church, however, did not have to wait long to see God put an end to the plotting of her imperial foe.

Within months of the fourth edict Diocletian came down with a terrible disease. He became extremely weak and wasted away to such an extent that he was unrecognizable. Galerius came to visit the invalid, but not to wish him a speedy recovery.

'You must resign now,' the younger man demanded. 'Unless Maximian and yourself step down there will be trouble between us.'

The weakened emperor bowed to the demand and promised to raise Galerius and Constantius to the supreme power. Galerius also demanded the right to choose the two new Caesars.

'I want Severus and my friend Maximin as Caesars.'

'Severus, the dancer!' Diocletian exclaimed in horror. 'But he's a notorious drunkard – do you really imagine that the citizens could be brought to respect such a ruler? What about Constantius' son Constantine, who is stationed here in the military camp right now? He is popular and all the soldiers are expecting him to become a Caesar.'

'I couldn't care less,' said Galerius. 'My wishes are more important than the ignorant whims of the masses!'

When the day for the appointment of the new emperors and Caesars came, the army was astounded at Galerius' announcement. Constantine himself hid his feelings, but from that moment on knew that Galerius was keeping an eye on him. When news arrived that Constantius was dying, Galerius was overjoyed.

'With him gone I can promote my friend Licinius in his stead.' The three other rulers would thus be Galerius' stooges – and he alone would reign supreme.

Constantius soon sent a message to Galerius, requesting that his son Constantine might visit him before his death. There was nothing the tyrant wanted less.

'If he goes to his father the army will make him Caesar whether I like it or not.'

For a time Galerius delayed, making various excuses for not permitting Constantine's departure. In the hope of disposing of his problem, he arranged a tournament in which the soldiers could prove their skills in combat with wild beasts. Galerius commanded Constantine to take part in the dangerous exercise and was infuriated to see his foe leave the ring not only uninjured, but possessed of even greater glory in the eyes of the soldiers after a valiant and muscular display. After long stalling, the emperor finally gave in.

'You may leave for your father's province tomorrow. See me first thing in the morning and I will give you a number of letters for delivery to the western provinces along your route.'

Galerius, of course, was already planning to ensure that Constantine never made it. When the young man left him he sent a trusted servant with a message for the dancing drunkard Caesar Severus:

'Constantine will be passing through your realm on his way to Gaul. Stop him at all costs.'

Fortunately, Constantine did not trust Galerius one iota. Instead of waiting for the next morning he went straight to the imperial stables, took a horse for himself, released all the rest, and with his speedy mount headed for the west at breakneck pace.

Post-horse stables were positioned at appropriate points along the Roman highways. An imperial messenger with an urgent despatch could thus travel a long distance at consistent high speed, regularly exchanging his exhausted horse for a fresh one. At each stable Constantine changed his own mount and set the other horses free, hoping thereby to slow anyone the emperor might send after him.

Galerius stayed in bed until noon the next day, hoping to delay Constantine's departure as much as possible. When he finally called for Constantine, he learned too late that his treachery had been defeated. His agents were sent in pursuit, but without fresh horses they could never hope to catch the fugitive. Constantine stayed one step ahead of his foes the whole way and reached his ailing father just in time.

'My son!' The old man was delighted and soon called an assembly of the soldiers.

'I am about to go to the other world,' he told them, 'and I ask you all to respect my son as you have respected me.'

'Long live Emperor Constantine!' cried the soldiers. 'Long live the emperor!'

And with that, Constantius passed away.

From that moment on, the empire was a scene of chaos. Maxentius, son of the retired Maximian, decided to emulate Constantine and proclaimed himself emperor. He gained a formidable military following and captured a large part of Italy, including the city of Rome itself. When Severus marched against him, the dancer was defeated and killed. Galerius also suffered a defeat at the hands of Maxentius, although he managed to escape alive.

Galerius further complicated matters by advancing his friend Licinius to the imperial purple. The Caesar Maximin was disgusted that someone had been promoted ahead of himself, and out of jealousy he proclaimed himself emperor also. Matters became even more confused when Maximian came out of retirement and tried to recapture his old province. Rome now had more emperors than one could easily poke a sceptre at.

But busy as the pagans were killing each other, the persecuted church knew little relief. Only Constantius and Constantine showed any tolerance, and Christians living under the other rulers suffered ten long years of affliction. Maxentius ended the official persecution in his own province, but his rule was so cruel to all subjects, Christian and pagan alike, that the church had little cause to celebrate the truce.

EUSEBIUS, *CH* 8.1–15; LACTANTIUS, *DEATHS* 7–32

The Tyrant Maximin

Maximin, who ruled over Egypt and Syria, was the most bloodthirsty of all the imperial persecutors. Urbanus, one of his Syrian governors, was particularly cruel, and among his many victims was Apphianus, a teenage student recently graduated from the great Greek school of Beirut.

The persecution was already three years old when Urbanus ordered the whole populace of Caesarea, men, women and children, to assemble at the idol temples to offer sacrifice. Any who refused were to be promptly executed as enemies to the gods. For Apphianus this was the final straw.

'Something has to be done!' he told his friends. 'Someone must confront Urbanus and Maximin with their error. If we could get through to them what the message of the gospel really is, they would have to see that we are their friends, not their enemies.'

His fellow believers were not convinced.

'It is best to stay low until the persecution is over,' they told him. 'Hide out and hope for the best. If you are going to be realistic about it there is nothing you can do but pray.'

Apphianus was not satisfied with such a path, and he went to the city's main idol temple the next day. Urbanus himself was there, just about to sacrifice, when Apphianus burst through the crowd of soldiers surrounding the altar and grasped the governor by the hand.

'Stop this evil!' he cried. 'You are sacrificing to "gods" who have no power to save. Turn away from their deceit and embrace the true religion of the Living God!'

Urbanus and his men were furious, and Apphianus was seized and subjected to the most horrible tortures. He was thrown into prison half dead, only to be brought out the next day and even more severely punished. Nothing, however, could break the martyr's spirit. Apphianus' feet were wrapped in oily rags and burned to the bone, his sides were cut until his organs and bones were visible, but with his every breath he continued to profess his faith in Christ. When every device of cruelty was exhausted,

Urbanus ordered that the student be thrown into the depths of the sea.

Apphianus was taken out from shore in a boat and, still breathing, was cast overboard, but even as he disappeared beneath the water there was a terrible blast of wind, and land and sea alike were shaken by an earthquake. The startled executioners took to the oars with desperate vigour, and those viewing the martyr's death from the shore stood stiff with horror. They looked from the churning waters in front, to the trembling city behind, and wondered where on earth they could run.

A freakish wave appeared in the distance, growing mightily as it surged for the coast. The watchers scattered, the wave hit the land with a dreadful crash and immediately afterwards sea and earth became quiet. The wave had left behind it, lying before the city gates, the body of the martyr Apphianus.

Urbanus, inflexible as the martyrs themselves, was not warned by this event and refused to soften his policy. He did not, however, long outlive his innocent victims. He lost favour with Maximin, and after being dismissed from his position was dragged, weeping and begging for mercy, to his own execution.

But still the persecution raged. Those Christians who were not executed immediately were blinded, and with their ankles seared so that they could only limp they were sent to the mines to do hard labour. Still their bravery could not be destroyed.

'Can't we break these people?' asked the exasperated rulers. 'How do you fight someone who rejoices in injuries and seems to prefer death to life?'

The pagans decided on a new and sickening law. They banned the burial of the bodies of the Christians, and the city streets were soon filled with the dead.

'Surely this will scare them!'

It seemed inanimate nature itself had a richer vein of sympathy than the pagan heart, for while the streets of Caesarea were choked with decaying bodies the most astonishing thing occurred. All of a sudden, on a day of clear blue skies, the walls and pillars of the city were covered with water, running down like tears. Christian and pagan alike were struck with wonder.

'The earth itself, the very stones, sheds tears for our suffering!'

It is not surprising that each day saw more pagans, even at the risk of death, accepting Jesus and joining the church.

The persecution, as always, was particularly severe in Alexandria. The local bishop, Peter, managed to evade capture for several years – quite a feat in those times – but about 311 he was finally arrested by Maximin's officers. There was, however, something quite different in the reaction of his flock to this new tragedy. A strange feeling was in the air.

'We are winning!'

The whole Alexandrian church, believers of every rank, seemed to be hearing the same voice within. Somehow they felt that this persecution was actually the last gasp of the pagans, and that peace must come soon. This time, when news of the bishop's arrest and impending execution spread through the city, instead of producing shock and fear it revealed a new determination.

'To the prison!' the cry resounded. 'To the prison!'

The whole city was amazed to find that the execution had to be postponed.

'The Christians have surrounded the prison, thousands of them, and they won't let a soul through!'

The city officials met and determined that a large force should be sent to break through the crowd, with orders to kill all who opposed them. Horrified at the prospect of a bloodbath, Peter sent one of the most trusted elders to speak to his people.

'Bishop Peter requests that you go home immediately. He is willing to die for Christ's sake, but will not allow you to sacrifice your precious lives so needlessly. You must leave!'

'Never!' the people cried. 'They can have the bishop, but only over our dead bodies!'

Peter had to come up with another plan.

'Tell the military leaders that I am willing to save them the trouble of battling the protesters. Have them send soldiers to the back of the prison tonight. As there are no doors or windows no one will be guarding the area. I will tap on the wall to show where I am, and working quietly they should be able to make a hole in the wall without anyone noticing. We must ensure that they don't confront the people.'

Pleased with this information, the leaders arranged for a group of soldiers and stonemasons to follow Peter's instructions. Peter was in prayer the whole night, pleading with the Lord to take his life but spare his flock, and in answer a great whirlwind and rainstorm struck the prison and nobody heard the chiselling out at the back. All went as planned, and it was not long before Peter was pulled through the wall and led away.

The soldiers were completely awed and could not even bear to look at the bishop as they led him to execution. All burned red with shame.

'May we stop at the tomb of Saint Mark?' Peter asked. 'He is the founder of the church in this city, and I would like to pray there.'

'Do what you want, but try to be quick.'

Peter went down on his knees and poured out all that filled his heart. He pleaded with the Lord to make peace for the church and begged that his own blood might be a seal to end the persecution. Rising up he spoke to the soldiers.

'Do as you have been commanded.'

At that the soldiers began to argue amongst themselves.

'I'm not doing it!'

'Well someone has to.'

'What about you?'

'What about you!'

'The mob will come after us if we don't do it soon.'

'Well, why don't you do it then!'

Finally they decided to each throw five *solidi* (which was a considerable sum) upon the ground. Whoever struck the blow should have it all. Each looked greedily at the money, but then, looking unsteadily upon the bishop, remained frozen to the spot. After a few silent and uneasy moments one of the soldiers took his sword and, his teeth clamped upon his lower lip, struck the bishop and killed him. The executioner grabbed the money and almost ran from the scene.

The crowd was amazed to discover what had happened.

'How is this possible?'

A Christian woman who lived near the tomb of Saint Mark came forth to the grieving crowds. She had spent the whole night in prayer.

'My brothers and sisters,' she said. 'While I was praying to the Lord last night I heard a voice. "Peter was the first of the apostles," it said, "and Peter is the last of the martyr bishops of Alexandria."'

The voice had spoken truth.

EUSEBIUS, *MARTYRS OF PALESTINE*; 'THE GENUINE ACTS OF PETER'

'By This Conquer'

Soon after Peter's death, the Emperor Galerius fell ill. A great ulcer appeared around his belly, and it finally burst to leave a huge open wound which swarmed with repulsive worms. The doctors and magicians could do nothing for the emperor, and the stench of his rotting flesh became so foul that none could endure to remain in his room. Galerius, writhing in agony and aware that death was near, was tormented by the grim knowledge of his crimes against the church. In his despair he called for a scribe and dictated to him the words of a new law – his famous edict of toleration.

'Those Christians who have left the church must return to it immediately. There is no longer to be persecution of any sort against them. Most importantly, all Christians must offer prayers to their God for Emperor Galerius and for the good of his empire.'

The tyrant was dead within the month, but at least his life had seen one good deed. The other emperors accepted his new law, the prison gates were thrown open, and the persecution ground to a halt.

In one area, unfortunately, the new peace was not to be long lasting. Maximin briefly bowed to the wishes of the other emperors, but soon after Galerius' death he revoked the edict and reinvigorated the persecution in his own realm. It was soon evident, however, that his wickedness was not to go unpunished much longer. Tiridates the Armenian, hearing of the renewed persecution, attacked and defeated the treacherous emperor. A terrible plague struck at the same time, and severe famine followed. Clearly the days of this tyrant were numbered.

It was, however, to be another emperor, Maxentius, who would be first to fall. But before we hear about his fate, we must briefly backtrack to see what became of his father Maximian, the man who had been the original co-emperor of Diocletian.

Things had not gone well for Maximian when he proclaimed himself emperor for a second time. He failed to win back his old province, and he was finally forced to flee to Constantine. Constantine was married to Maximian's daughter and was the only emperor who would protect the older man.

'Constantine, my well-loved son,' said Maximian, 'you have shown yourself a truly noble soul by giving me your protection. I resign my right to be emperor and pledge never to give you any trouble.'

But Maximian could no more change his ways than the leopard its spots. A barbarian army soon entered Constantine's realm, and the young emperor was forced to take the field against them.

'Accept some advice from an old man,' Maximian offered. 'A large army against these barbarians would be more trouble than it's worth – take rather a small force to deal with them. Believe me, I have been leading armies since before you were born!'

Constantine took the advice, and within a few days was on his way to fight the Franks. His father-in-law did not waste a moment.

'Constantine is dead!' he told the soldiers who remained. 'He has fallen in battle with the barbarians and I, to my sorrow, must succeed him.'

Maximian, of course, now had control of most of the army and was sure that when Constantine returned, with a small and battle-weary force, he would be easily defeated. News of the treason, however, spread quickly and it was not long before Constantine himself was aware of it. He returned with lightning speed to confront his rival, and Maximian was horrified to see most of the army desert him immediately. With his few remaining followers Maximian shut himself up in the city of Marseilles and prepared to fight it out. When Constantine arrived at the gates he went up on top of the wall to speak with him.

'What is it that you want, Maximian, and why have you treated my friendship thus?'

'Damn you, Constantine!' Maximian yelled. 'I'll not answer any questions from such a beast as yourself!'

'That is not pleasant language for either an emperor or a father-in-law,' Constantine replied. 'If I were you I would not be making my enemy any more angry.'

'Your anger means nothing to me, you worthless scum!'

While this unedifying conversation was being conducted above, some of Maximian's men despaired of success behind such a fool and, secretly opening one of the city gates, invited the enemy in. Maximian was soon dragged before his victorious son-in-law.

'I am well aware how little you deserve it,' said Constantine, 'but today I forgive your treason and grant you your life.'

Maximian, rather than being filled with gratitude, was made only more spiteful by this generous treatment. He saw that he had little chance of winning over the people and decided that his only hope of revenge was through the assassin's dagger. He involved no one but his daughter Fausta in the plot, commanding her to help him gain access to her husband's chamber during the night.

'Leave the door open for me. You must help me remove the disgrace I have suffered from that vile man.'

Fausta's predicament was not enviable. She knew that she held the lives of both her husband and her father in her hands, and with a dreadful knowledge of the result she reported her secret interview to Constantine. That night Maximian was arrested in the act of attempted assassination and was executed as his crime deserved.

Maxentius was secretly pleased that his father Maximian was now out of the way, but he used the execution as an excuse to declare war on Constantine. Constantine responded swiftly. His army was inferior to Maxentius', but the prize for victory was a great motivation. Delay would cost him both his kingdom and his life, whereas if he struck quickly and lethally the whole of the west would be his.

Marching on Italy, Constantine was grimly aware of the difficulty ahead. Maxentius had already defeated two emperors in battle and Constantine felt sharply the need for an ally. Who could he turn to?

'My predecessors have relied on the gods,' he reflected, 'but that seems seldom to have achieved much good. How many emperors, believing the prophecies and promises of the priests, have met with an unhappy end!'

While his troops took a rest on the march, the emperor entered his royal tent for privacy.

'I have, however, seen a higher power, one which makes men, even women, bold to endure anything.' The emperor was confused. 'Perhaps the idols are powerless, as the Christians say, but how can I be sure of the truth of this?'

Falling upon his knees, Constantine prayed.

'If there is a God who can help me, I beg You to reveal Yourself, to stretch forth the right hand of Your power.'

The emperor heard an excited babble breaking forth outside.

'Look! The sun!'

The emperor hastened from his tent and directed his gaze to heaven. Above the sun, which was high in the sky, he saw distinctly a bright cross, in the form of a letter 'X'. Staring in wonder, the emperor and his soldiers saw the words 'BY THIS CONQUER' inscribed on the flaming sign.

Encouraged, though perplexed, Constantine pondered the meaning of the sign until nightfall. As he slept, he saw Christ stand before him. The dream figure showed him a sign, an 'X' with a 'P' rising through it, and bid him use the sign on his military banners instead of the traditional pagan military symbols. 'X' (pronounced 'Khi') and 'P' ('Rho') are the first two letters of Christ's name in Greek.

Awaking, Constantine summoned skilled workers in gold and precious stones and ordered them to make a battle standard like the one he had seen. When the 'Standard of the Cross', or 'Labarum', was finished it was carried to the front of the army and the banners of the 'gods' were cast away.

Constantine's army, led by the Labarum, marched through Italy towards the tyrant's Roman stronghold and, after a string of successful encounters with divisions of Maxentius' army, the whole force was exultant in the wonderful power that they felt surrounded them.

'Christ of the Labarum, Christ who was crucified, is fighting for us!'

Soon Constantine was at the very gates of Rome, ready to take on the whole force of his enemy. Unwilling to risk a fair battle, Maxentius came up with a stratagem to turn the tide in his favour.

'Build a bridge of boats across the Tiber River,' he commanded. 'I will lead the troops against Constantine, but will soon let him think he has the better of me and, faking a retreat, will lead my army back across the bridge. The boats, however, will be prepared so that they can easily be sunk and Constantine's pursuit will end on the riverbed!'

On the day of battle everything went as planned, until Maxentius himself was halfway across his bridge of boats.

'Prepare to sink them!' he cried. 'When we are across and Constantine has reached about the same place that I am now . . .'

But he didn't finish another word, for just at that moment the bridge broke up of itself and the tyrant of Rome perished in the depths of the Tiber. Constantine's men watched in amazement.

'Like Pharaoh of old,' Constantine proclaimed, 'Maxentius has perished under the waves. "He who digs a pit shall fall into it!"'

Constantine led his triumphant troops into the great city, and the people received their deliverer with rejoicing.

'The tyrant is dead! Long live Constantine!'

The conqueror soon commissioned a statue of himself to ornament the ancient city. Grasped in the marble emperor's hand was the sign of the cross.

'Through the cross I have triumphed. The future of the empire is in Christ.'

EUSEBIUS, *CH* 8.15 – 9.8; *CONSTANTINE* 1.26–40; LACTANTIUS, *DEATHS* 29–30

The Edict of Milan

After celebrating at Rome, Constantine departed for Milan. There he met with Licinius, and between them the two emperors drew up the famous Edict of Milan.

The new edict freed Christians from all forms of oppression and ordered the immediate restoration, at public expense, of confiscated church buildings and other property – 'for by doing this we can be sure that the divine favour we have already experienced will continue to the distant future'. Whereas Galerius' edict had offered mere toleration, the Edict of Milan promised protection, even friendship. The conference of the emperors at Milan in AD 313 marks the opening of a new chapter in the world's history – Christian Europe.

The emperors soon left Milan. Licinius, disturbed by reports from the east, was compelled to return to his province by rapid marches. Maximin, the only other remaining emperor, had seized upon Licinius' absence to invade his territory.

'Give me victory,' the tyrant promised his gods, 'and I will sacrifice every Christian in my realm!'

The outcome will be no surprise. Maximin's army was defeated and the tyrant barely escaped with his life to go into hiding in Tarsus. Licinius, however, was hot on his heels. Knowing that the end was near, the tyrant Maximin had a huge feast prepared.

'I must die, but first I shall enjoy myself!'

He gorged on fine food, quaffed wine by the jug, and finally ended the meal with a huge dose of poison.

A new schism afflicted the church in the wake of the Diocletian persecution. Just as the Decian persecution had caused the strict Novatian to form his own sect in Rome, the new persecution led to a similar problem in North Africa.

Diocletian had ordered all copies of the Scriptures to be handed to the authorities to be burned. Some Christians, pretending obedience, had actually surrendered fakes – in some cases heretical writings or even medical works! A strict African group, however, the Donatists, insisted that even pretending to obey the emperor was a sin. They believed that Christians should be eager for martyrdom and should not use deception to save themselves. Like the Novatians, they wished to excommunicate all who had been guilty of any compliance with the pagans.

Following the persecution, the Donatists appealed to foreign church leaders and to Constantine himself and urged the rest of the church to adopt their practices. They pushed for their leader, Donatus, to replace the bishop of Carthage, whom they accused of laxity with those who had surrendered Bibles or fakes. It was the Donatists themselves, however, who found their beliefs condemned by the church at large, and their opponent bishop became more firmly secured in his position. The Donatists left the church in protest and split the North African believers in two.

'At least I die rejoicing!' he slobbered.

But even that was not to be. His bloated stomach slowed the poison's work, and for four days he lingered in agony, writhing on the ground and stuffing handfuls of dirt into his mouth. Finally driven to madness by the searing pain, the tyrant began smashing his head against a wall. His skull cracked and both eyes crushed, Maximin collapsed blinded and gasping for breath.

'I see God upon His throne!' the crazed and blinded tyrant screeched to his remaining followers. 'He is surrounded by His servants, all those thousands whom I have put to death. No! No! I am not guilty, I've done nothing to the Christians! It was others. It was other people!' The tyrant was writhing and groaning like someone under torture, until with a wheezing sob, 'I confess!' he said. 'I did it, I did it all! I killed them all. Oh Christ, have mercy on me!'

And with those words he died.

LACTANTIUS, *DEATHS* 45–49

The Desert Monks

The church throughout the empire, as well as in neighbouring Armenia, was in a quite new position. Not only was it free from persecution, but it now had the powerful Constantine as its friend and defender. Only a few months earlier the emperors had been burning churches to the ground – now they were building new ones, huge and ornate cathedrals that dwarfed their earlier sisters.

It was during this season of celebration that a bishop by the name of Eusebius wrote what has become one of the world's most significant books – a history of the church's first three centuries. Eusebius' work is a treasure trove of the works of the Spirit, preserving dozens of stories that might otherwise have been lost. A glance at the earlier pages of this book will show just how much of our knowledge of the first centuries of the church comes directly from Eusebius. Eusebius, with great justice, is known as 'The Father of Church History'.

Also inspired by the triumph of the church was the growth of an alternative Christian lifestyle which, on the surface, might seem a strange paradox. The days of Constantine and Eusebius witnessed the appearance of the first Christian monks.

From earliest times the church has contained a degree of asceticism. Frequent fasts, celibacy, extended periods of prayer and meditation – all these features marked out the ascetics of the first few centuries. The church had not been the first to encourage these tendencies. Ascetic prophets, down to the time of John the Baptist, were not unknown in Jewish society. John lived in the desert, ate a simple and sparse diet, and appears to have been celibate.

During the first two centuries, Christian ascetics lived in the midst of 'normal' society. They were marked out from other believers only by their stricter self-discipline, and it was not until the worst days of persecution in the third century that some abandoned the cities altogether, fleeing to the wilds simply to save their lives. Some perished, but others managed to support themselves for long periods on the meagre fruit of the desert.

Many ascetics found a new peace and joy in lonely places, delighting in their isolation from the temptations of society.

With the end of the persecutions, the number of ascetics taking the road to the desert further increased. It might seem strange that the defection to the desert should gain speed just as conditions improved in the cities, but the ascetics had their reasons. With Christians at peace with Rome and countless thousands flooding into the triumphant church, there was much to be gained by striving for positions within the church. The door of prosperity was for the first time opened wide to the long-suffering church, and to escape the associated temptations many opted out of society altogether. Under persecution the church had been forced to rely on God alone for her sustenance and strength. Monasticism, the desert ascetic movement, was an attempt to maintain this high level of divine reliance in an age when the world wanted to shower the saint with privileges, not blows.

Antony was the father of the desert monks. Born in Egypt about the year 250, Antony's young manhood saw the early part of the 40 years' peace from Valerian to Diocletian. Contact with ascetics fired a love of the celibate life in his young heart, and at twenty Antony gave away all his possessions and embraced a life of voluntary poverty and constant devotion.

At thirty-five Antony determined to leave behind even the few conveniences that the city still offered him and to make trial of the hardships of the desert. For the next 20 years he lived in the ruins of an ancient fort, sustained by wild fruits and supplies of hard dry bread that he received a few times a year. In this barren place he sought to subdue utterly his worldly desires and to accustom himself to uninterrupted communion with God.

The Diocletian persecution burst forth towards the end of these first two desert decades, and Antony's retreat was soon crowded with fugitives from the city. Men of all ages made their homes in the surrounding hills, and many were inspired by the older hermit's example to eke a meagre living of their own from the sandy soil. Antony became a teacher to this new desert society, sharing whatever wisdom he had gained from two decades of battling with the devil and striving for holiness. City folk, seeking the monks' prayers in their troubles, soon began visiting the desert retreat. Frequent reports of divine healings served to heighten Antony's popularity further.

In the darkest days of the persecution under Maximin, Antony briefly returned to Alexandria. He encouraged the suffering, visited the prisons and in all ways infuriated the authorities, but his appearance and inner strength were so striking that none dared lay a hand on him. When the persecution drew to a close, Antony left the city unscathed.

In the wake of Constantine's conversion, as noted above, many more ascetics fled to the desert. For Antony it was all rather too much, and in a quest for the quiet he had lost the first monk set out even deeper into the desert. He found a mountain some three days' journey away, a site that invited with a small but regular supply of water and a number of wild fruit trees. He lived here for most of the next forty years or so, much less frequently visited by the outside world. He cultivated a small garden, mainly for the needs of visitors and wayfarers. When he finally came to die, at the age of one hundred and five, he called his followers to him.

'The Egyptians,' he said, 'embalm the bodies of good men, especially martyrs, and wrap them in linen cloths. Instead of burying them they keep them on couches in their houses, thinking this an honour to the dead. I myself have reproached them and urged an end to a practice so repulsive to biblical precepts, pointing out that all the patriarchs and prophets and even the Lord Himself, were entombed. Many have heeded my words on this matter, but I fear that there may be some inclined to attempt the preservation of even my own bones. I have stayed far from the cities even during my life. I don't want my bones to be sent from city to city once I am dead! Keep the place of my burial a secret.'

With that established, Antony exhorted his brethren to persevere in the ways he had taught them and committed them to the Lord's keeping. Having bid farewell to each with a kiss Antony looked intently at the blue desert sky, an expression of great peace and comfort spread over his features, and with a look as of one about to greet a friend his spirit passed from his body. In obedience to the monk's command his followers accorded him a secret burial and then departed to their own places.

Strange as many of its features may seem, the lifestyle that Antony inspired had many beneficial effects upon the church of his time. Few were prepared to follow the hard road of a hermit, but most admired the desert monks enormously and many in the cities were encouraged to adopt some of their practices. Thus prayer, fasting and frugality were put into the spotlight – an important development in an age of increasing wealth and power within the church. The monks were a flesh and blood sermon on the shamefulness of greed, a challenge and inspiration to the leaders of the church.

The monks were also important because they usually held to a simple faith – a fact whose importance will become very clear in the following stories.

ATHANASIUS, 'THE LIFE OF ANTONY'

The Council of Nicaea

Following Maximin's death, Constantine and Licinius did not long remain on peaceful terms. Licinius first angered Constantine by protecting a man who had fled to him after attempting to assassinate his fellow emperor. Licinius was still a pagan, and as the years went by he became increasingly suspicious of his Christian subjects – especially on account of their admiration for his imperial rival, who was lauded by many as a new King David. Licinius eventually established himself as leader of the dying pagan faction and in a fateful move supported a new outbreak of persecution.

The empire was now explicitly polarized between the old and new faiths, and when a dispute over the borderlands between the two emperors began in 324, Constantine, to the cheers of the church, invaded the territory of his rival. Licinius was defeated in two major battles, and the patron of idolatry was dethroned and later executed. Constantine was now master of the whole Roman Empire – a union that had not been seen for 40 years.

Constantine's standard, the Labarum, was by now famed throughout the empire, and with the symbol of Christ before them his soldiers felt assured of divine aid in every encounter. The Labarum would be carried into any division that was hard pressed by the foe, and its presence never failed to inspire fresh courage and vigour. Constantine himself told the story of one young standard bearer's fate. Carrying the Labarum in the thick of battle, this man was thrown into a panic by the near approach of enemy soldiers. Handing the standard to another he tried to flee, but no sooner had he let go of his charge than a dart struck him in the stomach and he fell dead. The man who received the standard saw this and determined not to prove to be a coward himself. He refused to seek cover although a shower of darts fell around him, and standing firm in the thick of battle he survived the day without a scratch. It was some time before he actually realized the wonder of his escape, later seeing that the thin pole of the standard had been virtually covered with darts!

'No standard bearer has been killed doing his duty,' the emperor would relate.

Constantine now ruled the Roman world in peace. Great churches were built and God's children rejoiced in the dawn of a new age. Chapels and streets alike resounded with Christian praise, and after the dark night of paganism the world itself seemed to sing for joy in the light of truth.

Would the peace under Constantine deepen and spread as the world drank in more deeply the purity of Christ's gospel? Unfortunately it was not to be so simple. A man named Arius had just raised his head, a man determined to start a new kind of war against the church. The days of persecution were not finished yet!

The Greek philosophers had practised the art of dialectics for centuries. Dialectics is, at its best, the search for truth through discussion and logical debate. The philosophers would develop ideas, whether on the nature of God, justice, morality or any other topic, and then seek to convince others of their opinions through argument. They prided themselves on believing nothing that had not been proved through some chain of 'deep' reasoning. Some philosophers liked nothing more than logical debate and would invent strange and absurd ideas to show off their dialectical ability to the best effect. A 'proof' that the moon is square, or that men are dogs, was the sign of a master of the art!

Arius applied the arts of the dialectician to Christian beliefs. Instead of accepting Christian teaching in faith, Arius endeavoured to make the church conform to the stringent logical demands of Greek philosophy. Through a series of increasingly erroneous arguments, he sought to undermine the Christian faith completely.

'If Jesus is the Father's Son, He must at some time have been "born",' Arius began. 'If He was born, He cannot truly have existed since "the beginning", since there was a time when there was a Father, but no Son. No doubt Jesus is the first thing that the Father made and therefore the highest level of Creation – but how can we call Him the true God, if once He did not exist? God is eternal and complete – nothing that has been made can be called eternal and complete. The Father made the Son out of nothing, just as He made the world out of nothing. Though the Son is above the rest of the world, he must yet be infinitely below the Father.'

This was shocking enough, but Arius kept a little more quiet about what he knew to be the necessary consequences of his ideas.

'Christ is lower than the Father. He can't possibly fully know and understand the Father, nor is He a perfect representation and revelation of the Father.'

With this, all that the church stood for was destroyed. The world, so Arius would have it, was returned to the darkness of the pagan world. God was again 'unknown' and 'unrevealed'.

A good many Egyptian Christians were befuddled by the first step of Arius' argument. It seemed reasonable enough that a 'Son' must somehow have been 'born' – but once Arius had led his listeners so far he proceeded to propel them over the edge of the chasm of unbelief into which he himself had fallen. Soon his teaching came to the attention of Alexander, bishop of Alexandria, and a council was called to deal with the problem. Arius, and all who agreed with him, were excommunicated – but that was not the end of the matter.

Arius and his followers refused to bow to the church's decision. They began to campaign for their ideas throughout the east, and many congregations were split by Arius' dialectical subtleties. The clamour of religious contention became so great that the emperor decided that the only way to heal the rift would be to summon the leaders of the whole church together in a massive council to discuss the issues through to a solution. This First Ecumenical (i.e., 'Universal') Council was held at Nicaea in 325.

Sabellius in the third century, and Arius in the fourth, were arguing on the opposite sides of the same problem. Christians had always believed Father, Son and Holy Spirit to be God, but also that there is only One God. The question of just how the two statements related to each other, in what sense God is One, in what sense a Trinity, did not become a major issue until the heretics made their challenges. Sabellius thought that if Christ and the Holy Spirit were God then they had to be identical with the Father. This meant that neither Father nor Son nor Holy Spirit really existed, but that the One God simply appeared in one or the other form at different times. Arius, on the opposite extreme, argued that if the three Persons of the Trinity were distinct, as the church had urged against Sabellius, then only One of them could be the true God. He still called the Son and Holy Spirit 'god', but in a pagan rather than Christian sense. Pagans believed in a supreme God above their many gods, and just so the Arians believed in three 'gods', with the Father at the top. The truth, of course, is that Father, Son and Holy Spirit are eternally and equally God. The three divine Persons are One God, distinct as to their respective roles, but one in will, power and substance.

The Council of Nicaea was one of the most unusual events in world history. A single glance at the bishops would have revealed that this was no ordinary group of men. Many of these Christian leaders carried visible scars from the persecutions, some limped and a few were missing one or both eyes. They might have looked like a group of old soldiers, and that was not far from the truth. They had served in God's army, and having survived the war with paganism they were now enjoying the peace. The historian Eusebius describes one such warrior, John, an Egyptian Christian who had been blinded in both eyes.

'It is hard to express the astonishment I felt when I once entered church to find John reciting the Divine Scripture. Hearing his voice I presumed he was reading like anyone else – imagine my surprise to come closer and discover that he was using only the eyes of his mind! He seemed like a prophet who had written whole books of Scripture, not on paper, but on his own eternal soul. It confirmed to me that true excellence does not lie in the body, but in the mind and spirit of a man.'

Imagine the scene at Nicaea! A few years earlier these men had been tortured, their friends killed, for professing the faith. Now they were being called upon to discuss their beliefs with the emperor himself! How often would so many who had suffered for Jesus have been gathered from such distant lands in one place? Arius and his followers, the Arians, knew that their only chance of victory lay in completely confusing the council.

'Most of the bishops don't understand our ideas,' said Arius. 'And that's a good thing.'

'What about Bishop Alexander and his supporters?'

'We must convince the council that they are attacking us unfairly.'

So the council became a battle between two groups – the Arians themselves and the few Christians who saw through their deceptions. Between the two groups were the majority of the bishops, a large middle party who had never before had cause to examine such matters. They would decide the victory at Nicaea.

The debate was intense. The Arians twisted and shifted throughout the council in an attempt to cover up the ultimate tendencies of their beliefs but, notwithstanding, the danger hidden in Arius' words slowly became obvious to all. One Arian was foolish enough to spell out the heretical belief too clearly, drawing up an Arian creed that he asked those present to accept. It was no sooner read than torn to pieces and trampled on the floor.

A creed is a short statement of Christian beliefs, designed to be learned by believers. It states only the basics, the ideas most important for converts to be clear on. The churches had used creeds since the earliest times, but in different areas they were worded slightly differently. The creed approved by the council was the one that had been used in Palestine, although it was lengthened and improved during the argument with the Arians, both during the council and afterwards, so as to disable their verbal trickery.

Arius' friends began deserting him. The council decreed by an overwhelming majority that all who denied the true divinity of the Son should be excommunicated.

'But the Arians do have one thing right. We need a creed for the whole church, one that will forever prevent the return of such a deception.'

At first the Arians fought bitterly against the proposed creed, though it was becoming clear that they could not possibly win. One by one they gave up the struggle for their beliefs, and each agreed to add his name to the new creed. Only four men went along with Arius to the bitter end and, infuriated at their stubbornness, Constantine sent them into exile. Confronted with the emperor's just anger, two of the four soon gave in and Arius was reduced, it seemed, to only two followers.

Had this council destroyed the Arians? Not by a long way. Most Arians had only accepted the creed through fear of losing their positions, and these men left the council deeply dissatisfied. It was clear that if opportunity offered they would drop the mask and return to their old sentiments – but in spite of this the victory at Nicaea was far from a hollow one. The creed had been established as a rock of truth, a beacon to future generations and, hardly less importantly, the duplicity and moral cowardice of the Arian troublemakers had been exposed for all to see.

The Council of Nicaea dealt with many other questions. Some of the bishops, inspired by the growing ascetic movement, proposed a law barring married men from the ministry. The staunchest opposition to their suggestion came from Paphnutius, a confessor who had lost one of his eyes during the persecution. Though himself unmarried, Paphnutius argued

The Nicene Creed, as it finally developed, is translated into English thus:

I believe in One God the Father Almighty; Maker of Heaven and earth and of all things visible and invisible.

And in one Lord Jesus Christ, the only-begotten Son of God, begotten of the Father before all worlds, God of God, Light of Light, very God of very God, begotten, not made, being of one substance with the Father; by whom all things were made; who, for us men and for our salvation, came down from heaven and was incarnate by the Holy Ghost of the Virgin Mary and was made man; and was crucified also for us under Pontius Pilate; He suffered and was buried; and the third day He rose again, according to the Scriptures; and ascended into Heaven and sitteth on the right hand of the Father; and He shall come again, with glory, to judge both the quick and the dead; whose kingdom shall have no end.

And I believe in the Holy Ghost, the Lord and Giver of Life; who proceeds from the Father and the Son; who with the Father and the Son together is worshipped and glorified; who spoke by the Prophets. And I believe in one Holy Catholic and Apostolic church. I acknowledge one Baptism for the remission of sins; and I look for the resurrection of the dead and the life of the world to come. Amen.

It is not hard to sense the care with which it is written. It needed to be very clear, a statement which no Arian could honestly agree to and which could be used to test those seeking to enter the ministry. It wouldn't hurt if a few more Christians today learned it.

strongly against the imposition of man-made laws.

'By forcing celibacy and denying legal marriage, you will create a terrible evil,' he said. 'Marriage itself is honourable and pure, whereas ministers forced to abstain from it will instead be tempted to secret sins. You are proposing a yoke too heavy to bear.'

Thankfully Paphnutius' voice prevailed, and a unanimous vote rejected the proposal.

The council also tried to end the Novatian schism. Constantine invited Acesius, a Novatian bishop, and when the council concluded the emperor asked him whether he would accept its decisions.

'The council has decided nothing new,' said Acesius. 'The definitions in the creed and the agreed date of Easter are teachings which my church has always held.'

One problem solved by the Nicene Council related to the date of Easter. Easter Sunday falls on a different day year by year, and the way to calculate it is quite complex. From the days of the apostles onwards some areas followed a slightly different way of calculating Easter, and this meant that Christians in different towns would often be celebrating Easter on different days. This went on unquestioned at first, but from the mid-second century onwards many Christians desired to sort out the difference. The council provided an opportunity to do just that.

The date of Easter is calculated as follows: Easter Sunday is the first Sunday *after* the full moon *on or after* the March equinox. It can be any date from 22 March to 25 April.

'What reason then do you have for separating yourself from the fellowship of the rest of the church?'

'Because,' said Acesius, 'since the time of Decius the rest of the church has shown itself willing to forgive those who have succumbed under severe trials, or have fallen into serious sin. Such people might be forgiven by God if they are truly repentant, but the church should never readmit these tainted ones to its fellowship.'

'Build your ladder then, if you will,' said the disappointed emperor, 'and climb up to heaven all alone!'

EUSEBIUS, *CONSTANTINE* 2.7–9; SOCRATES, *CH* 1.3–11

The Conversion of Ethiopia

In the early fourth century a Tyrian philosopher named Meropius, a student of foreign cultures, made a journey by boat along the African coast. Taking with him two Christian nephews, Frumentius and Edesius, the philosopher embarked on what was to become a most unlikely missionary journey.

All went well until the return journey through the Red Sea, when Meropius' ship ran short of drinking water. When they put in at a harbour the crew and passengers were caught off guard by a sudden attack from the local inhabitants. Unbeknownst to the captain, the local people, the Ethiopians,

had just thrown off an alliance with Rome and were greatly
inflamed at the sight of the innocent foreigners.

'Kill them!'

The Romans were overwhelmed by the sheer number of their
attackers, and all but the two boys were murdered.

'Keep them as a gift for the king.'

Doubtful as it might have seemed at the time, however, the
Lord was watching over his young ones. He softened the heart
of the king of Ethiopia towards them and both were appointed
to honourable positions. Edesius became royal cupbearer, while
Frumentius was eventually put in charge of the financial records
of the royal court.

When the king died he left a young son, Ezana, to take his
throne. The royal widow, having become acquainted with the
wisdom and honesty of the two young Tyrians, asked them to
train her son and to help govern the kingdom while he was in
infancy. Raised to such a position beyond all expectation, the
brothers put their fortune to good use. They made a search for
other Christians living within the kingdom of Ethiopia, or
Axum as it was then known, and gathered them together to
establish a regular fellowship. They ensured that Roman visitors
were well treated and eventually built a number of churches for
the use of both locals and foreigners. A small number of
Ethiopians were converted by the example and testimony of the
royal servants.

When Ezana came of age, Frumentius and Edesius quit their
high positions and requested permission to return home. The
king urged them to stay, but when the brothers remained firm in
their resolve he gave them his blessing. Once back in the empire
Edesius headed straight for Tyre and a reunion with family and
friends. He remained there and was eventually ordained a priest.
Frumentius, on the other hand, went to Alexandria. He
informed the bishop, Athanasius, of all that had happened and
urged him to send missionaries to Ethiopia immediately.
Athanasius considered the situation and came to an easy
decision.

'You, Frumentius, are the best person to lead any new

mission. If you are willing, I would like to ordain you as the first bishop of the Ethiopians.'

And so it was. Frumentius' return was welcomed with rejoicing, and the king and a great many of his people were soon converted. Archaeologists have uncovered several coins from the reign of King Ezana, and these mutely tell the same story. Coins of the king's first years show pagan signs and inscriptions; those of his later years bear nothing but a cross.

SOCRATES, *CH* 1.19

Athanasius and the Arians

Athanasius was very young, still in his early twenties, when he became bishop of Alexandria. This remarkable man seems in fact to have done many things at an early age.

Athanasius came to the attention of Bishop Alexander while still a child. While out for a walk, Alexander noticed a group of boys playing a strange game beside the river. They seemed to be imitating a church service, and as Alexander watched he was surprised to see everything acted out with complete correctness – the boys even baptized pagan children. Alexander made inquiries and found that it was Athanasius who had started the game and that it was his memory that provided the details of the ceremonial proceedings. The other children called him 'bishop'.

'Now there is a promising lad!' Alexander said to himself, and from then on he kept a special eye on the child bishop. Athanasius' zeal in no way abated over the years, and in his late teens he was raised to the deaconate. At the Council of Nicaea his young voice and sharp wits were outstanding in the battle with Arius, and at Alexander's passing Athanasius finally became the real bishop of Alexandria!

The supporters of Arius, meanwhile, were working behind the scenes to facilitate the heresiarch's ('father of heresy') return from exile. Some, who had the emperor's ear, began urging Arius' case with great vigour.

'Arius has been misunderstood,' they said, 'and his enemies

have slandered him grievously. His true opinions are quite in accord with the decisions of Nicaea, if only the emperor would allow him to express them clearly. It would be a great glory to your majesty if you should heal this rift completely, by returning Arius to his city.'

Arius himself wrote to Constantine, claiming complete agreement with the Council of Nicaea and pleading for mercy. The emperor, convinced by his evil counsellors, gave his approval for the heretic's return to Alexandria. Athanasius, however, stood firm.

'I refuse to stand idly by while this wolf returns to the fold! The emperor has been deceived by fine sounding words that mean nothing.'

Constantine was infuriated at the bishop's resistance, and the heretics began plotting against Athanasius.

'Athanasius will ruin everything. We must get rid of him.'

The Arians laid charges of bribery against Athanasius, but these were no sooner laid than proved unfounded. They next accused him of plotting against the emperor, but when Constantine tried the bishop on these charges and found them to be completely untrue the Arians were horrified to see Athanasius dismissed by the emperor with great honour. Arius' plight was now worse than at first.

'We must take a different approach,' said the heretic. 'We need charges less easily disproved.'

'We could get a woman to accuse him of indecency.'

'How about a charge of wizardry?'

'Why not both?'

'Perfect!'

The Arians employed a harlot to accuse Athanasius of rape, and they also cut a hand from a corpse.

'We found this embalmed hand in the bishop's house. It is the hand of Bishop Arsenius, whom Athanasius accused of heresy and subsequently murdered. He uses it in pagan magical rites.'

The Arians had sent their friend Arsenius into hiding, with orders not to show his face until the enemy was dead. Constantine immediately summoned a council so that the 'crimes' of the bishop could be tried. What could Athanasius do? The bishop chose a friend to help him.

'Timothy, you must accompany me to the council. With your help I can clear my name from the charges of that crazy woman. I don't believe that I've even seen her before – and that is exactly how I will trap her! But I don't know what to do about Arsenius. Only the Lord can prove my innocence there.'

The Lord wasn't slow to help his servant. Constantine decreed that the council should be held in Tyre, the very city, so it happened, in which Arsenius had gone into hiding. Word of the impending trial came as a shock to some of the locals, who had several times seen Athanasius' supposed victim in a city tavern. The governor was informed, a search was made, and the living corpse was soon in custody. Arsenius at first denied his identity, but the governor summoned Bishop Paul of Tyre, who knew Arsenius personally, and the fact was established. The stage was set.

The council gathered in Tyre a few days later. Athanasius delayed his entry to the last moment, when he and Timothy burst into the hall and, before anyone could speak, cornered Athanasius' main accuser, the Arians' harlot.

'Woman!' Timothy cried. 'What madness has led you to accuse me of a shameful deed? I have never even seen you before.'

'How dare you deny it!' the woman screamed, snarling as she pointed a finger at Timothy. 'I could never forget your face! This is the man who robbed me of my chastity!'

'Are you sure?' Athanasius himself asked, standing beside his friend with a grin across his face.

'I certainly am,' said the harlot, adding a string of filthy curses, while everyone but the Arian leaders burst out laughing.

'Good show, Athanasius!'

But the best was yet to come.

'Wait a moment,' said Athanasius, as the anguished Arians scurried about. 'You can't just take that wicked woman out of here. Bring her back this moment so that we can learn who has put her up to this deceit!'

'Not on your life!' said the Arians, leading the woman out before turning in fury on their enemy. 'Rest assured that we don't need her testimony to cook your goose! Eyes, not ears, will send you to the grave!'

With that the Arians produced a box, containing the revolting embalmed hand.

'The hand of your victim, Arsenius!'

With that the room was in an uproar, and it was some time before Athanasius could hush the crowd enough to make his defence.

'Do you know Arsenius personally?' he asked his judges.

'We did know him! That is, before you had your wicked way.'

'Good,' said Athanasius, before calling out loud, 'come in, Arsenius!'

The room was silent as the 'dead' man entered, his hands hidden in his garments. The Arians shuffled nervously as Athanasius approached the new arrival. Many of the other bishops thought that Arsenius really would be missing one hand – the evidence, after all, was right there on the table in front of them.

'How did you come to be maimed, Arsenius?' one asked aloud. 'Was it really Athanasius, or some accident?'

Athanasius smiled at the question. Arsenius shivered.

'I'm glad you could come,' Athanasius said with mock seriousness. 'The man I murdered and mutilated! He looks well, don't you think?' With that Athanasius pulled one of Arsenius' hands into view, silently staring at his enemies before exposing the second to gasps of surprise.

'Excuse me, friends, but where do you believe the third was attached? In my ignorance I always supposed that the good Creator had only given us two!'

It seemed that the bishop had defeated his enemies, and if the Arians had been blessed with any decency or shame they would have prayed that the earth would open up and swallow them, but unfortunately for Athanasius the Arians were not at all put off by the exposure of their lies.

'Kill him!' they cried, lunging at Athanasius with fists flying. 'He's not fit to live!'

Constantine was not present at the council, but he had sent officers to ensure the smooth operation of justice. These men now had to rescue Athanasius from the Arians' clutches, and with all speed they withdrew the bruised bishop from the hall and put him on board a ship. With no hope of justice from the Arians, Athanasius set sail for Constantine's capital, Constantinople, to put his case before the emperor himself.

Once he was firmly established as sole emperor Constantine had begun to look for a new capital – a city from which he could rule the whole empire more effectively. In spite of its great military success over the centuries, Rome was not a particularly well-positioned city. Geographically speaking, the ancient capital was quite exposed to attack, and in an age when the barbarians were pushing their assaults ever deeper into the provinces, this was becoming an increasingly urgent problem.

A Greek town named Byzantium took the emperor's fancy. Sitting on the Bosphorus, the southern mouth of the Black Sea, and surrounded by water on three sides, Byzantium was both centrally placed and easily defended. Indeed a more central location is hard to imagine, situated at the meeting place of the Black and Mediterranean Seas and the Asian and European continents.

In 330 Constantine officially moved his residence and began the construction of a new city, which he named Constantinople, on the site of the original town. Rome was famed as the city of seven hills, and Constantine's new city was also spread over seven hills. For many years both Rome and Constantinople, 'New Rome', had the status of capital, though as time passed the newer city slowly gained over its rival. Christians rejoiced at the sight of this first city to be officially Christian from the day of its foundation, a city untainted with idolatrous sacrifice.

Constantine, riding on horseback and surrounded by courtiers, was making his entrance into his capital city when a small group of men burst forward and stopped his procession.

'Who are these fools?' the emperor asked hotly. He was soon informed that they were all Christian ministers, with Bishop Athanasius of Alexandria at their head. At that the emperor urged his horse forward and did not even deign to look at the suppliants.

'Emperor, I beg audience with you!'

Constantine ignored the request, but the bishop followed him, repeating his request loudly until finally the emperor turned to him.

'You are supposed to be on trial in Tyre,' Constantine said sternly. 'I have no intention of speaking with you.'

The emperor was about to order the intruder's removal, when Athanasius stopped him dead:

'I seek only justice from you. I have already appeared at Tyre and, these men can confirm it, was almost murdered by my foes. I ask only that you summon the council to reconvene in your capital, that your own justice might decide the case.'

Constantine was momentarily thoughtful, before turning to Athanasius with a kinder countenance. 'As you wish.'

The Arian bishops were still deliberating in Tyre, passing resolutions against their enemy in his absence, when a letter arrived from the emperor. The Arians were thrown into panic by the order to reconvene in Constantinople, especially when they read that Athanasius was already there, and most of them refused obedience and slunk home to their respective cities. A few of the most vicious leaders of the heretical faction went to the capital to rescue the situation and gained a secret audience with Constantine.

'Athanasius' reports about our council are lies and slander,' they insisted. 'Beware, for Athanasius has told many that he will rebel against your government if you find him guilty. He is planning to incite his city to refuse to pay their taxes. You must not give him a chance!'

The Arians brought several witnesses to this new accusation, and when their voices were joined to those of Constantine's Arian counsellors the Alexandrian bishop's fate was sealed. Athanasius was exiled to Gaul without an opportunity to defend himself.

Now was the time of triumph! Arius, his enemy defeated, was called to meet the emperor.

'Will you agree with the teaching of the church for once and for all?'

'Emperor Constantine, I swear to you that I hold the same faith as the rest of the church!'

'What about the ideas which you were excommunicated for?'

'I swear that I do not hold any heretical opinions.'

'Very well,' said Constantine. 'If you hold the true faith, you have done well to clear your name. But if you have now sworn to me a lie, then may God condemn you for your lie and your false beliefs. Today is Saturday and I give you permission to attend church with me tomorrow.'

Arius left the emperor's presence that day and paraded through the streets like a champion who had won a great victory. His followers gathered around him and they congratulated each other that finally their leader was restored to the church.

'To the church at once,' one of his followers cried. 'To the church!'

With a shout the Arian mob changed direction, and a few moments later they were crowding around the entrance of the city's major church. Alexander, bishop of Constantinople, was waiting for them.

'Come no further!' he cried, resisting their entry. 'The slanderer of Christ shall never enter Christ's church!'

The Arians were halted by the bishop's boldness. After threatening him, they backed down for the moment.

'Enjoy your afternoon, Alexander,' they said contemptuously, 'but Arius will take his seat in church tomorrow whether you like it or not.'

The Arians left and Alexander retreated into his church in great distress.

'Oh Lord!' he wailed, throwing his hands aloft in prayer. 'What days are these?'

Along with his friend Macarius, Alexander fell down on his face upon the ground.

'Lord, if You intend that Arius should desecrate Your church, then I beg that You allow me to depart. Take my life rather than let me see these evil days! But Lord, if You will spare Your church, and I know You will, do not give us over to contempt and disgrace. Hear the words of the Arians against You and Your servants and take away the wicked Arius instead. If Arius enters the church his heresy will enter with him and the foolish will mistake his impiety for piety!'

While the bishop was in anguish the Arians continued congratulating themselves.

'This is only the beginning,' said Arius. 'Soon we will conquer and no longer will we need to hide behind deceit!'

But even as he spoke a terrible pain gripped the heretic's belly. With a gasp he rushed off to the toilet and there he was shortly afterwards found dead. For centuries afterward the scene of this bizarre judgement would be pointed out by the citizens of Constantinople.

'That is the spot,' they would say with a shudder, 'where Arius' insides burst right out of him!'

Arius may have rejoiced that he could fool the emperor, but he forgot that the eyes of God were still upon him.

ATHANASIUS, *DEFENCE*; LETTER 54; SOCRATES, *CH* 1.15–39

The Soldier Monk and the Blind Author

By the time that Arius met his end a huge change had taken place among the monks – a change set to forever alter the face of the church and empire. It all began with a soldier named Pachomius.

Son of a pagan family, Pachomius served for some years in the Roman army and during that time developed a great admiration, and then love, for the Christians. When the imperial troops were stationed in Thebes the local believers would come to serve them, providing food and doing simple tasks, even washing the weary soldiers' feet. Pachomius was not alone in discovering through such practical expressions that these people really did have something special, and when he left the army and had to think about his future, he soon felt a divine call on his heart.

Pachomius met some Christian monks and with their guidance began to follow the harsh life of the desert. But he was not satisfied.

'Surely there must be more than this? Fasting is good discipline, living in the desert does at least keep one far from sin and danger, but is there not a risk in taking this asceticism so far? Are we not too concerned with our own salvation, too little concerned with the good of others? Could we not be doing something more useful?'

From these internal struggles the idea of the monastery was born. Rejecting the desert solitudes, Pachomius encouraged his followers to live together in small settlements. The first of these came into being about 325, but the idea caught on with such alacrity that, by the time of Pachomius' death a little more than two decades later, his followers numbered more than three thousand, gathered in nine separate establishments.

Pachomius' military background prepared him well for the oversight of such communities. He knew the high value of discipline and obedience, and the code of conduct which he composed for his followers shows a great deal of wisdom and care. Prayer and meditation were still the high callings of the monk, but Pachomius' followers were also required to spend considerable time in physical work. They made handicrafts to sell, cared for travellers and the sick and, unlike most people of their time, were encouraged to learn to write. Writing, in fact, became one of their most important tasks.

In an age when books were wholly handmade, an arduous and time-consuming business, the growth of an army of monkish scribes was nothing short of a revolution. Whatever else they may have done for themselves and their era, the monks' most significant ongoing contribution was that of preserving the literature of the ancient world through their unwearying and highly accurate copying. Without the labours of the monks our shelves of classic literature would be very thin indeed.

Another Christian of this period also became famous for his work with books. Didymus was appointed by Athanasius as head of the great catechetical school of Alexandria. What made Didymus stand out from other scholars of his time was that he was completely blind from infancy.

The challenges in the path of a blind man at that time were

enormous. All of Didymus' early education had to be acquired by listening alone, and in spite of his handicap Didymus not only mastered the major sciences, but also managed dramatically to outshine his fellow pupils. His brilliance in mathematics especially, having never seen a diagram or an equation, astounded his contemporaries.

Later in life Didymus determined to master reading and writing as well, and using a plate of engraved characters he learned the shapes of all the letters. Such plates could be used as a form of Braille, but Didymus' main desire was to learn how to write the characters. He was soon able to write as clearly as any man.

For sixty years Didymus the Blind led the great Alexandrian school. Christians came from across the empire to sit at his feet as pupils, or simply to see this extraordinary individual for themselves. While visiting Alexandria to lend his support to Athanasius in the battle with Arianism, the great monk Antony met with Didymus and was highly impressed with the blind man's skill in argument with the heretics.

'You, Didymus, should never sorrow for the loss of your bodily eyes. Rats, mice and all the lowest animals possess eyesight, but you are rarely blessed in the possession of keen eyes of the mind! Within you have the eyes of an angel and with them see God Himself.'

ANONYMOUS ABBOT OF TABENNENSIS, 'LIFE OF PACHOMIUS'; SOZOMEN,
CH 3.15

Safety in the Lion's Den

Monasticism spread swiftly from Egypt along the Mediterranean coast into Palestine, Syria and Asia Minor. Malchus, a native of Mesopotamia, came to Syria in the early fourth century and there joined himself to a monastic community. His story really begins, however, when after many years in the desert Malchus began to think of leaving his fellow monks and visiting his homeland once more.

'My mother is old,' he explained, 'and I want to see her one last time.'

Secretly, Malchus wished to ensure that he received the family farm when the old lady died. 'There is nothing wrong with that,' he told himself. 'I will sell it and give some of the money to the poor and start a new monastery with the rest. Who will blame me if I also keep a little over for myself?'

Malchus' fellow monks tried to stop him.

'It might sound like a good idea,' they said, 'but we know that monks who temporarily return to the city usually give up the desert altogether.'

'After so long in the desert you will be swept off your feet by the city. You will be in danger of becoming one of the worst of sinners.'

Malchus, however, was determined to hear no advice, and he soon set out for home.

The desert highways were dangerous roads in those days. The Arabs were renowned for their brutality, and many bands roamed the burning sands in search of plunder and slaves. To make themselves a little more secure people usually travelled in large groups.

Malchus was no exception, and reaching the main road back to civilization he joined a travelling party of about seventy. Against the Arabs, however, not even such a large group could consider itself safe. A few days into Malchus' journey, his companions spotted a large group of men riding horses and camels.

'Arabs! Here comes trouble!'

Trouble was an understatement. The Arabs, or Saracens, rode fiercely, their long hair streaming out behind them. Armed with bows and spears, they charged straight into the group of travellers and the helpless companions were soon scattered and beaten. Some were seized as prisoners, while those whom the Saracens considered useless were left behind to survive as they could. The captives were soon divided between the raiders, and the thieves then led their new possessions home. Malchus and a female traveller were both claimed by the same master.

'You two will serve me well! You as a shepherd, the woman as a cook.'

On the long journey to their new home the slaves were offered nothing to eat or drink but half-raw meat and camels' milk. Malchus now had a great deal to complain about.

'I sought freedom from the monastery, but instead found slavery to a Saracen!'

Once settled in his new home, however, Malchus quickly came to terms with the life of servitude. As a shepherd he was free to roam with the flocks, rarely seeing his master or fellow slaves, and he exchanged a diet of half-raw meat for abundant fresh cheese and milk. Such a life was not unpleasant, and Malchus spent his days in prayer and psalm singing.

'Thank You, Lord! The monk who was nearly lost through his own free will has become a monk again without his choice!'

But trouble returned from the strangest direction.

'You have worked well,' his master addressed him one day. 'Indeed you have astounded me, for I have never caught you stealing a thing! I wish you to take this woman as a reward.' With that he pushed forward the woman who had been enslaved along with Malchus. The monk took a step back.

'I am sorry,' he said, 'but I am a Christian. I cannot marry this woman since her husband, from whom you stole her, is still alive. One of your friends owns him to this day.'

'Swine!' the Arab bawled, drawing his sword and lunging for the poor monk. Malchus would have been struck dead immediately, had he not dodged about furiously and finally grabbed the proffered woman's arm.

'All right!' he cried. 'I'll take her!'

Clearly the woman was no gift, but a bribe to ensure that the useful shepherd would not think of escape. The Arab was satisfied with the match he had forced on the monk, but as the day wore on Malchus himself began to wish that he had allowed his master to kill him. When he was alone with his 'wife' he shared his thoughts.

'I am a monk and have vowed to God never to marry. Poor me! I had thought that I was no longer in any danger of breaking my promise, now that I am growing old and grey. I would rather take my own life than abandon my vow.'

'Have no fear Malchus,' the woman answered, 'for neither do I wish to marry you. I also am a Christian and a married woman, and it would be wrong of me to marry again. But listen to me. Let us not risk our lives by angering the master, but let us pretend to have accepted each other and then see what God will do.'

Malchus was overjoyed with the woman's answer, and the two followed the plan for some months, until Malchus was sitting alone one day thinking about his old life. As he daydreamed, he noticed a colony of ants.

'Look how they labour together,' he said to himself. 'Solomon spoke well when he told us to look at the ants to gain wisdom! They busily store food for winter and are ever helping each other with their burdens. I myself am like an ant, only I am alone and useless. If only I could return to the nest, where I could be surrounded by others like me!'

That evening the woman noticed that her friend was sad.

'What's wrong?'

Malchus told her how he felt and then begged her to join him in escaping.

'I have a plan.'

There were two huge he-goats in Malchus' herd, and the monk now killed them, prepared some of their meat, and from their hides made two watertight bags. All was ready, and as soon as it was dark the Christians fled into the night.

'We must go straight to the river,' said Malchus. 'It is ten miles distant, but we have a good head start. No one will be looking for us until at least the middle of tomorrow morning.'

Reaching the river, Malchus directed that they should inflate their goatskins.

'We can use them to keep afloat. The river will carry us downstream, and anyone crossing the river after us will lose our tracks completely. Let's go!'

The pair floated more than a mile downstream before pulling themselves from the moonlit waters. A nasty surprise was in store.

'We lost some of our meat in the water,' Malchus groaned.

'And some of what's left is waterlogged and ruined. We have only enough for about three days.'

'Let's forget it and get going.'

'First,' the monk insisted, 'drink from the river until you are ready to burst. We might not see water for days.'

Soon the friends were running into the night, headed, they hoped, for home. Two days went by. They ran most of the night and took what little rest they dared during the day, always looking behind them, panting painfully in the heat and dreading the approach of Saracens. On the third day they spotted two riders on camels, charging towards them at great speed.

'The master has seen our tracks,' Malchus cried. 'We are dead!'

Looking about in despair he noticed a cave entrance.

'Let's go in!'

'But in this heat,' the woman sobbed, 'it will be full of scorpions and snakes and who knows what else, seeking the shade.'

'We've no choice.'

Just inside the entrance of the cave there was a small dark pit.

'Let's hide in there,' Malchus said. 'We won't go any further. In fleeing death we might run straight into its arms in there!'

'If the Lord wishes to help us,' the woman said firmly, 'we now have a place of safety. If He is abandoning us as unworthy sinners, then at least we have here a tomb.'

In a prayerful and terrifying silence the Christians sat and waited. Soon the master and a fellow slave appeared in the cave's entrance.

'Go in and get them.'

'Come out Malchus,' the slave cried, walking past the cowering Christians and deeper into the cave. 'You're dead! Why not give up and get it over and done with? The master waits!'

In a flash, a lioness burst from the depths of the cave and caught the slave by the throat as he spoke. He did not even whimper as the beast dragged him back into her lair.

'Where are you?' the impatient master called. Bursting into the cave with sword drawn and a violent shout, he cursed his

slave's stupidity and cursed the two runaways for resisting him.
'You all need a thrashing!' He had not even passed the pit when
the lioness again sprang forth, and the Saracen was unable to
raise even the faintest struggle.

'They're dead,' Malchus whispered, 'but how do we avoid the
same fate?'

All that day and night they sat in silence, shaking with fear
and awaiting their chance. In the earliest morning they almost
gave up all hope, as they heard the mighty creature softly
padding towards them. She passed by and out of the cave, and
they saw that she was carrying a cub with her teeth. Obviously
the old home had become a bit too busy for her tastes! Still the
Christians lacked the courage to make a move.

'She could be close by. Out in the open we won't stand a
chance.'

Hearing nothing from outside for the rest of the day, Malchus
decided to risk making a break for it in the late afternoon. There
was no sign of the lion outside, and he found both dromedary
camels peacefully chewing the cud nearby. With a mount each
and plenty of food in the master's saddlebag, the Christians set
out for home. After ten long days in the desert sun, they came to
a Roman camp. It is not hard to imagine the stir their story
created among their countrymen.

'You can sell your camels here,' said the Roman commander,
'then you will be your own masters again! May you always be
so blessed!'

The pair now made their way to a place called Maronia.
There they stayed and, until extreme old age and death, lived as
the closest of friends, Malchus with the monks of Maronia and
his sister in Christ with a community of female ascetics, or nuns.

JEROME, *LIFE OF MALCHUS*

The Persian Persecution

Christians had lived peacefully in the Persian kingdom for many
years, but that was set to change now that Rome, the traditional

enemy of Persia, had become Christian. For many years the Persian priesthood grew in hostility towards the church, but it was ultimately the hatred of the Persian Jewish community that set the ball rolling. In about AD 340 an embassy of Jewish leaders voiced their concerns in the court of Sapor II.

'Mighty Sapor, we are compelled by our love to your government to bring some grave facts to your attention. We would not dare speak, but we cannot bear to stand silent while daily we see your kingdom slowly disappearing!'

'What foolishness are you speaking?' the king demanded angrily.

'Live forever our king!' the Jews exclaimed. 'No foolishness at all! What we mean is that every person who becomes a Christian might as well be a professed traitor against the nation, for it is clear that as soon as war should fall out between ourselves and Rome every one of them will betray you. O King, you must stop them!'

Sapor listened to the advice of the Jews, and after consultation with the Magi began to oppress the Christians with heavy taxes. Soon discovering, however, that such mild persecution only inspired the church to greater zeal, the king was enraged and commanded the closure of churches and execution of ministers.

The Persian bishop, Simeon, was tried in the king's presence and sentenced to death. As he was led away to prison, Simeon happened to pass Usthazanes, the manager of Sapor's palace. Usthazanes was a Christian, but he had fallen away at the threat of his master and performed an act of idolatry. Now, at the sight of his bishop, Usthazanes rose from his seat at the palace gate and bowed: 'Good day Bishop Simeon.'

'Don't bow to me,' Simeon thundered, turning away his face. 'I don't even know you.' Usthazanes was horrified.

'If a man so long my kind and familiar friend treats me thus for denying Christ, what must I expect from the One I have denied Himself!' Casting off his official robes and dressing himself in the mourner's black, Usthazanes sat beside the palace gate, publicly displaying his grief and tears. It was not long before King Sapor sent for his aged servant.

'Usthazanes, tell me, has some tragedy struck your family?'

'O king, nothing has happened to my family! I myself am the tragedy! I mourn that I am alive, for I have kept my life only through deceit and treachery. To please you I have denied my Lord, Jesus Christ, and have falsely worshipped your god!'

Sapor was not inclined to use harshness with his aged servant and counsellor, and with smooth words he tried to turn Usthazanes from his course.

'Think! You are joining yourself with the enemies of the nation!'

But the king's shock turned to anger when he found his servant's resolve to be as firm as the Rock upon which it was based.

'King Sapor, I can never again deny my Lord!'

Sapor was infuriated by such a radical change of heart, and he ordered his friend's immediate execution. The servant made one last request of his master.

'From my youth until now I have served your father and yourself with all diligence. As a reward I ask only one thing, that you tell the whole kingdom that Usthazanes has not been executed for crime or treason, but for loving the name of Christ!'

'Very well,' said the king, 'nothing could please me more. The announcement that I will not even spare the master of the palace will be a terror to every Christian in the realm!'

Sapor, however, did not know the Christians as Usthazanes did. The king's servant knew that his evil example had caused many Christians to fear, and Usthazanes hoped that by proclamation of his repentance many might be strengthened to become imitators of his zeal. From the cell where he still awaited his own execution, Bishop Simeon gave thanks for the glorious change.

The following day Simeon and all of the other gaoled ministers, about one hundred men, were led forth to execution. The chief of the Magian priests offered the men freedom on condition of worshipping the sun, but as none were prepared to buy life at such a cost they were beheaded one by one. An elderly presbyter named Anannias was one of the last victims of this outrageous carnage. Seeing that the old priest trembled as the executioner approached, a leading servant of Sapor, Pusices, spoke out boldly:

'Old man, close your eyes for a moment and be of good cheer, for soon you will open them to behold the light of Christ!'

Anannias heeded the advice and quietly surrendered his life, while Pusices himself was dragged before the king. When questioned on his own beliefs Pusices boldly proclaimed his faith before Sapor, and the exasperated monarch ordered his execution amidst the most disgusting tortures.

In the wake of this massacre the church enjoyed a respite of about a year, but when it became apparent that the destruction of the ministry had not stopped the church's growth Sapor gave his priests authority to exterminate Christianity utterly. The persecution that followed was as gruesome as any that Rome had endured. Some sixteen thousand Christians are reported to have perished throughout the nation, and many more might have died had it not been for the death of one Azades, a personal friend of Sapor. Convicted and executed for his faith by the Magians without the king's knowledge, Azades' death filled Sapor with sorrow and regret – but unfortunately not with real repentance. The king lifted the threat of death from the shoulders of ordinary Christians, though he left the bloody decree against the ministry in place. This royal attitude to the church was to have major ramifications over the following centuries, but we shall return to that much later.

SOZOMEN, *CH* 2.9–14

Emeralds and Sapphires

Returning to the empire, we note some of the dangers involved in what was perhaps the most powerful Christian movement of the fourth century.

The lives of the monks and other ascetics, both men and women, inspired many Christians. Prayerfulness and frugality flourished, but so did hypocrisy and many extreme and troublesome practices.

It is not hard to see how a life that stresses self-denial can lead to very ugly consequences. Many monks took fasting and other vows to extremes and became virtually suicidal. They saw hunger and thirst as the keys to holiness and entered a world of continual and voluntary pain and suffering. More concerned about looking good before men than about truly being close to God, they strove with each other to show a more spectacular indifference to the agonies of the flesh.

No less dangerous were the many hypocrites who publicly professed the strictest principles of self-denial, but in secret engaged in every indulgence and sin. And, as Malchus' friends had warned him, there is no worse sinner than a fallen monk. A few examples will paint the picture – many, fortunately, have a happy ending.

One Alexandrian woman, raised in great wealth, was an example of hypocrisy. Calling herself an ascetic and dressing in humble clothes, she delighted in being seen as one who had given up everything for Christ. To the beggars who frequented her door she could offer nothing but words.

'No, no. I am afraid I cannot give you a cent. I no longer live in this world and use the money of the market place. All I can give you are my prayers!'

Hidden away, however, she retained a stockpile of gold larger than she could ever reasonably spend, flattering herself with the thought that she only kept the money to do kindnesses to her relatives. A monk named Macarius, hearing rumours of the woman's great wealth, wished to test the report. Macarius had once been a jeweller, but he had left his trade to run a hospital for those who were crippled. He visited the wealthy woman and cast a line.

'What would you know, but I have just inherited a package of emeralds and sapphires. You can probably imagine how odd it is to see such jewels again after so long in poverty. I used to have a real love of gemstones, but now I scarcely know what to do with them!'

'Really?' the woman asked, excitement rising in her voice. 'What are they worth?'

'A very great deal, so far as I can tell. I would almost say priceless. But I don't even want to waste my time selling them. A moderate price, less than the real value of even one of them, would more than satisfy me.'

'Then you need go no further for a buyer!' the woman cried. 'I will take them now.'

'Well you must come and look at them.'

'Just get them for me!' she gasped, throwing her money at the monk's feet. Macarius took the money and gave it to the hospital.

Months dragged by, and Macarius acted as though nothing had happened. The woman was at first too embarrassed to bring up the subject of the gems, but finally her impatience got the better of her tongue.

'Oh, your money,' said Macarius. 'Yes, I invested it in the gems immediately. They are in the hospital if you want to look at them. If you don't like them you can have your money back.'

'Take me there!'

When they arrived at the hospital Macarius asked whether the woman would like to see the emeralds or the sapphires first.

'Whatever!'

Macarius took her upstairs to the women's ward.

'Behold your sapphires!' he said, pointing out the rows of crippled women. He then took her downstairs and introduced the male 'emeralds'.

'Just ask if you want your money back.'

The woman was shocked speechless. The colour left her face, and with her head spinning she crept away from the hospital. An agony of grief for the loss of her money, however, eventually collapsed into an agony of repentance. Seeing clearly the sinfulness of her conduct, now that it was exposed before the world, she came to Macarius with tears of thanks.

'Thank you for rescuing me from the fate of Ananias and Sapphira.'

There were many other stories of proud, greedy and selfish monks.

A monk named Paul was a slave to pride. Each day he sat in a public place with three hundred pebbles in his lap, one by one dropping them to the ground as he said his prayers. He never did a scrap of work and lived on the most meagre of rations.

'Three hundred prayers every day!' he would congratulate himself. 'The world has never seen such a prayer warrior!'

But one day Paul received some troubling news, and in a state of great anxiety he went to see a friend.

'I am greatly vexed,' he said. 'I have heard about a nun who for 30 years has eaten only on Saturday and Sunday, and who says fully seven hundred prayers. My own three hundred prayers now seem pitiably inadequate, but for the life of me I can't manage any more.'

'I myself,' his friend replied, 'feel no guilt for the number of my own prayers, not even in comparison with yourself or this "wonderful" nun you mention. If you pray three hundred times and yet your conscience condemns you, then clearly you are not praying with purity of heart. Stop trying to please men. Who are you praying to, after all?'

Paul's friend had not really meant his last sentence as a question, but it struck Paul speechless nevertheless.

'Who am I praying to?'

Scattering his pebbles and retreating to the privacy of his cell, Paul practised a new type of prayer. For the first time no one heard him, save only the God-Man beside the Father's throne.

A lady named Melania also needed a lesson in humility. Wishing to make a large donation to the church, she visited Pambo, a famous monk.

'I wish to dedicate my goods to the work of God,' she said. 'May I leave them in your hands?'

'Surely,' said Pambo. 'May God reward you for your good intention.' He then directed his assistant to distribute the gift to those who most needed it. Melania became very impatient.

'Sir, you did not even look at my gift,' she said. 'It was more than three hundred pounds of silver!'

'Really?' said Pambo, without even looking up. 'The One to whom you give this gift has no need of weights and measures. He knows the weight of the mountains themselves. If the gift is for me, then tell me its weight. If it is for God, who accepts the widow's two mites as happily as all the wealth of Rome, then be silent.'

Others had to learn their lessons in humility a harder way. A monk from Palestine, Valens, believed himself the holiest man in the world. He refused even to accept friendly greetings.

'Have a good day Valens.'

'Do you insinuate that your blessing could conceivably make my day any better? If you knew to whom you spoke you would rather ask a blessing than give one!'

Valens began to see angelic visions and boasted of them to all who would listen. His fellow monks were convinced that he had been given over to the devil on account of his arrogance. The last straw came when Valens refused to receive communion.

'I have no need of it! I have already seen Christ today!'

Exasperated, the other monks put Valens in chains and had him imprisoned. After a year he was set free, cured of both his arrogance and visions!

Monks were often called upon to become bishops, and many of the greatest leaders of those times spent some part of their lives in the desert or monastery. But not all responded well to the call of duty.

A monk named Ammonius, when offered the position of bishop, bluntly refused to sacrifice his peace and quiet for the temptations and troubles of the city. When his refusal was not accepted and his visitors threatened to take him to town by force, he cut off one of his ears with scissors and then threatened to cut out his tongue as well!

'Will you take a maimed bishop, eh?' he asked. 'Even if you will, how will you go with a dumb one?'

Even some of the more respectable monks were quite extreme. When Pior fled to the desert he vowed never again to set eyes on his family. He lived like this for 50 years, until finally his sister, old and close to death, heard that he was still alive.

'I must see him once before I die!'

Messengers were sent to Pior, and grudgingly he went to his sister.

'Here I am,' he said, 'I'm not staying, so have a good long look.'

Pior himself kept his eyes tightly shut.

'I vowed never to look on you again,' he explained, 'so this is the best I can do.'

At least we can admire him for not breaking his vow – although it would be more admirable to avoid such a foolish vow in the first place!

PALLADIUS, *LAUSIAC* 6–39

The Arian Persecution

Constantine died on the day of Pentecost AD 337, and the empire was divided between his three sons. Athanasius, as it was now well known that he was innocent of the accusations of the Arians, was permitted to return to Alexandria as bishop.

The Arians, unfortunately, had not taken a warning from the death of their leader. They made the most of the change in government and soon convinced Constantius, one of Constantine's sons, to support them. At this time Arianism openly raised its head for the first time since Nicaea, and the heretics sparked a series of new councils, hoping to overthrow officially the decisions of Nicaea. For some time there was much confusion and strife, with the Arians seizing all opportunities to advance their cause and harm their enemies, but it was not until the death of Constantine's other two sons, when Constantius became sole emperor, that real trouble began. The Arians now had free rein.

Athanasius was leading a church service when an army of five thousand heavily armed soldiers arrived, with commands to arrest him and set up an Arian in his place. The soldiers surrounded the building so that Athanasius could not escape. What could he do?

'After this reading from the psalms,' he announced, 'everyone is to leave the church and go home immediately.'

Soldiers were already pushing into the church as the people

began to leave, but Athanasius refused to flee in the crowd.

'I will not risk the safety of the congregation to ensure my own escape. If God grants me opportunity I will leave after the others are safely out.'

When nearly the whole crowd had departed in an orderly manner Athanasius and his deacons followed them. The soldiers, as though blinded, did not even realize what was happening and silently allowed Athanasius to pass as they began the search of the empty church! As the congregation disappeared into the streets Athanasius himself slipped into a side alley and made his escape.

The Arians also turned their attention on the empire's other leading bishops. Paul, bishop of Constantinople, was exiled and later strangled, while Liberius, bishop of Rome, was summoned to Constantius' court.

'You must condemn Athanasius,' the emperor commanded. 'You can maintain your position only on condition that you promise to have nothing more to do with that impious man.'

'I will happily do so,' answered Liberius, 'when you prove that he is an impious man.'

For this answer Liberius also was exiled.

More famous was Cyril, who became bishop of Jerusalem in 351. Soon after his ordination, on the day of Pentecost, a strange event shocked his city. A bright cross appeared in the sky, hanging over Golgotha, and the whole city was filled with awe and terror. The market came to a standstill, as pagans and even Jews joined the Christians in flocking to the churches. The wonder was reported throughout the world, especially by the many visitors in Jerusalem at that time, and Cyril's name was held in high esteem, as it seemed that God had shown his approval of the new bishop.

Cyril might have been in favour with God, but he could not long stay in favour with Constantius. He refused to submit to the Arian leaders, and they began to look for a way to ruin him. When famine struck they had their chance.

Unable to provide food for his starving congregation, Cyril decided to sell some of the fine materials and ornaments that had been donated to his church over the years. It was just what the Arians had been waiting for.

'Cyril has plundered the house of God!' they cried in Constantius' court. 'Good people, including your father, have donated beautiful things to God, only now to find that Cyril is making profit from them and flogging them off for any old whore to wear! It is an outrage! Cyril must go!'

Now that they had the upper hand the Arians should have been free to establish their own creed in opposition to the Nicene, but their internal quarrels soon plainly revealed that shifting sand is no foundation for a church. A series of Arian councils each came up with a slightly different modification of Christian teaching. Each promoted a creed of its own, missed out some words or added others to the creed established at Nicaea. On one wing were Semi-Arians, who agreed with the whole of the Nicene Creed, save only that they wished to soften the statement that the Son was of the same essence with the Father, preferring to say that He was 'like' the Father. They thought that they might thus make peace between the two parties. Vain wish.

On the other wing were extremists, who said that Father and Son had nothing in common; one was the infinite God, the other was merely a creature. A dialectician named Aetius, nicknamed 'Aetius the Atheist' by the Christians, led this group. With years of strife and contention amongst the leaders of the church, many ordinary Christians no longer knew who to follow or what to believe.

But the Arians, especially the more extreme faction, did much more than make heretical creeds. As they slowly took over the churches during the reign of Constantius, the face of the empire was darkened and then turned blood red.

'Not even the pagans persecuted with such savagery!'

It was no exaggeration. In the cities where the true faith was strongest the Arians launched themselves at the Christians with demonic fury. George, Athanasius' replacement as bishop of Alexandria, was a fiend as cruel as any persecuting pagan emperor, delighting in the invention of new tortures. He arrested a great many nuns and threatened to burn them unless they should renounce their faith, and when they stood firm he ordered that they be stripped and beaten until they were unrecognizable. Later he arrested 40 Christian men and had them whipped with thorn branches until they were unconscious. Some died from the pain, while others needed years of surgery to remove the thorn points one by one.

The Arian assault hit the Novatians as well as the mainstream church. The persecution actually brought the main church and the Novatians closer together, and they would probably have been reunited permanently had not a faction of stubborn ministers intervened. Regardless, the Arian supremacy created a greater degree of sympathy and understanding between the two groups.

The Arian Macedonius replaced Paul as bishop of Constantinople, and after a brutal assault on the mainstream church he rounded up and arrested the Novatians as well. When they refused to take communion from him Macedonius subjected them to severe beatings and then, forcing their mouths open with stakes, shoved the unwanted bread and wine down their throats. A number of Novatian women were forcibly rebaptized, and those who made any complaint had their breasts crushed in vices and sawn off.

But even such ill treatment could not crush their spirits. Macedonius ordered the destruction of all churches in which the true creed prevailed, but when his agents arrived at the church of the Novatians in Constantinople they found themselves greatly outnumbered by a combination of Novatians and mainstream Christians.

'The emperor is with us,' the Arians menaced. 'Don't mess with us!'

But the Novatians and their allies did not appear even to notice them.

'Get to work!' the Novatian bishop cried.

With that they began, brick by brick and beam by beam, to tear down their own house of worship. Women and children bent their backs for the task, and their mainstream brothers and sisters were equally eager in the work. The Arians sat back and watched the proceedings in disbelief.

'Oh well,' they said, 'I guess they're not disobeying!'

The masonry and woodwork were carried away and put down some miles out of the city. There the church was carefully rebuilt, and there it stood throughout the persecution. The bemused Arians did not dare a second assault.

But few church buildings, or people, were so fortunate during these difficult times, and the persecution showed no signs of abating until an unexpected event changed the whole government.

ATHANASIUS, 'DEFENCE OF HIS FLIGHT'; *ARIAN HISTORY*; SOZOMEN, *CH* 2.34 – 4.20; THEODORET, *CH* 2.4–14

Julian the Apostate

The unexpected event was the death of Constantius, the friend of the Arians, and the rise to power of his cousin Julian. The Arians no longer had a friend in authority, their power to persecute was immediately gone, and their innocent victims were allowed to return from exile.

Julian, however, was not a Christian. A nephew of Constantine, Julian was a devotee of the traditional Roman paganism, with a fair slice of Neoplatonism thrown in. He was called 'the apostate' because he had always publicly pretended to be a Christian and only revealed his real beliefs when established as emperor.

Julian led pagan Rome's last attack on the church. The church was weak after years of suffering under the Arians, but Julian was still cautious. He didn't want to attack too suddenly, as he knew how poorly persecution had always worked in the past. He permitted the return of the mainstream church leaders not for any love of their teachings, but rather because he hoped to encourage a bitter civil war within the church. After witnessing a decade of Arian strife he hoped that he might be able to inspire the church to self-destruct completely.

Julian's first open move against the church was to ban Christians from attending the schools. Literary education was still mainly based upon the writings of the great pagan poets and orators, and Julian decreed that no one should be permitted to study pagan literature unless he was willing to worship the pagan gods. For centuries Christians had studied pagan literature, with its myriad tales of corrupt and immoral gods, and had thus been empowered to expose the falsities of pagan religion in argument. As Julian himself said, he wished to 'blunt the tongue' of the church.

The empire still had a massive and frustrated pagan population, and things quickly heated up when they saw the new emperor's attitude. Pagan mobs began troubling the church in the major cities, a development that delighted the emperor.

'I needn't even get my own hands dirty!'

But it was Athanasius who first egged Julian to open imperial persecution. Julian heard that the Alexandrian bishop was still busily preaching the gospel and had recently baptized several leading pagan ladies. The infuriated emperor sent soldiers to remove and execute the great leader, and the dismayed Alexandrians were yet again confronted with imperial soldiers at their cathedral door.

'Have no fear!' Athanasius encouraged his people. 'It is only one cloud which will soon vanish away.'

Athanasius escaped from the city and took a ship headed along the Nile deeper into Egypt, but he had not gone far before second thoughts took hold.

'Let's turn back,' he told his friends. 'Why should we flee? We can be more useful in Alexandria than in hiding.'

'Have you gone crazy? Your enemies are hot on your heels. If we turn back they will catch us in no time.'

'Trust me.'

Sure enough, within twenty minutes of turning back, the Christians met with their pursuers.

'Have you seen Athanasius?'

'Yes indeed!' Athanasius himself replied.

'How far off is he?'

'Closer than you would think!' Athanasius said cheerily. 'If you're quick you will catch him.'

With that the soldiers continued up river, while Athanasius returned to the city and continued his work without fear, as the imperial forces were sure that he had escaped in the other direction!

Julian's imperial letters read like a bizarre comedy. The emperor saw clearly the inability of paganism to defeat the church, but rather than bowing to the divine power of the gospel, Julian explicitly set about imitating it. It would be sad if Julian had been mimicking the church without realizing what he was doing – instead it is ridiculous to examine the seriousness with which he treated the task of defeating the church through modelling idolatry upon it:

'Paganism is not as prosperous as we might hope – mainly due to the conduct of the pagans themselves . . . why is it that Atheism [the name with which the emperor labelled Christianity] gains so much ground – is it not because of the kindness, charity and dignity of the Christians? Obviously we must imitate their daily conduct if we desire the idols to come back into favour. Our priests must be made to act more like Christians, they should cease visiting strip shows and taverns and should be discouraged from engaging in crime. We must establish pagan hospitals and hostels in every city . . . let us not be exceeded in piety any longer.'

Julian also instituted a new pagan priesthood, based upon the structure of the Christian ministry. Apparently he did not understand that it was only the power of God that made the lives of the Christians different. It is appalling to study the apostate's depth of self-deceit. This was a man who scrutinized the church with evil intent and never managed to see the divinity within. He eventually came up with a plan that must rank as one of the most peculiar ever concocted by an enemy of Christ.

'The Christians all point to Jerusalem as a fulfilment of prophecy. They insist that the temple lies in ruins as a divine punishment for the Jewish rejection of Christ. Not a difficult boat to sink, I should imagine.'

The empire's Jews were overjoyed with the news that the emperor had ordered the immediate rebuilding of their temple.

'Finally we have our city back!' they said. 'The temple will rise again!'

From across the empire they came to the city of their fathers, and the rebuilding began immediately. Many Christians were deeply shocked.

'How can this happen? Are these evil days the punishment for our sins? Doesn't the Bible make it clear that the temple will be destroyed on account of the sins of the Jews?'

Bishop Cyril, who had recently returned from exile, was not worried.

'Trust the Lord to stand up for Himself,' he told the people. 'If He wants the temple to be a ruin, a ruin the temple will be. What can man do against Him?'

The next night the bishop's wisdom was proved true.

'Earthquake!' the cry rang out in the dark. 'Run for your life!'

Several of the nearby buildings that housed the Jewish builders collapsed on their occupants, and the survivors returned to the temple site in the morning to find their foundations completely shattered. They stared on in frustration, surrounded by a great crowd that had come to see the damage. Just as they were deciding how to get back to work a terrible noise was heard and fire spontaneously broke out amongst the building materials and tools. Many labourers perished in the blaze, and the screaming crowd scattered as great fireballs erupted from the foundations. Fire engulfed the whole site and burned until nightfall. Not a tool remained, but even this was not the end. Strangest of all was a dark sign that many of the builders found marked on their clothing.

'A cross!'

And with that surprise, many came to believe in the sign of the One their fathers had murdered.

THEODORET, *CH* 3.1–15; SOCRATES, *CH* 3.1–20; JULIAN, LETTER 22

'You Have Conquered'

Julian was determined to restore Rome's ancient military splendour along with her gods and only a year into his reign, buoyed by the flatteries of his friends, he declared war on Persia. His pagan admirers assured him that he would lead a triumphant army across the world, and in his own mind Julian was already someone great. He dreamed of equalling the military campaigns of Alexander the Great.

Before marching on Persia Julian determined to rid his army of Christians, or at the very least to corrupt those who remained. He came up with a cunning way to do so.

It was the custom for each soldier to receive his pay from the commander singly, the whole army marching by in a simple ceremony. Julian, hoping to fool his men, placed a bowl of incense and an altar before his throne, that each soldier might burn a handful of incense to the gods as he took his pay. Relying on the simplicity of the soldiers he arranged for a large group of pagans to lead the line and hoped that the rest would follow the procedure without even thinking about it.

The plan was a success. A few men refused to burn incense and were expelled without pay, but most didn't even consider what they were doing. Later, when the soldiers had gathered in an inn, one of them began to speak of Jesus.

'Jesus, you say?' called a voice from across the room. 'How dare any of you mention the Lord! You should be ashamed of yourselves – a mob of wretched idolaters!'

The soldiers looked at each other in dread.

'What have we done?'

In an instant the inn was almost empty and the soldiers were streaming back into the emperor's hall.

'Take your tainted money!' they cried, showering their gold coins around the startled emperor's feet. 'Do to us what you will, but don't expect to deceive us and get away with it!'

Julian was furious, but loath to give the affair publicity by the fame of a mass martyrdom, he could satisfy himself only with casting the soldiers out of the army. That done and, ironically, his purpose largely achieved, the emperor was soon crossing the Persian frontiers with a massive and mostly pagan force.

Libanius was the leading pagan teacher of the age and a good friend of Emperor Julian. He was delighted with the change of government and hoped that paganism would soon recapture the hearts and minds of men. He could not restrain himself in conversation with a fellow teacher, a Christian.

'Do tell me,' he said triumphantly, 'how is the carpenter's son now employed? Has he thought to change trades yet?'

'The Creator,' said the other, filled with the Spirit of prophecy, 'whom you derisively call carpenter's son, is right now making a coffin.'

'What does that mean?' Libanius snorted. 'Do you think the emperor close to the grave? Don't count on it!'

Julian, meanwhile, was already deep in Persian territory, having captured several important towns and taken a great many Persians prisoner. These defeated foes pleased Julian's ears with the assurance that a decisive thrust into the centre of their country would win him a complete victory and, though his generals warned against too sudden an advance, the emperor chose to heed the more flattering advice.

'Shall I be a coward? I will not relent until I see the Persian king grovelling at my feet!'

The Romans were accompanied by a large fleet, which had followed their course along the broad Persian rivers.

'These ships are making the men into cowards,' Julian told his counsellors. 'They talk of their usefulness if we should need to retreat, but I tell you that so long as I rule, the Romans will never retreat! Burn the ships!'

The orders were immediately carried out, and the army looked on in horror as the fleet went up in flames.

'There is now no retreat!' Julian cried. 'Romans – conquer or die!'

Just at this moment some of Julian's generals, clearly panicked, ran up to the emperor.

'Emperor, we have just tortured those Persian soldiers who convinced you that victory was near.'

'Yes?' said Julian in surprise. 'What good did that do?'

'They confessed to having deceived you. The Persians are in a much better position than we thought, and we ourselves have been led into an area where it will be impossible for us to find food and water.'

Julian was silent for a moment, before signalling a quick change of plans.

'Put out the fire!' he screamed. 'Save the boats! We are betrayed!'

But it was too late to do anything for the boats, and the unhappy Romans began to grumble against their leader for throwing them into such danger.

'Do not fear,' Julian encouraged them. 'There is a rich Persian farming area not far from here. We will march there and find plenty of food.'

But even this wasn't to be. The Persians were well aware of the Romans' next move, and they torched all of the crops. With their path blocked by the blazing fields, the Romans were forced to sit in camp for several days.

Now the Persians really had the upper hand, and day after day they launched attacks upon the famished Roman troops. Aware that the Romans were superior fighters, they were determined to wear them down slowly. The spirits of the Romans were as low as possible. Julian ordered his priests to seek signs from the gods, but every message they received was bad. The Romans could not hold out much longer. Must the whole army perish just for one man's grandiose dreams?

The answer soon came. Under a vigorous Persian attack Julian himself fought near the front lines, hoping to encourage his soldiers with his presence. A Persian spear thrown at random into the Roman ranks brushed Julian's arm and struck right through his ribs and penetrated his liver. The apostate clutched at the spear and tried to remove it, but he only managed nearly to sever his own fingers on the weapon's sharp edges. Sure that the wound was fatal, the apostate looked to the sky in fury.

'Man of Galilee,' he cried, tossing a handful of his blood into the air, 'You have conquered!'

SOZOMEN, *CH* 5.17 – 6.2; AMMIANUS MARCELLINUS, *ROMAN EMPIRE*, 24.7 – 25.3

Valentinian and Valens

Julian's death was the death of Roman paganism. Jovinian, a Christian who treated with Persia to enable the Romans to retreat from enemy territory with safety, succeeded him. Jovinian died soon after the army's return, but he was followed by Valentinian, also a Christian.

Valentinian had only recently been recalled from exile. As a leading military commander in the western empire he had once been forced to accompany Julian on a visit to a pagan temple, but when the idol priest sprinkled the worshippers with 'holy water' and some fell on Valentinian's cloak, the gruff soldier could not hide his repulsion.

'Get away!' he growled, knocking the priest aside before hacking off the offending section of cloak with a dagger and flinging it to the ground in disgust. 'That's what I think of your rites!'

The apostate's fury can well be imagined, but rather than create a stir by publicizing the real nature of the commander's offence, Julian sentenced Valentinian to perpetual exile on a false charge of military misconduct.

As emperor, Valentinian followed the established custom of dividing the empire in two, taking the west for himself, while his brother Valens assumed control of the east. All may have worked out well, had it not been for the fact that Valens was a friend of the Arians. It was not long before the fires of persecution were rekindled in the east.

Again Athanasius was the first target. For 40 years this bishop had stood against Arians and pagans alike and done everything in his power to protect the beliefs of the church. His enemies had repeatedly sought his life, but God's hand had never failed him. His flock loved and revered him, and it is a measure of his popularity that in all those years of secret hiding places he was never once betrayed by a false friend.

Athanasius enjoyed a final victory against Valens. Hearing that the emperor wanted his blood, the bishop went into hiding and spent four months shut within his family tomb! His flock, however, were not going to suffer the arrogant Arians in silence a second time. They protested violently against the emperor and Valens, fearing full-scale rebellion, had no choice but to allow Athanasius' return. For the rest of the great bishop's life the Alexandrians had peace.

Many other Christians were not so fortunate. The persecution was even harsher than that under Constantius, and the exasperated believers soon sent a delegation of 80 church leaders to speak with Valens.

'Emperor Valens,' they pleaded, 'profess which creed you will, but you must restrain the hands of the Arians from injustice. Your reign has become a reign of blood!'

Valens was infuriated, but he was too fearful of public opinion openly to punish such revered leaders with death. He sentenced them to exile, but secretly added instructions to their guards.

'Find an old ship in which to transport them and once you have them beyond sight of land you must set the ship alight. Take a second ship with you, make your escape in that and ensure that the deed remains completely secret.'

All went smoothly until the sailors abandoned the prison ship. It was then that a violent storm arose, and the burning ship, without a pilot, was sent flying before the gale until it came within view of the shore. Nothing could be done to save those on board, but with thousands of witnesses it was not long before the whole empire learned of their fate.

'The Arians must go!' the people lamented. 'What will happen next?'

Shortly before this tragedy, mighty earthquakes and extreme hailstorms had rocked the empire. These events had been taken as a sign of the divine displeasure with the new emperor, and a terrible famine that began almost immediately after the assassination of the 80 ministers only further served to confirm the general opinion.

But the emperor was not to be intimidated so easily. Passing through Edessa and hearing that the city had a beautiful church dedicated to St Thomas, Valens determined to see it for himself.

But when he learned from the governor that the worshippers at that church were bitterly opposed to Arianism, the emperor fell into a blind rage. He struck the governor in the face.

'Is not your job clear? The Edessenes will accept an Arian creed, or they will die!'

At Valens' command the governor prepared a force to attack the church, though secretly he sent a warning to the believers, informing them of the time of his arrival and urging them to stay away.

'I will tell the emperor that I came to the church and found it empty. He will be gone next week and things will be back to normal.'

The offer might have sounded reasonable enough, but in Edessa, a city whose king, two centuries before, had been the first ruler to embrace the gospel, not a single Christian was prepared to take it. The next day dawned and the believers crowded into St Thomas'.

The governor had no choice but to advance on them. As his men approached at a slow march, a woman dragging a child by the hand pushed her way through the ranks of soldiers. The governor, astounded at her boldness, ordered that she be brought to him.

'Wretched woman! Where are you going in this crazy manner?'

'To the church like everybody else,' she replied.

'Don't you know that the governor is about to kill everyone he finds there?'

'Yes I do,' she said. 'That is why I want to be there!'

'And why are you taking your child?' the governor asked in amazement.

'That he also may be ranked among the martyrs!'

When the governor saw her determination he ordered his soldiers to withdraw and informed the emperor that the whole city was prepared to die.

'Surely you can't expect me to kill everyone?'

Valens, grudgingly, backed down and thus Edessa was saved. Even children were well aware of the struggle going on.

Lucius, whom the Arians had made bishop of Samosata, was riding his ass through the city streets one day. The Christians ignored him, neither treating him with the respect due a bishop nor the contempt due a heretic. Lucius might never have known how much he was detested had not some boys been playing with a ball.

'Oh!' one of the boys gasped as he dropped the ball. He turned to retrieve it and saw it roll between the feet of an ass, but when he looked up and saw Lucius upon the ass he reacted with horror.

'Polluted!' he groaned under his breath.

'Polluted!' the other boys cried. 'What can we do now? Gregory has ruined the ball!'

Gregory gingerly picked up the ball and returned to his friends.

'I'm sorry.'

'That's all right,' one of the older boys said seriously. 'I know what to do.'

Lucius was greatly taken aback, but not wanting to seem too concerned he called one of his assistants and gave him orders.

'I am going to keep on my way,' he said, 'but you stay here and watch. Tell me later what they are up to.'

The boys by this time were piling up firewood and soon had a small fire going. Lucius' assistant watched in amazement as the boys tossed the ball to each other through the orange flames.

'Burn off the heretic filth!'

'Clean the Arian ball with fire!'

'Make it good and hot!' one boy shouted. 'Hot as the Arians in hell!'

SOCRATES, *CH* 3.22 – 4.18; THEODORET, *CH* 3.12 – 4.13

Martin of Tours

But the battle with Arianism was not the only concern of the fourth-century church. Paganism still reigned in many areas and, whatever other duties and problems Christians might face, the mission to those who had not heard the gospel must always take a high place.

Martin was born of pagan stock in the early fourth century. At the age of ten he heard a Christian preaching the gospel. It was a fleeting encounter, but one which changed his life.

'This is incredible!' he told his parents. 'The man spoke as though he was filled with the power of God Himself! We must become Christians!'

Martin's parents were not at all happy with their son's new ideas.

'What is the world coming to?' his father, a military man, complained. 'You are Martin – you are named for Mars, god of war. You will be a pagan and a soldier whether you like it or not!'

But Martin's soul was not to be squashed so easily, and only a few months later the youth ran away from home and took shelter in a Christian church.

'Make me a catechumen,' he pleaded. 'I am young, but I already know that my life belongs to Jesus.'

Martin's parents soon tracked the runaway down and forced him to return home with them. For the next few years Martin gave his parents a grudging obedience, and at fifteen he was compelled to enter the army.

Roman soldiers were usually provided with servants to perform their menial tasks. Martin, desiring to increase in humility and obedience, determined to treat his own allotted servant as a friend and equal. While other soldiers rested and their slaves cleaned their boots, Martin would often clean both his own and his servant's boots. At meals the men sat as equals, serving each other. To the other soldiers it was an odd spectacle.

Most Roman soldiers were much given to drink and worse, but Martin stayed clear of even the vaguest hint of scandal. He became known for his charity and care for the poor and eventually won the respect of his fellow soldiers.

Martin and his comrades once passed through the city of Amiens. It was in the middle of a severe winter and Martin had only a cloak to cover him, having given the rest of his clothes to beggars he had met along the road. The winter was so harsh that many paupers had died from exposure, and Martin could not bear the sight of any worse dressed than himself.

'Something for a poor and naked man?' Martin heard the beggar's faint call as he passed through the gates of Amiens. 'Have some pity for the love of God!'

Martin looked, and there indeed was a man who was almost naked, sitting out in the snow and slowly freezing to death. The other soldiers, though they had plenty of spare clothes, rode by without even looking down. Seeing that the poor man's necessity was left to him, Martin stopped and took his sword from its sheath.

'My brother, I share with you the little I have.'

With that he stuck his sword through his cloak and cut the garment in two equal pieces.

'God be with you,' he said, handing half to the beggar.

Many of the soldiers laughed to see Martin dressed in only half a cloak, but those with more sense blushed for shame. What they had refused from their wealth, Martin had given from his poverty. The following night, rolled up asleep in his half-cloak, Martin saw a vision of Christ seated in heavenly glory, surrounded by multitudes of angels and arrayed in the portion of cloak he had given the beggar.

'Martin, who still awaits his baptism, has clothed me with this robe.'

Martin awoke the next day quite sure of what he must do next. Instead of being puffed up on account of this gracious revelation he had a deepened feeling of his own inadequacy and his need for the sign appointed by Christ to mark true spiritual rebirth. Hastening to a church he requested baptism. He was now determined to abandon the military profession, though a friend's plea caused him to delay.

'If you wait until I can quit my position,' said his friend, 'we will leave together. I also want to become a Christian.'

After nearly two years had dragged on in this manner, a barbarian army invaded the empire and a large force was assembled to confront them. Before battle the soldiers were summoned to receive a bonus from their commander, Julian, who was later to become emperor and acquire the name of 'apostate'. As was the custom, the soldiers went forward singly to receive their pay directly from the commander and Martin, seizing what seemed a good opportunity to leave the army, withheld his hand from the proffered gold and spoke submissively to his general.

'Commander, I should not receive this money. I have served you many years as a soldier, but I now desire to become a soldier for God. Let those who wish to fight receive their pay, but as a soldier of Christ I no longer want to battle with worldly weapons.'

Julian was furious.

'Coward! Don't you pretend to religion with me. It is fear of the enemy that makes you speak thus.'

'If you think I follow Christ from fear,' Martin answered, 'then test me. I will happily stand in the front line tomorrow, without weapons, trusting only in the name of Jesus to save me.'

'Just as you wish,' Julian laughed. 'Throw him into prison and do to him everything he has said.'

Martin spent that night alone in prayer. 'Lord, I know that You alone can save and I put my trust in You.'

Early the next morning, ambassadors came from the barbarians.

'Let there be no fighting between us,' they pleaded with the Romans. 'We promise surrender, if you will but spare our lives.' So there was no fighting that day and no front line for Martin to stand before.

Martin now left the army and for some time lived with Hilary, bishop of Poitiers, in Gaul. Hilary was a leading theologian and an outstanding opponent of Arianism. His theological writings and a period of exile for his beliefs won him the name of the 'Athanasius of the West'. In his company Martin made great progress in Christian living and learning and was appointed to the office of exorcist.

In time another striking dream roused the young Christian. He dreamed of his parents, far away in Italy and still trapped in idol worship, and heard a voice that commanded a return to his homeland. Martin could do nothing but obey, though it was not without trepidation.

His fears were quickly realized, and journeying home across the Alps the traveller was set upon by a band of thieves. Martin was bound and taken aside to be guarded and searched by one of his captors.

'Who are you?' asked the thief.

'I am a Christian,' Martin answered.

The thief shook his head in surprise. 'Why do you act so boldly? Don't you value your life?'

'I value my life,' Martin answered, 'and if I'm bold it is only because God is with me. The Lord's mercy is always present, but especially so in times of trouble. I fear more for you than I do for myself, since your crimes put you far from Christ.' Martin went on to explain the gospel to the thief and called upon him to repent.

The thief trembled when Martin spoke of judgement and salvation, and after looking about to ensure that his comrades were not watching he untied Martin and sent him on his way.

'Pray to your Lord for my soul,' he called, before tears suddenly filled his eyes. 'No, that's not enough!' he said. 'From this day forth I too will follow your Jesus!'

Martin continued on his way and, descending from the mountains, was soon in the city of Milan. Passing on from there he encountered a stranger travelling in the opposite direction.

'Where are you off to at that bright pace?' asked the stranger.

'I am hastening to the service of my Lord.'

'The Lord!' said the stranger with a snort. 'His service is a struggle too great for you! Wherever you go, whatever you do, the devil will fight you!'

'But the Lord is my helper,' Martin replied, 'and I shall not fear.'

At the words of Scripture the stranger vanished and Martin was left alone.

'Surely I have seen the devil himself!' he said in amazement. 'Lord, deliver me from evil!'

Pavia, his parents' home, was only a short distance south of Milan and Martin was the next day reunited with his family. To his great joy Martin soon saw his mother freed from idolatry, though his father remained impervious to the preaching of the gospel. Martin's teaching and purity of life inspired many of the other townsfolk to accept Jesus.

Martin eventually moved on and embraced the life of a monk. He established a monastery in Italy and later another in Gaul. He became a widely respected teacher, and his outspoken opposition to Arianism saw him suffer public floggings at the hands of Auxentius, the barbarous Arian bishop of Milan. He was one of the most loved Christian leaders of his time and the Lord worked many signs through his hands.

A catechumen once visited Martin's monastery in Gaul, eager for the holy man's instruction, but after only a few days there he developed a severe fever and died. Martin, who had been absent on business, returned home to find the young man laid out ready for burial. Under a powerful impulse of the Spirit Martin asked to be left alone with the body. He bolted the door and stretched himself out upon the young man as the prophet Elisha once had done. He next gave himself to urgent and passionate prayer, until a feeling of certainty grew within him that the Lord was going to act. He sat back expectantly and noticed a slight tremor pass through the body, then the young man opened his eyes and burst out into praise of God.

The whole region marvelled at the event and Martin's name became greatly revered. When the bishop of Tours died the people refused to have anyone but Martin over them, and thus he became bishop of one of Gaul's great cities.

Martin was among the most industrious and energetic bishops the western empire had yet seen. Though the cities of Gaul were now mostly Christian, the countryside remained largely untouched by the gospel and Martin made the small pagan villages his great priority. He spent many years in travelling and preaching the word, and with the aid of his new converts he led the destruction of the ancient idol temples.

Once, following the destruction of a pagan temple, Martin

commanded that a certain pine tree nearby be cut down. Some local pagans, who had quietly allowed their temple to fall, complained furiously about any attack on the tree.

'We must cut it down,' Martin insisted. 'It was dedicated to the demon of the temple and so long as it stands will be a snare to simple souls.'

'If you trust your God,' one pagan cried, 'and think Him more powerful than the "demons", then we will happily cut down the tree ourselves. Only you must stand beneath and catch it as it falls!'

With that the pagans gave a great laugh.

'Prove your God! If your attack on sacred things is the work of a mighty God, prove it!'

'Very well,' Martin called over their noise. 'Do as you will!'

The pagans verily skipped for joy.

'The loss of a tree is nothing, compared to the destruction of an enemy of the gods!'

Martin was tied and made to stand beneath the tree. The old pine was sharply bent, and it was easy to predict the path of its fall.

'Goodbye bishop!' the pagans cried as they attacked the tree. 'A little more to the right, if you please. Ah, that's just right!'

With a great creak the tree began to fall. Martin's friends looked on in horror as they awaited the inevitable, until suddenly the falling tree spun like a top and crashed down on the opposite side to the bishop, sending the pagans themselves scattering from its crushing weight. The Christians praised God and wept for joy, while the astonished pagans came to the bishop's feet and begged forgiveness. Only two or three from the whole region refused to receive the name of Jesus.

At a later time Martin wished to destroy a temple in another area, but he was prevented by resistance from a pagan mob. He retreated and spent three days in prayer and fasting, in sackcloth and ashes begging the Lord to free the pagans from slavery to their demons and priests. At the end of this time he saw a vision of two angels dressed as though ready for battle.

'We will deal with the idolaters. You deal with the temple.'

Martin immediately returned to the temple and began to knock it down. The pagans surrounded him in a mighty crowd, but all were frozen to the spot as the demolition took place. When the last brick was overthrown the pagans could again move and, realizing what had happened, they praised the name of Jesus.

'The True God has done this to us,' they said. 'Our idols could not even help us save their own temple. They are useless!'

As bishop Martin also had to deal with Christians who acted foolishly. There was a certain place which many Christians treated as a holy place, commemorating it as the resting place of some ancient martyrs.

'They were holy men,' the people said, 'and we should not forget them.'

Martin tried to discover the martyrs' names, or the time of their suffering, but found nothing more substantial than a few vague rumours. Unwilling to prevent the people from congregating there if it truly was a martyr's tomb, and equally unwilling to allow a dubious practice to spread, the bishop attempted to come to a definite decision.

Martin took a group of elders to the revered site and pleaded with the Lord that the truth might be revealed. As the bishop's party prayed, a shadowy figure appeared to one side of the tomb.

'What are you?' asked the bishop.

'A robber, beheaded for my crimes and buried here, though this is not my home. My home is below, where punishment is my lot.'

Those who stood by heard the voice, though only Martin saw the vapoury form. Needless to say, the 'holy' site was promptly covered over and the robber's grave pronounced off-limits.

Several other visionary experiences were reported of the great bishop, the most striking of which was an appearance of purple light, in the midst of which Martin saw a man dressed in royal garments, with a golden crown upon his head. Martin was dazzled, and after a long silence the apparition spoke.

'Acknowledge me Martin. I am Christ, and descending to

earth I have made myself manifest to you before all others.'

Martin was speechless, and the visitor repeated his declaration.

'Except I see the marks of your suffering,' Martin replied in the Spirit, 'I shall not believe that Christ has come.' At that the stranger vanished, leaving behind a foul smell which left Martin in no doubt as to his real character.

Divine healings, the casting out of demons and a multitude of other stories added to Martin's fame – though none ever outshone the halving of the cloak, which remained one of the favourite themes of Christian art for centuries to come. Martin shepherded his flock for 25 years and finally passed away in his eighties, widely esteemed as one of the great men of his time.

It was in the early hours of the morning that Martin died, and his friend Sulpitius Severus, a Christian author who lived many miles away, had just dozed off upon his couch. Suddenly the dreamer saw Martin in front of him, though he could scarcely look upon the bishop, whose eyes and face were dazzling with a heavenly fire. Martin blessed his friend, before to Sulpitius' astonishment he was taken up into heaven. Clarus, a friend of Martin who had recently died, also appeared to Sulpitius and he too was carried up into the clouds.

'When I saw that,' Sulpitius wrote in a letter to his friend Aurelius, 'I also wanted to go up where they had gone. I began striding, but could make no progress through the air and the disappointment of my vain efforts woke me. I lay still a while, mulling over my vision, when suddenly a serving boy came in, a sad look upon his face.

"What news could be so gloomy?" I asked.

"Two monks," he said, "have just arrived from Tours. They have brought word that Martin is dead!"

'At that I burst into tears. Though I know there is no reason to mourn a man who has gone to a better place, crying is natural to one who has lost a friend, and while I rejoice for his happiness, I weep for myself.'

SULPITIUS SEVERUS, *THE LIFE OF MARTIN*; LETTER 2

The Downfall of the Arians

In the year that Martin became bishop of Tours, the Arian bishop of Milan, Auxentius, died. The people were in an uproar and, gathering in church to elect a new bishop, there was an explosive confrontation between the Christians and Arians.

The governor of the province, Ambrose, hastened to the church. Making himself heard above the cries from both sides, he pleaded for peace and with great patience and wisdom slowly silenced the fierce contention. The fighting died down, but still no solution to the original problem had presented itself, when suddenly a child's voice rang out.

'Bishop Ambrose!'

There was a moment of thoughtful silence, before the whole congregation began to cry out, 'Ambrose must be our new bishop! Only Ambrose can give us peace!'

'I am a governor, not a priest,' Ambrose insisted over the racket. 'I have not even been baptized yet! A catechumen can't be a bishop!'

The people were not interested in Ambrose's complaints, and the gathered bishops immediately had the governor baptized. They then prepared to ordain him bishop.

'You mustn't,' Ambrose insisted. 'The people don't know what they are asking!'

The bishops sent a message asking the judgement of Emperor Valentinian (Milan was now the western imperial residence), and they soon received the response they wanted:

'Ambrose has obviously been called by God to this position. Tell him to have no qualms about accepting the vote of the people.'

It was not long before the new bishop of Milan showed the truth of Valentinian's words. Ambrose served for more than twenty years as bishop and was one of the greatest Christian authors and ministers of his time. He gained fame as a hymn writer and several of his hymns are still found in modern collections (among them 'O Jesus Lord of Heavenly Grace', as translated into English by J. Chandler). We shall hear more of Ambrose later, but for the moment we return to the eastern emperor Valens.

An extended delay of baptism was common in the fourth century and many, including Constantine himself, did not receive baptism until shortly before their death.

For centuries catechumen had been encouraged to delay baptism for up to three years, to ensure that their conversion was sure. In the fourth century a variety of reasons led some individuals to extend this traditional delay further. Some, especially government officials, delayed baptism from fear of incurring guilt in the course of their office, for example by involvement in unjust executions, and desired to be able to take baptism on retirement as a divine cleansing from any fault they had committed. Others, cynically, delayed because they were not yet sure that they wanted to abandon their lusts and crimes. They knew that baptism washed away sins and that you could only be baptized once, so they superstitiously postponed the rite in case they needed a thorough cleansing later in life!

The folly of such delay should be obvious. True faith should teach us to receive baptism and then rely on the power of Jesus to preserve and redeem us. The waters of baptism are not a magical detergent, but a symbol of the change that Christ makes in our hearts. Nevertheless, the foolish practice of postponement remained common until more than a century after Constantine. It then disappeared only because it became irrelevant, as Christianity had won most of the empire and most Christians had adopted the practice of infant baptism.

The superstitious delay of baptism, in fact, was a major cause of the universal adoption of infant baptism in the early church. Prior to the fifth century, the church practised both adult and infant baptism. Many parents baptized their children as babies or infants, as a pledge of their commitment to train their children as Christians, while others postponed baptism until the child should be of an age to desire it for themselves. A substantial number of the latter delayed from fear that their child might fall into grave sin later in life and were thus actuated by a similar motive to the delaying pagan converts. To end this excuse and pretence for sins, most ministers began to support infant baptism. It is noteworthy that many of the leading figures of the fourth- and fifth-century church (e.g., Gregory Nazianzen, Augustine, Chrysostom) had pious parents who practised adult baptism, but themselves came later in life to reject that position and support infant baptism.

Valens' realm, already shaken by natural disasters, was now threatened by various barbarian attacks. In this grim state of affairs the Arian emperor greatly dreaded a revolution, and when a report reached him that certain men of high political standing had used divination to discover the name of his successor, he launched a rigorous and bloody inquiry.

The most bizarre conspiracy was soon uncovered. Several leading pagans, desirous of a return to idolatrous rule, had performed an elaborate magical ceremony, the focal point of which was a ring suspended by string from a tripod, with a metal disk engraved with the letters of the Greek alphabet beneath. With a gentle push and the appropriate incantations, the ring could spell the answer to any question.

'Who shall succeed the emperor?'

The ring's dance touched the letters TH E O D, and at that the pagans raised a cry of delight.

'Theodorus shall reign!'

Theodorus was a leading pagan statesman, and word of this pleasing prophecy soon spread in the upper-class pagan circles of the east. Valens was terrified by the revelation and all involved in the ceremony, along with Theodorus himself, were savagely tortured and executed. The emperor's fears did not end here, however and with Theodorus dead he turned his attention on other leading figures whose names began with the fateful letters. Several were executed, while others changed their names and laid low until the storm should pass.

The superstitious emperor soon afterwards ordered the execution of all with any manner of involvement in pagan magic. This was a fairly broad brush since most philosophers, including the broad group known as the Neoplatonists, at least dabbled in the occult and Valens' cronies needed only the slenderest grounds to mount an attack. It became dangerous merely to wear the philosopher's cloak or possess 'suspicious' pagan writings and hundreds of ancient manuscripts, indeed whole personal libraries, went up in flames as desperate pagan intellectuals destroyed the evidence of their interest in Greek literature. Great works of poetry and philosophy perished alongside the outlawed magical tomes, and it is very likely that some important ancient works were lost forever at this time. But not all the scourgings, beheadings and bonfires in the world could save this emperor from the fate that hung over him.

Valens' next moves were against the church. Basil, bishop of

Caesarea, was one of the leading defenders of Christian truth. After establishing Arian bishops in many other cities, Valens travelled to Caesarea to deal with this enemy in person. Upon arrival he summoned the local governor.

Basil had been a monk before becoming bishop. He shows us contemporary monasticism at its best, a man who lived a strict and frugal life but did not at all lose his desire to help others, or his joy in the world's beauties. He is famous for a series of sermons on the six days of creation, all of which show his great love for nature and fascination with the complexities of God's world. His fourteenth epistle also, written soon after he became a monk, shows his aesthetic spirit and paints an achingly beautiful picture of his retreat.

'God has given me a home perfectly suited to the life of a monk, and I now see before my eyes such a scene as I have always dreamt of. There is a lofty mountain covered with thick woods, watered with cool and crystalline streams. The plain beneath is surrounded by tall trees, a natural fence, and is so secluded that it seems to be an island. Deep valleys fall away from it on two sides, the river runs by the third, and the mountain blocks any entrance from the north. There is only one way into my "island", and few find it. The stream behind my hut is full of fish and is the most rapid I have ever seen, bubbling and boiling as it courses over the rocks. The air is fresh and clear and the breezes from the river exhilarate. Others might spend their whole time just in observing the multitude of flowers and singing birds, but for me the greatest excellence of the place is silence for meditation. Calm and quiet is the most pleasant fruit that my retreat bears, and as yet I have not met another soul save only a chance hunter. The place abounds in deer, wild goats and hares and happily is unvisited by bears and wolves. How could one leave such a place?'

A pure and unidolatrous appreciation of nature was yet another good that Christianity brought into the world.

'If Basil refuses to accept an Arian creed he must be exiled,' Valens told the governor. 'We must, however, act with caution, to prevent any possible uprising in support of him. You approach him first and we shall see his response.'

The governor visited Basil and, treating him with great respect, tried to win the holy man's confidence.

'The emperor promises you his friendship if you bow to his wishes,' he said. 'Surely you would not risk everything for the sake of a couple of words in the creed?'

'Such talk,' said Basil, 'is fit only for boys. True Christian men would not abandon an atom of truth for all the money in the world and would rather suffer torture and death than deny their God. The emperor's friendship is a wonderful thing, but only if joined with true religion. Otherwise it is a deadly poison.'

'You are mad!' spat the governor.

'Maybe,' Basil answered, 'but I hope always to suffer the same insanity.'

The governor began to threaten, but the bishop was unmoved.

'Threats or no threats, I will believe tomorrow what I believe today.'

The governor took these replies to Valens, and the emperor listened in silence. Without a word he left the governor and returned to his quarters. He was greeted with a wail.

'Your Majesty!' sobbed a servant. 'Your son Galates has taken ill. You must come and see him straightaway.'

'Emperor Valens!' a maid cried, running to him. 'Your lady the Empress Dominica sends me. She must see you immediately!'

The bewildered Valens was led directly to his wife's chambers.

'My husband,' Dominica began, 'after seeing our son's sickness this afternoon I fell into a swoon. I have suffered the most terrible dreams, dreams that I feel have a message for you. I think that Galates is ill because of your treatment of Bishop Basil.'

Valens did not answer, but rushed to Galates' room in bewilderment. Seeing the boy's terrible state, he had no choice but to send for his enemy.

'Ask the bishop to come at once!'

By the time Basil arrived, the emperor had regained his composure.

'Do you still refuse to become an Arian?' he asked.

'I do,' Basil replied.

'Then prove your faith,' said the crafty emperor. 'Pray for my son's health.'

Basil was no fool. 'Believe the truth yourself, reunite the church in peace and the boy will recover.'

'Never!'

'Then you will see God's will executed on your son,' he said firmly, and a few days later his words were proved true.

Valens was now completely in awe of Basil and for a while dared not attack him. His Arian advisors, however, were not so affected and they persevered in their slander until Valens was led into fresh folly.

'Basil must be exiled,' they insisted. 'If he stays, the whole empire will consider you a coward.'

Valens finally agreed, and finding Basil still impervious to any threats or offers he wrote up a decree of exile against him. As he tried to sign his name to the document, however, his pen broke in two.

'Bring me another pen,' he commanded.

The same thing happened to this pen, and when a third pen had snapped in his hand the emperor cursed loudly and demanded a fourth. Now, however, trembling seized him as he prepared for the difficult task of signing his own name, until with a grunt he cast the pen away and tore the decree to pieces.

'No more complaining,' he growled at his attendants, 'not another word about Basil of Caesarea. Your lives are not worth it!'

Athanasius was another who had long been immune to the effects of Valens' cruelty, but at this time the worthy old bishop passed on and the heretics seized their chance to capture Alexandria. An Arian named Lucius was soon established as bishop of the great Egyptian city. Lucius, however, unable to win the ear of his congregation, soon turned an evil eye on the Egyptian monks.

'If they were out of the way the common people would be without spiritual leadership and could be led into Arianism in spite of themselves.'

Lucius had the monks dragged from their retreats, herded onto a ship and sent into exile. The place chosen for their prison was a small and savage island that had never before heard the preaching of the gospel.

The monks spent their time on board the ship in prayer. They pleaded for God's blessing on the Alexandrians, on their persecutors and on the people of the strange island to which they were headed. As they came near to shore their prayers were answered in most unusual fashion. The daughter of the island's chief priest became entranced and, overturning anything that stood in her way, she ran towards the sea, wailing with the voice of a demon:

'Woe to us! Christ's servants have chased us from cities and towns all over the world, casting us out even from mountains and desert places with their prayers. Even this island, which we thought beyond their reach, is now to be made their own. Here, servants of Christ, you have been sent by your persecutors, though not for your harm, but ours. Woe to us!'

With that the girl was violently convulsed and thrown to the ground senseless.

'Who are these strangers?'

The monks saw what was happening as they disembarked and hastened to the girl's limp body to pray over her. The girl suddenly took in a deep breath and the monks helped her to her feet and presented her to her parents in her right mind.

'We have seen nothing like this before!' said the islanders, and falling at the strangers' feet they begged them to explain who they were and what was this new power. With thanks to God the monks shared the gospel story, and it was not long before the island's idols were shattered, its temple converted to a church and the whole tribe baptized into the Christian faith. When news of these events reached Alexandria, Lucius found it impossible to stem the people's rage.

'Look at the blessing which everywhere follows the monks,' the Christians complained. 'Only Lucius could be such a fool as to bring the guilt of rejecting them upon our city. Down with Lucius!'

Lucius was cowed into inviting the monks' return, and the unwitting missionaries soon left behind them a thriving island church. But conditions under Arian rule continued to worsen. The idolaters did not stand idly by while the Arians were in control, and seeing the Christians now hated even by their own supposed bishops, they began violent uprisings against their enemies wherever opportunity arose.

'Avenge the honour of the gods!' was their cry, and if anything could be more horrendous than the Arian assaults, this was it.

In many towns Christians were seized and tortured, and the Arians delighted to see their work being done for them. Pagans attacked and ransacked the churches, defiling the holy places with acts of idolatry and indecency, the houses of prayer resounding with horrendous blasphemies.

But in spite of all this, the gospel message pressed on in its mission to the world. Valens' army had recently been engaged in bloody warfare with an Arabian tribe, but peace came suddenly when Mavia, princess of the Arabs, was converted by a Christian named Moses.

'I will agree to a truce with Rome,' Mavia told Valens' ambassadors, 'if he will arrange for Moses to be ordained as bishop of my people.'

The Romans were pleased with this request and Moses was sent to Alexandria for ordination. Coming into the cathedral, however, he was infuriated to see Lucius preparing to lead the ceremony.

'God forbid that you should lay hands on me!' said Moses. 'The Spirit will not give me power for my duty at your calling upon Him!'

'What are you saying?' asked Lucius in confusion.

'I am only saying what everybody knows. You slander the doctrine of the apostles, and your lawless deeds are a match for your words. Which pagan has not had a hearty laugh at the troubles you have brought upon the church? Who could number the pious men you have exiled? The frenzy of your crimes puts the most savage barbarian to shame!'

At that Lucius literally hissed with fury, but he knew that he was powerless to act. Moses demanded to receive ordination from true Christian bishops, and once his request had been met he left for his new home. Such firmness and purity were an inspiration to all who heard of it, and Moses went on to train Mavia's people well in the ways of Christ.

The tribe of the Goths was not so fortunate. Many were converted at this time, especially by a missionary named Ulphilas, and at first all was well. It was when the Goths tried to establish friendly contact with Emperor Valens that affairs took a disastrous turn.

'Are you Arians or false believers?' asked Valens. 'We can have peaceful relations with none but Arians, as Arianism is the true faith and the belief of our whole empire.'

The Goths knew nothing of such controversies, so Ulphilas spoke for them.

'I have heard talk of this trouble within the empire, this Arian conflict, and it seems to me a storm in a cup. We wish to be at peace with everyone . . .'

'Then you must be Arians,' Valens insisted, 'or there can be no peace between you and me.'

Living amongst the barbarians, Ulphilas had been largely isolated from the currents of theological controversy and he was probably quite ignorant of the issues at stake. In a fateful move, he bowed to Valens' demands and from that day forth the Goths named themselves Arians.

Friendly relations with the Goths did not long endure. They, along with many other tribes, were soon pushing into Valens' territory and claiming the land for themselves.

'Valens is too weak to resist us!'

Terence, one of Valens' best generals, was sent to a trouble spot in the east, and when he returned victorious the emperor sent him congratulations and offered the choice of a boon.

'Ask anything, good Terence, and I will grant it.'

Terence put his request on paper and presented it in person:

'Emperor Valens, I request only that the Christians might be allowed one small church in the city, where they can worship without fear of persecution.'

The emperor tore it to pieces in front of him. 'Ask for something else.'

Terence, picking up the pieces of his petition, answered calmly.

'I need nothing else, since I already have my reward. God will judge my intention, and that is enough.'

Terence's victory was the last of Valens' reign. When another general, Trajan, was defeated by the Goths, Valens accused him of cowardice and stupidity.

'Do not mistake events, Emperor Valens,' Trajan said boldly. 'I have not been defeated, but you have. You have taken up arms against the church of God and the approval of God is now with your foes!'

By now the Goths were within striking distance of Constantinople itself. The citizens of the endangered capital were infuriated at Valens' military mismanagement, and when he attended a major sporting display the crowd exploded in protest against him.

'Should an emperor watch the games while an enemy is at hand?' they taunted. 'If you will not defend us, give us arms and let us look after ourselves!'

Valens was furious, though the justice of the complaint was painfully obvious.

'I will deal with your enemies,' he promised, 'but when I return I will destroy this mighty city of yours and make it a paddock! Constantinople will be capital no longer.'

A Christian named Isaac approached the emperor.

'Give us our churches,' he said fearlessly, 'and God will give you victory.'

'Put this fool in chains until I return,' Valens commanded. 'I will deal with him then.'

'You will not return at all if you refuse to give us back the churches.'

With these words ringing in his ears Valens turned and left the city and immediately marched on the Goths.

His elder brother Valentinian had died almost three years earlier, and Valentinian's son Gratian now ruled the west. Gratian warned his uncle not to fight until he should arrive with extra forces, but Valens, confident of success, disdained sharing the glory of victory with his junior colleague.

Unfortunately for Valens there was to be no glory in this battle for anyone but the barbarians. After a violent clash, the Roman forces were routed and scattered and Valens himself, along with some attendants, fled from the field of battle and hid in a large and well-fortified cottage. Certain Goths passing the cottage were shocked by a sudden volley of arrows from the second storey, and unable to break down the door they tried to smoke the enemy out instead. They set to work rather overzealously and soon had the whole structure alight. Only one Roman escaped alive to inform them of the prize they had destroyed.

'You have burned the Emperor of Rome!'

Gratian arrived too late to benefit his uncle, but just in time to appoint a successor to his throne. His eye ranged over the leading men of the whole Roman realm and finally rested upon a leading Spanish general – Theodosius!

Theodosius was a true believer, cause in itself for rejoicing, but because of Valens' rule Arians and Semi-Arians now held most of the church's highest positions. To remove them would mean war.

Gregory of Nyssa, a brother of Basil of Caesarea, was one of those who returned from exile at this time. A letter to his friend Ablabius describes the scenes that greeted his return to his bishopric.

'The road homeward lies beside a river and passes through a string of small villages on the bank. Because of this unbroken line of habitations all the road was full of people, some greeting us briefly, others accompanying us the whole way, all mingling tears with cries of joy. There was a light drizzle, not unpleasant, just enough to moisten the air, but as we drew nearer home it developed into a shower and consequently our entrance into town was almost unnoticed. When, however, we entered the church's portico and our wheels were heard on the dry ground, the people of a sudden appeared in shoals, almost as though by mechanical means (I know not how nor wherefrom) and flocked around so closely that it was impossible to alight from the carriage. After we had persuaded them to clear a space to let us get down and allow our mules to pass, we were so crowded on every side that the excessive kindness all but made me faint. As we neared the entrance proper we saw a stream of fire flowing into the church, as a choir of virgins, wax torches in hand, entered ahead of us and made the whole area into a blazing splendour. Once within I rejoiced and wept with my people – for I experienced both emotions from witnessing both in my flock – and as soon as I had finished prayers I wrote this letter to inform you of my arrival. Now, under pressure of extreme thirst, I must bid you farewell.'

Happily the Christian leaders whom Theodosius brought home from exile were men of peace. They did not attempt to purge the church of Arians, but were content to allow a slow and peaceful return to normality. No clemency, however, could mollify the Arian resentment.

'We can't lose our grip! We must get Theodosius' ear, for without military backing our teaching is doomed.'

Their efforts to influence the new ruler did not go unnoticed, and a bishop named Amphilochius determined to make an unusual protest against the resurgence of heresy.

It was a state occasion and the emperor was seated with his son Arcadius beside him. A number of bishops came forward to be introduced, and all followed the court protocol of bowing to both Theodosius and his son. Amphilochius, however, bowed only to Theodosius, and instead of treating Arcadius the same way he playfully roughed up his hair.

'And how are you dear boy?'

At that the emperor reddened with rage.

'Throw this crazed old man out of here!'

The bishop was seized and forcibly led away, but turning he cried out boldly:

'Consider the Heavenly Father's wrath against those who refuse to respect His Son as Himself! Even you, my Emperor, consider dishonour done to your son as dishonour to yourself.'

Theodosius was taken aback, and recalling the bishop he apologized and confessed the justice of the comparison. From that time onwards he refused to give ear to the Arians, and their fate was sealed.

The great work for the church now was to rescue the many common folk who had been ensnared by Arianism. Decades of persecution had almost entirely destroyed the true Christian witness in some cities, and in places such as Constantinople most of the population now professed an Arian creed. Something must be done to strengthen the Christians who remained and to lead the thousands of stray sheep back to the fold.

Basil of Caesarea died shortly after the downfall of Valens, but his closest friend, Gregory Nazianzen, was now summoned to Constantinople to take the bishopric of the capital. Gregory, like his friend a brilliant teacher of Christian truth, received nothing but detestation from the Arian commoners, though more for his lifestyle than beliefs.

Basil and Gregory Nazianzen had studied together in Athens as boys. Athens was still a great centre of learning and pagan culture, but unlike most of their fellow pupils, Basil and Gregory were not at all interested in the pagan amusements of the city. As Gregory said in later years: 'In the whole city we knew but two streets, the one to church and the one to school. The streets to the theatre, the games and the unholy amusements, we left to others. All we wanted was to serve God.' Unfortunately, many others educated in Athens were ensnared by the lures of paganism, among them one of the boys' fellow pupils, Julian the Apostate.

'What sort of leader is he?' they scoffed, marvelling at his humility of dress and conduct. They were used to Arian bishops, who made a great show of luxury and pomp.

At first Gregory and his small congregation were savagely persecuted. His church was even stormed by the Arians, who spread filth on the altar, poured real blood in the communion wine and attacked the bishop himself with clubs and stones. But Gregory was undaunted. He continued to do his duty, preaching the saving message of Jesus Christ at every opportunity, and slowly but surely hearts were opened to the despised teacher. The Arian teachers were powerless in the face of the gospel, now that they had lost the power to exile and execute!

In 381 Theodosius summoned a second universal council of the church. Already the work of Gregory and other ministers had ensured that Arianism's main strongholds were shaken, and under the leadership of Gregory Nazianzen and Basil's brother Gregory of Nyssa, this second council, held in Constantinople, reunited the church in the true faith. The decisions of Nicaea were reaffirmed, and the countless Arian creeds and doctrines of the fourth century were consigned to the dustbin of history. The Arian problem was finally at an end.

'The Fathers of the Church' is a name given to the leading Christian authors of the first seven centuries. Many of the greatest of them lived in the fourth century: Athanasius, Basil, the two Gregories, Hilary, Ambrose and Cyril of Jerusalem, to name a few. Their writings are among the church's most precious treasures.

Almost. Arianism was never again a problem in the empire, but it had left its name behind. Even with Arianism defeated in Rome, the Goths and other barbarians kept the name that they had once adopted, and it would be many years before these new Arians disappeared. But as with all heresies, the disappearance of Arianism, though delayed, was inevitable.

SOCRATES, *CH* 4.19 – 5.8; SOZOMEN, *CH* 6.24 – 7.9; THEODORET, *CH* 4.5 – 5.9

Roses of the Desert

The great brothers, Basil and Gregory, came from a family with a long history of devotion to Christ. Their great-grandfather had been martyred, and their grandparents also had endured persecution under Diocletian. Their parents had ten children, five boys and five girls, and all were renowned for their commitment to Jesus.

The eldest sister, Macrina, was one of the great Christian women of her time. Even as a young girl she had been an enthusiastic and inspiring Christian and had helped to train her younger brothers and sisters in the faith. Her siblings loved her dearly and forever remembered with gratitude the ways in which she had kept them on the right paths.

Macrina was engaged young, but her fiancé died before the couple could be married. From then on Macrina refused to consider marrying another, insisting that her fiancé was not dead but rather more fully alive than ever, dwelling in the presence of God. In time she became the leader of a community of nuns, a service for which she was well fitted. Her brother Peter also became head of a monastery, as was Basil himself prior to entering the ministry.

One role of the monasteries was to accommodate travellers. Men would stay with the monks, women with the nuns, and they would receive Christian instruction in addition to food and shelter.

A couple once visited the communities of Macrina and Peter. They were travelling with their baby daughter, who suffered from a severe eye disease, and the nuns insisted that mother and daughter stay with them for a meal, while the monks did likewise with the father. Macrina, noticing the baby's eye, gently kissed the infected spot.

'Do us the honour of eating with us,' she said, 'and I will show you a medicine which I believe will cure this illness.'

The mother, overjoyed, sent a message to her husband of Macrina's promise.

After the meal the couple resumed their journey. Both were in a state of great spiritual excitement, bubbling happily about everything they had heard. The husband first recited Peter's sayings over the meal, and his wife followed with a similar report about Macrina.

'Macrina simply brims with wisdom and kindness. Throughout the meal she spoke on the things of God and spent a long time praying for our daughter. But, do you know what,' she groaned, 'I totally forgot to ask for the medicine when we left!'

Her husband was annoyed and commanded a servant to return to Macrina, but just then the baby awoke and fixed both eyes upon her mother.

'Stop,' the woman whispered in awe, 'now I understand!'

'What do you mean?'

'The medicine she used was prayer!' She passed the baby to her husband, who saw that not a trace of the infection remained.

Many other great monks brightened the life of the Roman Empire during the dark reign of Arianism.

Some served the church and their fellow monks in very practical ways. Dorotheus spent his life collecting stones and building simple shelters for monks who wished to live in the desert but were themselves unable to build. Apollonius, a retired merchant, spent 20 years travelling among the desert retreats, carrying medicines and healthy food to any who might be unwell. When he died he left his stores to another monk who carried on the work after him.

Ephraim the Syrian, a desert monk, was a brilliant author and became especially famous for his hymns – in Syria he is still remembered as 'the Guitar of the Holy Ghost'. In his old age a severe famine struck Syria, and Ephraim visited Edessa to preach against the wealthy.

'Beware, you who refuse your pity to the starving. The gold in your pocket is a passport to hell!'

The rich men of Edessa were terrified by the warning, but knew not how to help the poor.

'We can't just throw money at them – someone must look after them properly. But none of us could be trusted with such funds!'

Ephraim solved the problem by offering his own services, and with the rich men's money he established a temporary hospital with three hundred beds. With his own hands he tended the sick, strengthened the weak and buried the dead. He remained in Edessa until the famine ended a year later. When his work was done Ephraim returned to his desert cell and died only a month later.

Paesius and Isaias, sons of a merchant, both became monks. Paesius immediately gave all he had to the needy, and for the rest of his life supported himself in a humble trade while devoting his time to prayer and fasting. Isaias, by contrast, kept his money and used it to start a monastery. He and his monastic brothers welcomed the destitute, fed the hungry, treated the sick and each day walked the streets to gather all who needed their hospitality.

When the brothers died there was an argument about which brother was the better man. Some said that Paesius had better followed Jesus' command by giving everything to the poor, while others said that Isaias had shown more wisdom in keeping his money for the greater benefit of the needy. The contenders asked the famous Pambo for his opinion.

'Do not criticize either man,' was his answer. 'Paesius exhibited the self-denial of Elijah, while Isaias showed the hospitality of Abraham.'

Another great monk of the time was Sarapion. He did not leave the city behind, for he longed to help the many city people whom he saw living in sin. The pagan theatres were still showing immoral plays, and actors and actresses were famous for their wicked lives. Sarapion desperately wanted to reach out to these people with the love of Christ but found it hard to get close enough to them to make a difference. Finally he found a way.

'There's only one way to get into their homes.'

Sarapion arranged that he be sold for twenty pieces of silver to an actor and actress couple. As a household servant he would wash his masters' feet and perform other menial tasks, doing all with a relish and refusing to take anything but bread and water for his sustenance. Day and night he spoke of God, reciting Scriptures to himself and explaining Christian ideas to the other servants, and his words soon proved infectious.

'I have never before had the chance to hear these doctrines explained,' the actor said to him one day. 'I am very interested in what you have to say.'

Soon the whole household was led to Christ. The couple gave up the stage and both were baptized. Joining together in holy marriage they began a new life together.

'You have freed us from the most terrible slavery, slavery to sin,' they said to Sarapion, 'and in return we wish to make you a free man.'

'I am not a slave.'

'We know that you are free in Christ,' said the woman, 'but we wish to liberate you from human slavery.'

'I have never been a slave,' Sarapion said with a smile. 'I am a free man from Egypt, a monk, and when I saw you both I pitied your souls. Here is the money you paid for me, I have kept it all the time. Take it back and let me depart, so that I may help others.'

The couple were astonished and, filled with thanks to God,

they pleaded that Sarapion would stay with them as a father and teacher. Sarapion insisted that he must move on, so the couple were satisfied with a promise that he would return to see them at least once a year.

'Take the money and give it to the poor,' they said. 'It was money well spent, for it has bought our salvation!'

GREGORY OF NYSSA, *THE LIFE OF MACRINA*; PALLADIUS, *LAUSIAC* 2–40

The Confessions of Augustine

Life could be tumultuous for children of mixed marriages. One such child was Augustine, born in North Africa in 354. Monica, Augustine's mother, was a Christian, but his father Patricius was a pagan.

As a child Augustine listened to his mother's teaching about Jesus, but as he was growing up he made many pagan friends. It was eventually these friends who were the main influence on his life. In his early teens he would stay out late on the streets, a classic opportunity for mischief. Bad 'friends' have changed little through history.

'Listen,' a friend whispered one night. 'There's a pear tree just over the fence from Augustine's father's vineyard, heavily loaded with fruit. Let's say we help ourselves!'

'You're on!' the others agreed, and a few minutes later they were shaking the branches and clambering up the trunk.

'Don't leave anything on it!'

'But the fruit's not even ripe. How could we eat so much?'

'Eat them? We're going to throw them to the pigs!'

And so they did. It was an episode, oddly enough, which stuck in Augustine's mind for the rest of his life – a sin with no motive but the thrill of mischief itself. Foolish pranks were only the beginning.

Monica was horrified by Augustine's changing character. She was losing her position in her son's life, and he was soon living like any pagan. At fifteen he accompanied his father to the public baths, and the pagan gentleman was greatly amused to see his son flirting around. He later told his wife with a chuckle that they might not have to wait long to be made grandparents!

Monica was torn by the news. She urged her son to withstand temptation until he should be ready for lawful marriage, but Augustine dismissed her words as 'feeble womanish fears'. He soon found himself a mistress, a young girl of the lower classes, and at the age of only seventeen he became father to a son named Adeodatus.

Patricius died at this time, having become a Christian just before his death. Augustine also began thinking about religion, but not his mother's Christianity. The reading of pagan literature had inspired him to embrace the philosophical search for truth, and his first stopping place was in the exotic doctrines of the Manichaeans. Monica, feeling powerless to help her son, spent agonizing hours in prayer.

'Only God Himself can lead Augustine back now. Lord help him!'

One night she dreamed of an angelic youth, who asked the reason for her tears. She explained her problem and the stranger encouraged her.

'Have faith, Monica. Where you are your son will be.'

Monica told Augustine of her dream, but he had his own interpretation.

'Shall I become a Christian? Surely it is as likely to mean that you will become a Manichaean!'

'No,' Monica said firmly. 'You will come to me. He did not say I would come to you.'

Augustine was a little taken aback by that.

'I wasn't shocked by the dream,' he later wrote. 'It was the power that made her so sure of things, when I myself had no certainty about anything.'

Monica was sure, but that did not stop her prayers and tears, and she still tried everything she could to change Augustine's heart. Knowing herself unable to argue with her son on the subtleties of Manichaeism, she pleaded with her bishop to talk with him.

'We must leave him for the moment,' said the bishop.

'Augustine is now puffed up with the novelty of his heresy and delights in arguing the case for his beliefs. In spite of his error he is an exceptionally bright young man and has already perplexed many who thought to reason with him. It is best for the moment just to pray for him and to trust that he will discover the impiety of his heresy for himself. My own mother educated me as a Manichaean and without any argument from anyone, simply by studying their books deeply, I came to see that there is no power in that false religion and that only Jesus can save. Pray that Augustine also will make that discovery.'

Monica, not satisfied, continued to plead with the bishop. With tears running down, she begged him to argue with Augustine.

'Monica, have no fear,' said the bishop. 'The son of such tears will never be lost!'

Monica was silenced by this answer, struck as though by a voice from heaven.

'Thank you bishop,' she said, and with that left, rejoicing in the sure knowledge that God would call Augustine.

For the moment this seemed a long way off. Augustine was not only on the wrong path, but he was leading others astray as well. His closest friend, like Augustine himself, had been inadequately trained in Christianity as a child, and Augustine was able to convert him to the teachings of Mani. The friend, however, fell sick and as he lay in bed close to death, some old Christian friends came to visit. As it seemed that the young man might not recover, the Christians decided to baptize him, in spite of the fact that he was feverish and unaware of what was happening.

'Let us baptize him and leave him in God's hands,' they said. 'The Lord knows what to do with him.'

Augustine did not argue with the Christians. 'He doesn't even understand what's happening,' he thought. 'He is a Manichaean whether they like it or not.'

When the fever passed Augustine spoke with his friend about what had happened.

'You're one of the redeemed now!' he laughed. 'The

Christians have baptized you – made a saint of you! Shall I enlist you in their choir?'

Instead of joking, however, his friend shuddered at him as though he were an enemy.

'If you want to be my friend,' he said, 'do not scoff at my faith.'

Augustine was amazed at this transformation, but he kept his thoughts to himself. 'When he's better I will lead him back to reality,' he decided. 'I'll leave him for now.' But a few days later the young man relapsed and died. God had saved him from his 'friend'.

Augustine was troubled by this, but even more so by his deeper studies in Manichaeism. The more he studied the less sense it seemed to make, and he began to long for a mentor who could help him over the hurdles. When Faustus, the empire's most renowned Manichaean, came to town, it seemed that his wish had come true. Speaking to Faustus, however, only made things worse. Faustus' flimsy answers to Augustine's deeper questions convinced the young thinker that his faith was ill placed. So, breaking with the sect, a confused young man left his homeland to broaden his horizons in Italy.

Augustine ended up in Milan, where he met Bishop Ambrose. Ambrose was a brilliant teacher, and when Augustine heard him he came to see that Christianity contained deeper truths than he had ever realized – and that the arguments of the Manichaeans against it were hollow. But he was still a long way from putting his trust in Jesus.

A friend of Augustine's named Alypius had also moved to Italy. He was a sincere and upright young man, but one who had been raised to have a taste for the bloody entertainment of the pagan circuses. The philosophically-minded Augustine led his friend to see the vulgarity of such indulgence and he vowed to avoid them in future, but on a visit to Rome he met some old friends in the street.

'We're going to the amphitheatre, how about you?'

'I'm sorry,' said Alypius, 'but I don't go in for such things any more.'

'Come on, don't be stupid,' the others insisted.

'I'm serious!'

'We'll drag you there by force whether you like it or not!'

'Drag me if you want,' said Alypius, 'but you can't make me give my eyes and mind to the contemplation of such obscene cruelty.'

Alypius' friends were so shocked by his attitude that they actually did drag him to the show.

'You will thank us later,' they said. 'A bit of gore is good for you!'

Anyone who wants to know the spirit of pagan Rome must imagine for himself the horror of these displays. Dozens, sometimes hundreds, occasionally thousands, would enter the arena to be brutally killed, while tens of thousands cheered them on. Even 50 years after the death of Constantine, the church had still not managed to ban the pagans' favourite 'sport'.

Alypius sat with his eyes tightly shut, striving to ignore what was going on around him, but when the crowd suddenly burst into full voice he could not help but look. In an instant the sight of blood and thrill of the contest robbed him of his resolve, and with no power to fight his pagan desires he was soon enjoying the show and screaming along as insanely as everyone else.

Monica eventually came to visit her son in Milan and was delighted to find that Augustine had begun associating with Christian teachers.

'You must be a respectable man now,' she said. 'Find a nice girl to marry and settle down.'

Augustine, unenthusiastically, bowed to her wishes and Monica soon found a girl to be his wife. It was decided that the couple should marry two years later.

No one, of course, had asked Augustine's mistress what she thought of all this. Augustine was still living with the mother of his child and she, in Augustine's own words, 'was now torn from my side as an impediment to my legal and respectable marriage. My heart, so long joined to hers, was racked, wounded and bleeding from the separation and she soon returned to North Africa leaving our son in my care, vowing to the Lord Jesus that she would never know another man.'

Seeking consolation for his loss and unable to endure two years as a single man, Augustine soon added a new sin to all of his former ones by secretly taking a new mistress.

The whole affair shows Augustine in a very bad light, and Monica herself contrasts unfavourably with the poor abandoned mistress, whose name, a tragic and silent commentary on the injustice of her life and fate, is unknown to history. The greatest fault, however, lies with the culture itself and exposes the ugliness of a society in which men were permitted, and even expected, to take mistresses – lower class women whom it was quite inconceivable that they should marry. It is no exaggeration to say that one of the church's most radical and powerful teachings has been the assertion that male and female fornication and infidelity are equally sinful in the sight of God.

In spite of all, Augustine was genuinely searching for truth. A step in the right direction about this time was his rejection of pagan astrology. He was led to this by a friend named Firminius, who told him how his father and his father's close friend had been so fascinated with astrology as to plot even the horoscopes of their dogs! Once, when Firminius' mother and his father's friend's serving girl fell pregnant at the same time, the two astrologers determined to plot with great carefulness the exact moment of each child's birth. A messenger was sent running from either family at the very moment of birth, and the two heralds were amazed to meet each other exactly half way between the houses.

'One of those boys was myself,' said Firminius, 'the other is a slave to this day. Our lives have been completely dissimilar, though our horoscopes are exactly the same!'

Augustine, who had previously been much addicted to astrology, soon saw that a similar proof against the art could be found in the case of twins. The astrologers used the position of the heavenly bodies at the time of birth to foretell a child's future, and while twins usually have identical horoscopes, they often lead totally different lives.

A more stubborn intellectual issue with Augustine was the problem of evil. He could not understand how a good God could have made a world in which there is so much that is obviously not good. The Manichaeans sought to solve the problem by teaching that there were two equal and eternal gods, one good and the other evil. Augustine still believed this, and it had proved a great stumbling block on the path to Jesus.

Now, however, a new solution to the problem of evil occurred to Augustine. He was struck by the realization that good and evil need not be equal and opposite. On the contrary, good is eternal and absolute and everything that God has made is good, while evil is made not by God but by His creatures and is nothing more than the creature turning away from God in disobedience.

Augustine now had belief in God in his mind, though he still utterly lacked the power of Christ in his heart. In fact he was entirely miserable, and in his confusion he sought the advice of a renowned local Christian named Simplicianus. He told Simplicianus of his wanderings in pagan and heretical philosophy and mentioned his reading of Victorinus of Rome, a scholar who had translated many Platonic works into Latin.

'Of all the pagan writings,' said Simplicianus, 'none come so near the truth as the best of the Platonists, but even so they do not contain the word of salvation. When I was in Rome I became well acquainted with this Victorinus you mentioned. He was an important man amongst the pagans and once confided to me privately that he was a Christian. "I will believe that," I said, "when I see you in church." He was angry at that and asked me whether the walls of a church made one a Christian. Whenever I urged him to go to church he always said the same thing, "I don't need four walls around me to be a Christian." He was fearful of his friends, proud demon-worshippers, from whom he expected to suffer a torrent of scorn and rejection.

'So things remained, until Victorinus started to look into the Bible more deeply, and growing stronger in his faith he realized that if he did not confess Jesus before men then Jesus would not confess him in heaven. Suddenly the absurdity of his predicament struck him – he was ashamed to visit a church, though happy enough to go along and take part in repulsive idolatrous ceremonies. He came to me. "Let us go to church," he said, "for I wish to be made a Christian." But there was more. We offered to baptize him privately, but he chose instead to make the event as public as possible. Only the Spirit can give a man that strength. At first he thought it was simply a matter of mind and belief, but when the Spirit came, he had the power to act as well.'

Augustine was thunderstruck and, hungering for such faith and power, he became more assiduous than ever in his prayers, earnestly desiring this thing called the Holy Spirit for himself.

Soon afterwards Augustine and Alypius received a visit from a fellow African, a Christian, named Pontitianus. As the three sat down to talk Pontitianus picked up a book from Augustine's games-table and with delight saw it to be a volume of Paul's epistles.

'I thought I would have found you reading the philosophers!'

A conversation on the faith soon followed, in the course of which Pontitianus told the story of the desert monk Antony. Augustine had been completely unaware of the existence of the monks and was amazed that such a revolutionary religious leader should have been living and teaching so near his own time. Without fully realizing it, he had previously assumed that great spiritual leaders were a thing of the past and that mighty acts of God were a very distant thing. He was even more shocked to learn that there was a community of monks on the outskirts of Milan, supervised by Bishop Ambrose himself, and that two of Pontitianus' friends had recently abandoned their government positions to join the brotherhood. By the end of the conversation Augustine was almost drowning in inner turmoil. He took up his volume of Paul and went out to the garden, Alypius following.

He was now more than thirty years old, and the search for truth begun in his late teens had still borne no fruit. All his worldly wisdom had got him nowhere, and remembering his sins he now reflected with shame upon his feeble prayers. How often he had prayed for chastity, though always in his mind adding 'but not just yet!' He seized Alypius' shoulders.

'What is wrong with us? Our learning has got us nowhere, while others with precious little education are storming straight into the kingdom of heaven! Are we not ashamed?'

Alypius kept silent, and in his agony of soul Augustine prayed within himself, 'Let it be done now, let it be now!' But even as he formed the words there was a part of him holding back, and the thought of becoming a new man struck sudden terror into him. He thought of his mistresses, and they seemed to beg him to remain just as he was. His mind fumbled forward, offering a part of itself to God, but then shrinking back at the thought of losing control of his own future and forever abandoning 'sweet' sin. Finally he ran from his friend and, once out of sight and hearing, collapsed beneath a fig tree.

'Lord! Heal me now! Don't make me wait any longer!'

Through his tears he heard a voice, a child's voice, which seemed to come from a neighbouring house.

'Pick it up, read it! Pick it up, read it!'

The chant was repeated again and again, and Augustine became silent, reflecting that he had never before heard such an unusual child's game. His mind then turned to the story of Antony, who had once entered church as the words 'Go and sell what you have and give to the poor and you will have treasure in heaven and then come and follow Me' (Mt. 19:21) were read out and, struck as though by a personal command, had abandoned all to become a monk immediately. Augustine turned around and went straight home, opened Paul's epistles and read aloud the first words he saw.

'Not in rioting and drunkenness, not in lewdness and sin, not in arguing and envy. Clothe yourself instead in the Lord Jesus Christ and cease wondering about how you can satisfy your lusts' (Rom. 13:13–14).

He read no further, nor did he need to, for instantly a great light arose within him and the clouds of doubt that still clung to his heart were burned away.

'My friend, I am a new man!'

Alypius took the book from him, read the words which had opened his friend's heart, and then read the next words also, 'Receive the one who is weak in his faith' (Rom. 14:1). At that Alypius cried aloud with joy.

'I am that one!' he said. 'Lord, I pray that You will receive me also. I have been trying on my own too long!'

Both men went immediately to Monica, who rejoiced at the news and knew that her prayers had finally been answered. Filled with righteous disgust at his own unfaithfulness and impurity, Augustine's first act was to leave his new mistress and abandon his plans of marriage.

Herein lies one reason why so many Christians at this time were rejecting marriage. With Roman life, their own past life, so sinful and marriage so corrupted, many were moved to renounce 'normal' life entirely. The pagans thought nothing of adultery, and few families were free of its taint. Monica herself had for years patiently endured Patricius' adulteries, by her submission and piety eventually winning her husband's heart and finally his soul.

Augustine and Alypius, along with Adeodatus, were soon baptized. Much of the next few months had an almost dreamlike quality, as Monica and Augustine, finally reunited in heart, spent long hours in talking of the kingdom of God. The mother could not have been happier, or have asked for more.

'There is not much left for me in this life,' she told her son. 'For years the only thing that has kept me alive has been my hope that I would see you saved. God has granted my last wish, and I now know that my time will soon be done.'

It was only five days later that Monica developed a fever. As she lay sick her friends made lamentation for her, since it seemed that she would die and be buried far from her North African home.

'Why should I fear to be buried in Italy?' she asked in surprise. 'Do you think that God will forget where I am when the day of resurrection comes? My body can rest anywhere the Lord wishes.'

With those words Monica passed away, rejoicing in the love

of God and His kindness to herself and her son. Little did she know of what her son would become. Augustine was destined to be one of the most significant men this world has seen.

THE CONFESSIONS OF AUGUSTINE

The Massacre of Thessalonica

Theodosius' reign saw the destruction of the old idols all over the empire. The great pagan temples were knocked to the ground, and the dying gods themselves displayed to the world all too clearly the falsity of the old beliefs.

'The gods are hollow!'

Many indeed were. Some of the idols had 'spoken' to their followers for centuries – how could anyone doubt that they were truly divine? Now, however, as the temples were demolished, it was seen that these speaking gods were hollowed out so that the priests could hide themselves in secret passages and speak through the idols' mouths. Not a few pagans joined in the demolition when they saw the deceptions that had been played upon them.

The fall of the temples, however, did little to reform Roman habits. The pagans were far more addicted to circuses than temples, and to many it mattered little that the idols were ground to dust so long as the blood sports and brothels remained. In this turbulent period the city of Thessalonica witnessed a particularly gruesome 'sign of the times'.

A favourite charioteer was imprisoned, and when race day came the fans demanded his immediate release. The magistrates ignored them, the mob took to the streets, and by the end of the day several of the city's judges were dead. Grim indeed, but the response of the emperor himself would soon make it pale into insignificance.

Instead of searching out the culprits, the emperor demanded immediate and bloody vengeance on the whole city. No trial was held to discover the guilty – the emperor's soldiers simply launched themselves upon the unsuspecting city like ravenous wolves, and in one day as many as seven thousand perished in the 'Massacre of Thessalonica'.

In earlier times emperors could get away with actions like this, but now there was a new force in the state. Theodosius, journeying to Milan after the massacre, tried to attend church – but he was met at the entrance by Bishop Ambrose.

'Do not cross this threshold!'

'What on earth are you talking about?'

'Are you really ignorant of what you have done?' Ambrose demanded. 'Your anger has ceased, but how is it that your mind is still closed to your guilt? Can a man whose hands drip with a city's blood expect to raise them in prayer in the house of God? Go and do not mock God by dreaming that your power will protect you from His anger. Do not return until your heart is right with the Saviour.'

No pagan was ever treated like this by an idol priest! How would a mighty ruler respond to such an attack?

Theodosius felt the bishop's words burn him like fire, and with undisguised tears he turned his back upon the church and returned to his residence. He confessed his guilt and accepted his excommunication without murmur, and for many months he remained a penitent outcast. So things continued until Christmas, when the emperor was thrown into despair by the sight of the whole world celebrating the great festival.

'What on earth is wrong with you?' asked his minister Rufinus. 'It is a season of festivities, yet you sit at home whinging and bawling like a child.'

'It is no festive season for me,' said the emperor. 'The church's door lies open to every labourer and beggar, while to me alone it is firm shut. By my own fault I am handed over to the powers of hell!'

'Let me go to the bishop,' Rufinus suggested. 'I will put your case to him firmly, and he will surely remove the sentence against you.'

'He will not listen,' Theodosius shook his head. 'His judgement is true and deserved.'

'But this cannot go on forever,' Rufinus insisted, and he would not be silenced until Theodosius finally permitted him to take his request to the bishop.

The festival of Christmas first rose to prominence around the middle of the fourth century. How far back the tradition that 25 December was the birthday of Christ goes is impossible to determine, but in the fourth century it was almost universally accepted. There is some evidence that a record of the census held at the time of Christ's birth still existed in the late fourth century and that it confirmed the traditional date of Christmas, but as such a record no longer exists we can probably never be certain.

Prior to the introduction of the Christmas feast, the church had celebrated Christ's birth on 6 January, the Feast of Christ's Epiphany ('the showing or revealing'). This was held to be the date of Christ's baptism, but the festival was regarded as a time to celebrate each of the leading revelations of Christ's life and ministry: His birth, the visit of the Magi, His baptism and His first miracle, at Cana in Galilee. When Christmas became more popular, however, the celebration of Christ's birth ceased to be a major part of Epiphany.

December had been an important month to the Roman pagans. A series of festivals marked the winter solstice, the death of the old year and birth of the new. These festivals were highly prophetic, and the church urged that Christmas was a fulfilment of what the pagans had unwittingly performed for centuries. The Saturnalia, leading up to the solstice, was a celebration of a past golden age. The Romans believed that in ages past not Jupiter but his father Saturn had ruled the world, and under his sway humankind had lived in peace and luxury, with everyone attaining a great age and no one having to labour for a living. It was an echo of the Garden of Eden, a remembrance of better times before the institution of idolatry and also a preparation for the idea that even gods could be overthrown. The Romans believed that Jupiter had dethroned Saturn, and they were thus prepared for the revelation that Christ had 'dethroned' Jupiter.

Following the shortest day of the year, the Romans observed a festival of the sun. They believed that as the days shortened the great god of the sun had weakened and died, but had returned from the longest night victorious, again asserting his invincibility and rule over the heavens. The application to the crucified and risen One is obvious. In the festival of Christmas the church proclaimed to a straying world both the true 'golden age' and the undying power of the 'Sun of Righteousness', the eternal Christ.

'He will definitely give in to you,' said Rufinus. 'Give me a few minutes, then come to the church yourself.'

But Ambrose was not at all interested in Rufinus' request.

'You have the impudence of a dog! Indeed it was you who counselled the emperor to this massacre, and now wiping shame from your brow you make this request without so much as a blush.'

'Be reasonable,' Rufinus persisted, 'you must eventually give in. Theodosius is already on his way.'

'If he wishes to enter the church by force I cannot stop him, but it will be over my dead body!'

Seeing the bishop's firmness Rufinus sent a messenger to deter Theodosius from following, but the emperor was already well on his way when the message reached him.

'Be that as it may,' he said. 'Nevertheless, I will speak with Ambrose.'

The bishop was waiting at the cathedral entrance.

'Do you come as a tyrant, ready to ignore the commands of God?'

'No,' the emperor replied, 'I come in penitence, begging that you will forgive my crime.'

'Have you repented? What have you done to make amends for your sin?'

'I do not know how to make amends. You must tell me what to do.'

'Your crime was to make a judgement against people's lives while in a rage. You must ensure that such a thing never happens again. Put forth an edict to ensure a delay of 30 days before any sentence of death or the confiscation of goods is carried out. If the judgement has been just you may proceed with the sentence after the expiry of 30 days, and if the judgement has been foolish, a month should be ample time to calm down and reconsider.'

'Your advice is good,' Theodosius agreed. 'Such will be the law of the kingdom from this day forth.'

'Then, my son, I welcome you back.'

Now, readmitted to the church, Theodosius rose even higher in the people's esteem. Rather than attending church in imperial pomp he refused to stand, or even kneel, and instead, lying face down upon the ground, he repeated to himself the words of David: 'My soul has gone down to the dust! Give me strength with your Word!' (Ps. 119:25).

THEODORET, *CH* 5.17–22

The Triumphs and Death of Theodosius

In these troubled times even emperors were far from safe. The western emperor Gratian was assassinated in 383, and as his brother and heir Valentinian the Second was still but a boy, a Spaniard named Maximus managed to usurp control of most of the west. Only Italy remained to the rightful ruler.

Maximus was the first Christian emperor to punish a heretic with death. Priscillian, a Manichaean as well known for immorality as for heresy, had a large following in Spain. When the local church leaders found themselves unable to restrain his cult, one of them appealed to Emperor Maximus. The result was that in 385 Priscillian and several followers were tried and sentenced to death, a proceeding that created a storm of controversy in the church. Many Spaniards were well pleased with the outcome, whereas foreign leaders like Ambrose and Martin protested bitterly against Maximus' action, insisting that a bloody solution to a religious conflict was the way of pagans and Arians, not of Christians.

In 387 Maximus invaded Italy, and Valentinian fled to the court of Theodosius. The eastern emperor embraced the exile's cause, and after defeating Maximus the following year he raised Valentinian, now aged seventeen, to the sole rule of the west. Four years later, however, Valentinian himself was murdered and a pagan named Eugenius took the crown. Again Theodosius prepared to march to the west, but this time his counsellors advised against it.

'It would be grossly irresponsible to risk war at this time. There is trouble enough at home with the barbarians, and even if you should ally yourself with the Goths and incorporate them into your army, you could still not muster a force comparable to that of Eugenius. Fighting on his own ground you are doomed to fail.'

'I cannot take your advice,' the emperor replied. 'I refuse to fear Eugenius while my troops march behind the sign of the cross. He marches under a banner of Hercules and will suffer the same fate as his god!'

In 394 the eastern army, with a Gothic auxiliary, marched against Eugenius and the two armies met near a crossing of the Alps in the north of Italy. Theodosius descended from the pass to find himself confronted with a plain full of enemy tents, utterly dwarfing his own forces, but as it was late in the day the fateful battle was postponed until morning.

Theodosius spent the night in prayer, but close to dawn the troubled emperor dropped off into a brief sleep. In a dream he saw two men dressed in white and riding white horses, who told him to dismiss his fears.

'Prepare your men for battle and boldly face the foe. We are on your side.'

Theodosius asked the strangers' names, and they answered that they were John the evangelist and Philip the apostle. Immediately the emperor awoke, and uplifted by this assurance of God's help he returned to his prayers.

One of Theodosius' soldiers experienced the same dream that night and reported it to his centurion. The message was passed on to Theodosius himself, to whom it was no surprise.

'This dream did not come for my sake,' he said, 'but rather that none might believe that I invented the story of my own vision. The time is come to forget our fears and to trust to Christ and not the size of our army.'

Eugenius laughed out loud when he saw Theodosius' forces coming against him.

'Theodosius has a death wish! Perhaps he takes too seriously the promise of resurrection – and desires to be with his God all the sooner! Be careful to take him alive, that I may see him in a set of chains.'

In spite of his boasting, however, Eugenius did not face the enemy along with his troops, and instead he retreated to a safe position entirely screened from the field of battle.

Even so, as battle began, it seemed that Eugenius' boasts would soon become reality. The eastern troops, regardless of the assurances of God's protection, were greatly outnumbered and could not but approach the enemy with mingled hope and dread.

'God help us!'

The first volleys of arrows and javelins were discharged by the opposing armies, but before any had found their mark a fierce wind sprang up, blowing straight into the face of Eugenius' troops. Theodosius' arrows were carried deep into the enemy ranks, while with a howling wind against them the western marksmen were rendered useless.

Seeing the opening Theodosius' army charged the foe, and as the wind increased huge clouds of dust were blown along with them. Eugenius' troops were already half-blinded with grit when the eastern army fell upon them. They were soon reduced to despair and cast away their arms and begged Theodosius' forgiveness.

'Stop the fighting!' the emperor responded. 'Bring me your leader!'

Eugenius, safely hidden on high ground, was not surprised to see a group of his soldiers running breathlessly up to him.

'Victory!' he cried. 'Bring me Theodosius!'

'We are not bringing him to you,' the soldiers panted. 'We are taking you to him!'

With that they dragged the emperor from his seat, shackled him and took him to the conqueror. The last battle of paganism and Christianity was at an end, and Theodosius was sole ruler of the Roman world.

It was not long after this last great triumph that Theodosius became seriously ill. Knowing that the end was near he divided the empire between his sons Arcadius and Honorius and then devoted his last days to the business of the church and prayer. He died in Milan in 395, breathing his last in the embrace of his dearest friend, Bishop Ambrose.

THEODORET, *CH* 5.24–25; AMBROSE, 'FUNERAL ORATION FOR
THEODOSIUS'

Alaric

Here we prepare to leave the Roman Empire for now. With the death of Theodosius and the succession of his young sons, the

Goths again became hard to handle. They had effectively been kept in line since the fall of Valens, but now a Gothic general named Alaric proclaimed himself King of the Goths and launched a campaign of conquest within the weakened empire. It seemed that the fall of Rome might be fast approaching – but how would it happen and would God indeed allow it?

Two years after the death of Theodosius, Ambrose himself fell sick. When his people begged him to plead with God for a longer life the bishop was firm.

'My life is such that I am not ashamed of it. I do not fear to live longer, but neither do I fear death. We have a good Lord and He knows what is best for me.'

On the night of Good Friday, having spent several hours in uninterrupted prayer, Ambrose slipped into the better life.

The year was 397.

PAULINUS, *LIFE OF AMBROSE*, ch. 10

When the Story Continues

The death struggle of the Roman Empire with the barbarian invaders begins our next volume. We follow the slow birth of a new world, Christian Europe, and discover the great labours of Augustine and other Christian leaders. We will see Christianity spread from the wild North Atlantic Ocean and the Baltic Sea to the swelling cities of China and hear the inspiring stories of the great missionaries who carried the gospel into so many far-flung lands.

Summary

First century

- The church is born on the day of Pentecost, about AD 30, with the descent of the Holy Spirit on the followers of Jesus.
- Stephen, the first Christian martyr, is a victim of the Jews.
- The church at first preaches to Jews, until with Peter's vision and the visit to Cornelius, the mission to the Gentiles is born. Paul's travels are the greatest example of this ministry.
- The church is guided by the apostles and those appointed by them.
- The New Testament is written.
- Nero begins the first Roman persecution of the church.
- In AD 70, the Jewish temple and nation are destroyed by Rome.
- Domitian is the second imperial persecutor.

Second century

- Under Trajan, persecution becomes official Roman policy.
- The Jewish false Messiah, Bar Kokhba, persecutes the church.
- Complex heresies such as Gnosticism, a mixture of pagan and Christian ideas, develop. Marcion starts his cult, using his own 'bible'.
- The apostolic fathers defend the teachings of the apostles.
- Justin is the first Christian philosopher.
- Famous persecutions take place in Smyrna and Lyons.

- The false prophet Montanus appears.
- Irenaeus labours against the heretics.
- The first school of Christian philosophy, the catechetical school of Alexandria, is established.

Third century

- Origen heads the catechetical school while still in his teens.
- The heretic Sabellius teaches that the Trinity exists only in God's appearance.
- The imperial policy is variable. Emperors such as Alexander Severus and Philip the Arab favour the church, while Decius and Valerian attempt to annihilate Christianity utterly. Around AD 260–303 there is a time of relative peace between the church and pagan Rome.
- The Neoplatonist philosophers attempt to revitalize dying paganism.
- The Novatians break with the mainstream church on questions of discipline.
- The heretic Mani combines Zoroastrianism and Christianity to form a new faith, Manichaeism.

Fourth century

- Armenia is converted by Gregory the Illuminator.
- The Diocletian persecution, beginning in AD 303, is the most savage yet known. It ends in triumph for the church when Emperor Constantine embraces Christianity.
- Eusebius is the 'father of church history'.
- The first monks appear.
- Arius denies the genuine divinity of Christ. The First Ecumenical Council, at Nicaea, condemns his heresy.
- Ethiopia is converted by Frumentius.
- Followers of Arius continue to fight the church. Athanasius opposes them. Under Constantius and Valens, the Arians rule

the empire and persecute true believers.
- There is great persecution in Persia.
- Julian attempts to restore paganism and initiates a failed attempt to rebuild the temple in Jerusalem.
- Theodosius destroys the power of the Arians.
- Many pagan temples are destroyed.

Bibliography

Most works quoted can be found in the *Ante-Nicene Fathers* or the two series of *Nicene and Post-Nicene Fathers*, first printed in 1886 – but still available (*ANF*, *NPNF*[1] [First Series] and *NPNF*[2] [Second Series]) in reprints by Hendrickson (Peabody, MA, 1994) and Eerdmans (Grand Rapids, MI, 1985–87).

Some works not found there are in the more recent *Fathers of the Church* (*FC*; Washington, DC: Catholic University of America Press, 1947–).

Christian authors

Agathangelus is not available in English translation. However, the story of Gregory is told in some detail in A.S. Atiya, *A History of Eastern Christianity* (London: Methuen and Co., 1968).

Ambrose, 'Funeral Oration for Theodosius', *FC*, 22.

Anonymous Abbot of Tabennensis, 'Life of Pachomius' (not available in English, but A.S. Atiya, *A History of Eastern Christianity*, contains a useful summary).

Anonymous, 'The Acts of the Disputation with the Heresiarch Manes', *ANF* 6.

Anonymous, 'The Genuine Acts of Peter', *ANF* 6.

Anonymous, 'The Martyrdom of Polycarp', in *Early Christian Writings* (Harmondsworth: Penguin, 1987, 1968) and in *ANF* 1.

Athanasius – all works quoted are found in *NPNF*[2] 4.

Augustine, *Confessions* is one of the most popular books in history. There are translations published by SCM (ed. Albert Cook Outler; Library of Christian Classics, XIII; London, 1955); Penguin (Harmondsworth, 1961); OUP (Oxford, 1998); *NPNF*[1] 1.

Clement of Alexandria – complete works are found in *ANF* 2.

Clement of Rome – 'First Clement', in *Early Christian Writings* (Harmondsworth: Penguin, 1987, 1968) and in *ANF* 9.

Cyprian, *Letters* and 'The Life and Passion of Cyprian', *ANF* 5.

Eusebius, *The Church History*; *Martyrs of Palestine*; *Life of Constantine*, NPNF[2] 1; also *Church History* (tr. G. Williamson, Baltimore: Penguin, 1965).

Gregory of Nyssa, *The Life of Macrina*, FC, 58.

Hippolytus, *Against Heresies*, ANF 5.

Ignatius, *Letters*, in *Early Christian Writings* (Harmondsworth: Penguin, 1987, 1968) and in *ANF* 1.

Irenaeus, *Against Heresies*, ANF 1.

Jerome, *Life of Malchus*, NPNF[2] 6.

Justin Martyr – all works, including the account of his martyrdom, in *ANF* 1.

Lactantius, *The Deaths of Persecutors*, ANF 7.

Palladius, *The Lausiac History* (tr. W.K. Lowther Clarke; New York: SPCK, 1918).

Paulinus, *Life of Ambrose*, FC, 15.

Perpetua, 'The Martyrdom of Perpetua and Felicitas', *ANF* 3.

Prudentius, *The Book of the Martyrs' Crowns*, FC, 43.

Socrates, *Church History*, NPNF[2] 2.

Sozomen, *Church History*, NPNF[2] 2.

Sulpitius Severus, *Life of Martin*; *Letters*, NPNF[2] 11.

Tertullian, *The Five Books Against Marcion*, ANF 3.

Theodoret, *Church History*, NPNF[2] 3.

Jewish and pagan authors

Ammianus Marcellinus, *The Later Roman Empire: AD 354–378* (tr. W. Hamilton; Harmondsworth: Penguin, 1986).

Josephus, *The Jewish War* (tr. G.A. Williamson; Harmondsworth: Penguin, 1959).

Julian, *Works* (tr. W.C. Wright; Loeb; London: Heinemann, 1962–90).

Pliny, *The Letters of the Younger Pliny* (tr. B. Radice; Harmondsworth: Penguin, 1963).

Tacitus, *The Annals of Imperial Rome* (tr. M. Grant; London: Penguin, 1989).

Virgil, *The Eclogues* (tr. Guy Lee; Harmondsworth: Penguin, 1984).

Index